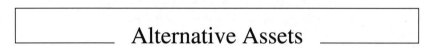

Alternative Assets

For other titles in the Wiley Finance series
please see www.wiley.com/finance

Alternative Assets

*Investments for a
Post-Crisis World*

Guy Fraser-Sampson

A John Wiley & Sons, Ltd., Publication

This edition first published 2011
© 2011 John Wiley & Sons, Ltd

Registered office

John Wiley & Sons Ltd, The Atrium, Southern Gate, Chichester, West Sussex, PO19 8SQ,
United Kingdom

For details of our global editorial offices, for customer services and for information about how
to apply for permission to reuse the copyright material in this book please see our website at
www.wiley.com.

A catalogue record for this book is available from the British Library.

ISBN 978-0-470-66137-6 (hardback), ISBN 978-0-470-97688-3 (ebk),
ISBN 978-0-470-98008-8 (ebk), ISBN 978-0-470-98009-5 (ebk)

Set in 11/13pt Times by Toppan Best-set Premedia Limited, Hong Kong
Printed in Great Britain by TJ International Ltd, Padstow, Cornwall, UK

Contents

Preface

The events of 2007 and 2008 have had many consequences, shattering as they have many of the old "certainties" by which the world's investors were happy to live out their lives. Fundamental questions are now being asked, throwing into question the very validity of much traditional finance theory. Even more fundamentally, we are being forced to confront disturbing new issues, such as the very meaning of words such as "return", "risk" and "value".

In truth, though, many of the world's investors were not even applying the precepts of traditional finance theory, though they may have paid them lip-service. The requirement for a properly diversified portfolio, for example, while a matter of simple common sense, was routinely ignored, even by those, such as UK pension funds, who had a legal, rather than simply a professional, duty to comply.

Yet it can be mathematically proven that what has become known as a "Yale type" approach (which really means little more than having a properly diversified portfolio), a concept much closer to that practised by North American pension funds, would have dramatically lessened the impact of the various financial shocks and stresses of the last quarter century or so.

Whatever the case, the recent financial crisis must surely have brought home to even the most obdurate investor that the "all your eggs in one basket" approach really is as foolish as it sounds, and that the imperative for a sensibly diversified portfolio of different asset types can no longer be ignored.

That means Alternative Assets, at least if we are going to apply that label (as most investors seem to do) to anything other than bonds and quoted equities, and here we run into an immediate problem. There is an old adage,[1] and a very good one, that you should never invest in

---

[1] Usually attributed to Warren Buffett.

anything you do not understand. Well, no real level of understanding of any Alternative Assets currently exists in the vast majority of the world's investment institutions. That means that unless they are going to invest blind in Alternatives then they need to gain such knowledge, and quickly. Those who actually possess that knowledge, particularly across various asset types, will cease to be regarded as mild eccentrics roaming the outer reaches of the investment world, and begin to be recognised as useful and, therefore, valuable individuals.

This book is an attempt to pass on at least some of that knowledge. Each chapter provides useful background knowledge on a particular asset type, including a discussion of whether a satisfactory beta return level exists and, if so, the different ways in which it might be accessed. While the author is a well-known advocate of Alternative Assets, it is in no way the intention to showcase their merits, nor to downplay their potential drawbacks. To suggest that all Alternative Assets offer exciting opportunities for all investors at all times would be nonsense. There are some that struggle to justify themselves on a returns basis, and others that offer significant difficulties of implementation. These issues can only be resolved by individual investors around the world having due regard to their own particular circumstances. There can be no valid "one size fits all" approach.

This introduction will be brief, not least because experience suggests most readers will have turned straight to Chapter 1, but four important points fall to be made.

The first is that all this book can do is to impart "knowledge", not experience. There is an important difference between the two. As a hugely successful investor[2] once pointed out, no fish can imagine what it is like to be a mammal. One day of walking around on land is worth two thousand years of writing about it. As business school students quickly realise when they go out into the world of investment, there are certain situations in which financial theory seems to work very well, and certain situations in which it seems not to work at all. Understanding that theory offers certain guidelines, rather than a rigid framework within which the "one right answer" can be calculated is an important step, and one which sadly many investors are never able to take.

The second is that readers will find certain issues popping up in more than one chapter. While it would have been preferable to split these out into separate sections of their own, this has not always been possible, since the same issue can impact different asset types in different ways, or raise different practical implications. Thus, while every effort has been made to discuss as much common matter as possible in Chapter

---

[2]Warren Buffett again.

2, there are some things which will regularly intrude. In particular, the issues around (1) counterparty derivative risk, (2) difficulties of physical possession and/or use of spot pricing, and (3) the inappropriateness of using a basket of operating businesses as a proxy for asset or project exposure.

The third is that, while what might be called traditional financial theory, which may be loosely described as everything and anything which is based upon the assumption that the risk of an investment and the volatility of its historic returns are one and the same, appears to the author to be, at the very least, open to many objections, its validity will be assumed for the purposes of this book. Thus, investors will be able to move freely within their chosen world, in which volatility is uniformly bad and liquidity is uniformly good, in which the past is always a good guide to the future, and in which normal distribution will always apply. Those who have been diligent enough to read this introduction will, however, be punished for their thoroughness by having these sentiments repeated in the body of the book. It is only fair to point out, though, that anybody who slavishly follows these precepts will find it difficult ever to countenance an allocation to many Alternative Assets.

The fourth and final point to record is that in this book there will generally be reference to "asset types" rather than "asset classes". In part this is a desire to avoid loose terminology. There are many who now question whether Private Equity and Hedge Funds, for example, are really "asset classes" at all. While this may prove a fascinating discussion, it is not one which we need to pursue between the covers of this book.

In part though, and more importantly, it is an attempt to bring home to readers that actually it almost certainly is not important what any asset is called. That is part of the human compulsion for classification, to apply a label to something and place it in its appropriate pigeonhole. A compulsion, incidentally, which has caused great problems in the area of Asset Allocation. No, what is really important is not what an asset is called, but how it might perform within an investor's portfolio.

Guy Fraser-Sampson
Cass Business School, City of London
October 2010

Acknowledgements

Leigh Bolton of Holmwood Consulting and Katherine Pulvermacher of African Rainbow Consulting (formerly Head of Research with the World Gold Council) kindly read in draft and commented upon the chapters on Energy and Gold respectively.

Valuable insight on various asset and fund types was provided by Paul Ogden of InProp Capital (Real Estate derivatives), Deborah Fuhr of BlackRock (Exchange Traded Funds) and Torquil Wheatley of Deutsche Bank (Active Currency).

However, all views expressed, and any mistakes which remain, are entirely my own.

1

What are
Alternative Assets?

The world of finance and investment is full of unfortunate terms and phrases. Unfortunate in that they are unclear, unfortunate in that they may actually be used in different senses in different situations, or unfortunate in that they evoke emotional responses which may not in fact be justified in the cold light of day. "Alternative assets" is one such term.

Dictionary definitions of "alternative" as a noun range among the following:

- "something different from";
- "able to serve as a substitute for something else";
- "either one of two, or one of several, things or courses of action between which to choose".

Yet the conjunction of "alternative" with "assets" suggests that it is here doing duty as an adjective (qualifying a noun, for the grammatical purists out there), in which cases dictionary entries would include:

- "different from and serving, or able to serve, as a substitute for something else";
- "of which only one can be true, or only one can be used or chosen, or take place at any one time";
- "outside the establishment or mainstream, and often presented as being less institutionalised or conventional";
- "ecologically sound and/or more natural or economical with resources".

In other words, as a noun "alternative" seems to be capable of at least three meanings, and as an adjective of at least four, which might be summarised as: "serving as a back-up", "mutually exclusive", "unconventional or non-traditional", and "green" (in its socio-political meaning). Of these, at least three are unhelpful, the first two in particular. There is no suggestion that we should invest in alternative assets *instead* of something else, or that they represent a mutually exclusive choice so that we may invest *only* in alternative assets. In any event, in neither case would we be able to make any sense of the situation unless we knew instead of *what*; what might the other alternative or alternatives be?

It is the third meaning that we are going to have to adopt, and yet even here we must be careful, for this usage would include overtones of being marginal, or even downright cranky such as when used to describe alternative medicine. Roget's *Thesaurus*, for example, offers "conventional" as an antonym, and "unorthodox" and "unusual" as synonyms. It is perhaps these overtones which can give weight to the pejorative resonance with which the phrase "alternative assets" is often uttered.

It is not even particularly helpful to look at the way in which the phrase is used in practice by investors, since there seems to be no common agreement on this. People can agree on examples (private equity, hedge funds and real estate (property), for example) but not on a universal definition. There seem to be at least three different ways in which the phrase is used to distinguish certain types of assets.

Illiquid

Many say airily "oh, alternative assets are illiquid. You know, not like bonds or equities – illiquid." However, this possible definition runs into trouble straight away.

For a start, not all bonds and equities are liquid, or at least not all the time. Anyone who may have tried to sell even good quality US corporate bonds in September 2008 will appreciate the force of this comment all too well. However, let that go. The definition still does not work.

Active currency rates are an alternative asset, and what could be more liquid than currency? Similarly gold, which many rightly regard as the ultimate defensive asset. Why? Precisely because one can take it anywhere in the world and turn it instantly into cash. In an Armageddon-type scenario one could even use it as a unit of purchasing power in its own right. So here are two "alternative" assets which we can identify straight away as being arguably even more liquid than bonds and equities.

Unquoted

This definition too runs onto the sandbanks as soon as we set sail in it. It is true certainly that private equity funds, or at least the limited partnership variety, are unquoted. However, all the commodities are "quoted" in the sense of having a price which is available for trading on public markets from one moment to another, as are energy assets, such as oil and gas, and of course currencies. We should also note, without necessarily having to pursue the point further at this stage, that adopting this definition would create some serious ambiguities which it might prove very difficult to resolve. How would you classify 3i, for example? As a private equity fund, or as a public company and major constituent of the FTSE 100 index?

Not Bonds or Equities

I have never heard this definition suggested, save in my own investment modules and workshops, but it seems to me to do the least violence to the situation, since it is both more difficult to attack linguistically and a closer fit for the instinctive attitude of most investors towards such assets. Certainly, one often sees a portfolio divided between "fixed income" (bonds), "equities", "cash" and "alternatives".

However, even here there are problems. For example, many investors include "real estate" (property) as an asset class in its own right and then have an allocation to "alternatives" alongside it. Some others include private equity within their allocation to "equities". There are even some who argue for a still more restrictive definition, which would only cover what one might term "exotics" or "collectibles" such as musical instruments, paintings, etc.

This is one of those situations where no sizeable group of people are ever going to agree on a common solution. It is, however, submitted that "not bonds or equities" is less open to debate than any of the other candidates, and will therefore be adopted for the purposes of this book.

ARE ALTERNATIVE ASSETS
REALLY "ALTERNATIVE"?

This may seem like a really pointless question to be asking, the posing perhaps of some arcane academic distinction, but it is not. On the contrary, it exposes a very serious and controversial issue.

The fact that these assets are commonly referred to as "alternative" reinforces the view that they are somehow peripheral to the whole business of investing or, even worse, that there is "proper" investing and "other" investing. "Proper" investing being of course bonds and equities, which should occupy the bulk of your time, and "other" being what you might take a quick look at if you have the time once the main business of the day is done. In other words, that alternative assets are somehow inferior to bonds and equities, which might be thought of as "mainstream". It would be unthinkable, under this view, for anyone to invest *only* in alternative assets, since they become by definition some-thing extra which one goes in for only if one has the time and inclin-ation after first setting one's allocations to bonds and equities.

With very few exceptions indeed, this worldview flows over into actual asset allocation in practice; it is for precisely this reason that we should take this issue so seriously. An automatic or unconscious assumption is being made which is capable of skewing decision making very badly indeed.

It became briefly fashionable during the dot com bubble to talk about "a whole new paradigm", or "a paradigm shift". By this was meant that as a result of the information and communications revolution brought about by the advent of the internet, a completely different belief system had come into being, and that it was necessary for finance and invest-ment thinking and practices to be brought into line with it. Should you, for example, be so square and un-hip to ask how a business with no prospect of earnings for many years could be worth several hundred million dollars, you would be met with a pitying smile and the news that "you just don't get it, do you?"

In fact, at the risk of being thoroughly un-hip, the use of the word "paradigm" was probably itself misguided. As used initially by Thomas Kuhn in his book *The Structure of Scientific Revolutions*,[1] it was con-fined to the scientific community. It was a system of scientific beliefs, and scientific only. What the internet pundits were talking about was actually not a paradigm at all, but an episteme.

An episteme, a concept coined by the flamboyant French thinker Foucault,[2] is a system of thought which embraces all aspects of culture and society, not just science. It also embraces the concept of "zeitgeist", the spirit of the times. In the sudden readiness of consumers to make purchases online, for example, we see not a new paradigm but a new episteme.

One of the features of an episteme which Foucault identifies is this very issue of unconscious assumptions. In the field of literary criticism, for example, Foucault's work had a huge impact, as people realised that it was impossible properly to analyse or comment upon a book without understanding the episteme within which the author lived and worked.

There is for example a very early Hitchcock film called *Murder*, made in 1930 starring Herbert Marshall and based upon a novel by Clemence Dane and Helen Simpson. It does indeed feature a murder, the title being a bit of a give-away here, the motive for which, it tran-

[1] Thomas Kuhn, Chicago University Press, Chicago, 1962.
[2] Michel Foucault, *The Order of Things*, Routledge, London, 1974.

spires, was blackmail. The information in respect of which the individual concerned is being blackmailed is that he is of mixed blood or, as he is dismissively described in the film, "a half-caste". A modern audience of course finds this incomprehensible. Many people today are of mixed race, and the fact that somebody is would not excite even comment, let alone prejudice or disdain. Yet we are not living in the 1920s and 1930s as the authors of the novel and the original audiences of the film were respectively. Clearly things must have been viewed differently in those days or there would be no point to the film, and Alfred Hitchcock was not the sort of man to make a film which had no point to it. So, it must have been the case that the prevailing episteme of those times included the unconscious assumption, no matter how incredible and objectionable it may seem to us today, that to be of mixed blood was somehow to be inferior, undesirable or untrustworthy, and certainly not the sort of cad to whom one might wish one's daughter to get married.

So, let us be aware of unconscious assumptions, and of the very important part which they can play.

For, just as with films and literature, we cannot properly understand investment practice unless we understand the episteme within which it takes place, since this will colour instincts, reactions, thoughts, discussions and decisions alike. It is here that we encounter the real problem with the word "alternative". While this is difficult precisely to articulate, it is part of a system of unconscious assumptions which includes elements of being "more difficult", "more risky", "dangerous", "cranky", "optional" and "unnecessary". No better evidence is required of all this than the very low allocations made to alternative assets relative to bonds and equities, at least outside the US.

The view is very much that bonds and equities are essential, while everything else is an optional extra, and quite possibly an unnecessary luxury. This has led in turn to some dramatically undiversified portfolios, particularly among pension funds who, ironically, are often the only class of investor actually to be under a legal duty to diversify their assets.[3]

The reader should therefore be aware that alternative assets in general are subject to a great deal of unconscious prejudice, and that their supporters are required to justify them both constantly and in great detail in a way which is never demanded, for example, of quoted equities.

At the other end of the scale, there are very few institutional investors who have eagerly embraced alternative investments as a source of

---

[3]In the UK, for example, see Pensions Act 1995 s.36(2)(a).

diversification across asset classes which hopefully offer lowly correlated returns. The Yale Endowment probably enjoys the highest profile
of these, and in recent years alternative assets have generally totalled
about 65% of their total asset allocation.[4] If only for this reason, the
question which serves as the section heading is clearly relevant and
valid. If alternative assets can make up about two thirds of the portfolio
of one of the best investors in the world, how can they really be said
to be "alternative" at all?

THOUGHTS ON CLASSIFICATION

Having established that we are going to assume that any assets other
than bonds and equities can be "alternative", let us see if we can identify some different asset types, and consider how we might further
discuss, and possibly classify them.

First and most obviously, if we are going to say that bonds and
equities are not "alternative", then what about things which are not
bonds or equities and which yet represent them, such as futures, options
and swaps positions over individual bonds or stocks (shares), or groups
or markets which include them? There is a yet further complication here,
of course, since hedge funds routinely deal in such instruments, and yet
by most people's reckoning are firmly in the "alternatives" camp.

It is probably best to treat these not so much as an asset type as a
way of investing, a means rather than an end. They are thus an investment technique, or a means of replicating or synthesising a particular
investment, rather than the investment itself. As we will see, it is in
fact often the case with the asset types which we will be considering
in this book that synthetic coverage of this nature is the only practical
path to take.

Private Assets

On one view, alternative assets fall for the most part rather neatly into
two separate categories, but with Hedge Funds hovering uneasily with
more of their weight on one side of the line than the other.

Many alternative assets are publicly quoted and highly liquid, thus
making it rather difficult to see what is really so "alternative" about
them at all. Commodities, energy, gold and currency assets all definitely fall into this category. On the other side of the dividing line
stand three which are very different: private equity, real estate (property) and infrastructure – we might term "private" asset types for two
important reasons.

---

[4]See for example the Yale Endowment Annual Report 2009.

The first and most obvious reason is that the things in which they invest cannot by any stretch of the imagination be described as quoted assets or instruments. Private equity funds may invest in shares, but the shares in a private company have few of the characteristics (as investments, not as legal instruments) of their quoted counterparts. They can neither be openly traded nor can they be offered to the public. There may even be important legal differences; in the UK, for example, the Takeover Code applies to public companies but not to private ones.

Real estate funds invest in buildings, which may well from time to time have an advertised price when they happen to be on the market for sale, but these periods are infrequent, and in any event there is no guarantee at all that even then the advertised price has any connection with the building's real value, however we might measure that. Property assets are illiquid, whereas bond and quoted equities are not. Property assets require care and maintenance, which bonds and equities do not, and their value can be enhanced by improvement or development, actual or potential.

As for infrastructure funds, these are perhaps the furthest removed from bonds and equities of all, since they invest in projects, albeit these might be legally structured for funding purposes into companies. On one analysis, an infrastructure fund is paying agreed capital sums in return for the right to share in a stream of future cash flows. What could be more illiquid than the contractual right to share in a project's income stream for perhaps the next 30 years or so? What could be further removed from the concept of legal instruments which can be traded instantly on the world's financial markets?

So, they are "private" asset types in the sense that their underlying investment entities are not publicly quoted. But there is something else as well: this is that the overwhelmingly popular ways in which such assets are accessed are themselves private. Yes, there are quoted private equity vehicles, such as 3i, and doubtless there will sooner or later be an infrastructure equivalent of this FTSE 100 monster, but the vehicle of choice for sophisticated investors has always been the limited partnership.

Real estate is more problematic in this regard, for there are of course hundreds of quoted property investment vehicles around the world ranging from mutual funds to REITs; this is, for example, how most European pension funds have chosen to structure their property exposure. However, private real estate (often wrongly and confusingly called private equity real estate or PERE[5] for short, simply because it employs a private equity type fund structure) has always been a significant part of American investment portfolios and recently

---

[5] Or even, still more confusingly, sometimes PERA.

crossed the Atlantic and seems set to be a growing part of the European scene.

There are of course those who question why anyone would want to access assets through a private vehicle when they could have the lower fees and comforting liquidity of a public vehicle. As we discuss elsewhere, however, this should increasingly be recognised as a double edged sword. First, that liquidity may be more imagined than real. Second, in turbulent equity market conditions such vehicles can easily give rise to both man-made volatility and man-made correlation as their unit or share prices ride up and down with stock market beta rather than necessarily with the value of the underlying assets.

So, we might classify as "private", those asset types which satisfy both these criteria. There will always be investors who seek out quoted private equity exposure, and for such people then there are certainly proxies such as 3i investing at the company level, or fund of funds equivalents readily available. The bulk of private equity capital is, however, deployed through private vehicles.

With infrastructure the problem is more complex since when investors talk of investing in "quoted infrastructure", they frequently have in mind buying shares in companies which undertake infrastructure activity, the drawbacks of which approach will be fully explored in later chapters.[6] "Quoted infrastructure", in the sense of listed funds which invest in projects, do exist, but given that the underlying assets (projects) are themselves illiquid, then something like a limited partnership will often be the vehicle of choice for any sophisticated investor looking to access this asset class too, not least because of various tax advantages. Stand-alone partnerships are also used by investors to access individual projects.

With real estate the situation is more problematic and "private real estate" is simply a sub-set of "real estate". However, something which is often overlooked is that many of the world's biggest investors choose to build their own direct portfolios of property assets, and this activity too would form part of private real estate. After all, what could be more "private" than simply buying something yourself and keeping it as your own personal property?

So, it does seem to be the case that there is indeed a category of alternative investments which we can classify as private assets, and these would comprise almost all private equity and infrastructure, and all that real estate investing which is conducted either directly or

---

[6]For what it's worth, some research carried out a few years ago in Australia, admittedly on very limited data sets, suggested that private infrastructure funds had strongly out-performed "quoted infrastructure" even after deduction of all fees. See the chapter on infrastructure for more details.

through unquoted vehicles. Perhaps the test should be that it is only here, with private assets, that true illiquidity (at least in the legal sense of the word) is to be found.

While it is always dangerous to make predictions, and this one may seem more perverse and controversial than most, it is entirely possible that in future a number of investors will begin actively to seek out private assets as a significant part of their portfolios precisely for the very illiquidity which they offer, no matter how counter-intuitive this may feel to most investors reading this book. This point will be examined and developed in the next chapter.

Commodity Type Assets

Another discernible category of assets would be those which are, or represent, some quantity of a physical object, such as an ounce of gold, a barrel of oil or 20 tons of pork bellies. This would embrace everything which we will be treating as "commodities" and "energy", as well as gold, which we will consider as a separate asset class for both historical and practical reasons.

These all share some obvious common characteristics. They can all be publicly traded from one second to another on financial markets. They all represent substances which can be used either as raw materials or as means of production by industrial companies around the world. They are all financial investments, but each in its purest form can be transmuted into physical ownership; those with long memories might, for example, remember the larger-than-life Texan businessman Bunker Hunt calling for physical delivery during his bid to corner the world silver market in the late 1970s.

For some investors they represent "defensive" investments. They offer the comfort of being able to hold physical assets rather than financial instruments. They offer the reassurance that a commodity must always have some intrinsic value, being unable to fall to zero as could the shares (stocks) of a bankrupt company, or even the bonds of a failed state. Perhaps they might even be believed to offer that most elusive holy grail of all, a source of excess return which is largely uncorrelated to global equity markets.

Of course, this is all a bit of an illusion. As we will see, it is usually precisely financial instruments that such investors end up holding, rather than the physical asset itself, since they cannot handle, and thus do not want, physical delivery. Even in the case of physical gold, it is usually a piece of paper rather than a gold bar which sits in the safe, or with your custodian. In the case of just about every one of these commodity type assets, what you get left with is not a quantity of the stuff itself, but exposure to the underlying futures contract, the price of which may or may not represent the future strike price at expiry and which, many argue, does not even have a particularly close relationship with the prevailing spot price.

It remains the case, however, that these asset types do seem to be recognisably different to private assets. Most obviously, they are liquid. Any futures contract, or an option in respect of it, can be bought and sold, and where these are exchange traded rather than dealt Over the Counter, then they carry only symbolic counterparty risk. So, liquidity is one thing which sets them apart.

Volatility and Valuation Issues

Volatility is another. Even measured on a year to year basis, which masks the true extent to which their prices may go up and down over shorter periods, this is high; both oil and gas, for example have a single standard deviation of about 40%, which means that if you were looking for a 95% degree of confidence you would have to allow in your modelling for them to go either up or down 80% in the course of any single year. Private assets, on the other hand, because they are held in private vehicles, tend to have relatively stable values which go up and down only either as assets are bought, sold or revalued, or cash flows are received and distributed.

It is only fair to point out that there is a strong counter-argument here, and one which gained in both topicality and urgency during the gathering whirlwind of 2008. It transpired that the framers of the relatively recent International Accounting Standards (IAS) governing the valuation of assets had never envisaged the sort of extreme market conditions which in fact occurred, and the situation was complicated still further by American accounting bodies attempting to impose some of their own domestic FASB[7] requirements on any businesses in the rest of the world having any links with the US (the reverse of the usual situation, where agreed IAS provisions are given effect by domestic accounting regulations).

The FASB provisions, however, seemed even less appropriate to extreme market circumstances than their IAS counterparts, as was dramatically demonstrated during September 2008 when, at one time, there was simply no effective market anywhere in the world for corporate bonds, for example. Some of these provisions seemed to be saying that an investor could only value an asset at the price at which they could actually sell it in the marketplace at that moment. Logically, then, if there was no buyer available at any price, the asset should be written

---

[7]Financial Accounting Standards Board.

down to zero. Given that this would have had a major impact on the balance sheets of banks around the world who were struggling, successfully or otherwise, to stay in business and out of liquidation, such views did not meet with universal approval.

In the event, some classic political fudges ensued, some of which even allowed accountants to treat certain types of assets as if they were something else entirely. Two principles of general application might usefully be noted here.

A People will usually try to change the data to fit the rules, rather than vice versa.

B If a rule leads to a ridiculous result, then it is usually because it was a ridiculous rule to start with.

Accountants at the time argued that there was a concept known as "fair value" which always existed and could always be measured. It is only fair to note (1) that they were always at pains to stress that this was not the same thing as calculating something which was "real", "true" or "correct" (surely another example of B above), and (2) that since the financial crisis many accountants have now changed their views and there is currently an active debate raging within accountancy circles as to whether there really is such a thing as universal "fair value" after all.

Even post-crisis, it is necessary to touch upon this point because it is both a sensitive and an important one. Many critics of private assets point to the issue of valuation as showing that the "value" of, for example, an interest in a private equity fund, cannot be accurately assessed or relied upon for audit purposes. One is tempted to respond as Brahms habitually did when people used to point out that a particular passage in one of his symphonies was remarkably similar to a few bars in one of Beethoven's: "any donkey can see that", he would say.

Nobody pretends, least of all anybody in the real estate or private equity industries, that an interest in a private vehicle which invests in private assets, can be accurately measured in the sense of arriving at some philosophical touchstone of finite, absolute value. Indeed, it is probably more correct to say that the real value of any such underlying asset can only be established for certain once it has been sold, and every last piece of the consideration realised in cash and distributed back to investors. Attempts, inspired by auditors and regulators alike, to "mark to market" such assets simply reveal a deep and disturbing ignorance of their true nature.

As Markowitz noted[8] more than fifty years ago, investors treat uncertainty as a bad thing and certainty as a good thing. This is true. Indeed,

---

[8] *Portfolio Selection: Efficient Diversity of Investments*, John Wiley & Sons, New York, 1959.

it is so self-evidently true that one wonders why anyone felt a need to say it in the first place. However, it does not go far enough. It is not just that investors prefer certainty (even apparent or illusory "certainty") to uncertainty. It is that most of them are completely unable to handle uncertainty in any shape or form, certainly in their decision processes. There has for example been much research into cognitive biases such as Ambiguity Bias (a heavily skewed bias towards an apparently more certain outcome) and Illusory Correlation (a bias towards seeking confirmation of an apparently more certain outcome from historic financial data, even to the extent of seeing patterns in the data which do not in fact exist).

This tendency is most marked in those who have what the Americans now call a "Type A" personality, people who believe strongly in one right answer and the ability of mathematics to calculate it. Such individuals tend to make very good actuaries and bond analysts, but very poor investors. The fortunes of any investment portfolio will always be prey to considerable uncertainty. Even if one constructs a portfolio composed entirely of long UK gilts one can only limit the type and extent of the uncertainty, not eliminate it altogether (you cannot accurately predict what is going to happen to inflation and interest rates over a 20 year period, for example). It is their belief that this uncertainty is somehow something which can be calculated or measured, as opposed to evaluated or assessed; an attitude which lies at the core of so-called Modern Portfolio Theory, and bedevils the world of finance.

There is a simple response to such an attitude, no matter how well rooted it may appear to be in mathematical theory. Uncertainty is a part of human existence and, since investment cannot occur except as a result of human interaction and decision making, thus also of investment. Either you are comfortable with that uncertainty, and can envisage outcomes occurring within certain parameters rather than as single, predictable events, or you are not. If you are not, then you have two choices: either to stay out of those areas of investment which seem to give rise to the most uncertainty, or to try to impose inappropriate mathematical methods upon them in an effort to make yourself feel better about the whole business. In fairness, most investors would greatly prefer the first option, but find themselves increasingly being pushed into the second.

Time Horizons

So, whether by reason of market mechanics or accounting and valuation, commodity type assets will tend to display much more volatility, on a year to year basis but also when measured over shorter periods.

This strongly suggests that they are likely to be more suitable for long term investors, who can within reason choose the moment at which they sell, rather than short term investors, who may be forced to sell when they would really rather not, in order to meet some pressing liability.

In practice, these days many investors divide their portfolios in two. The sorts of phrases you will come across are "risk reducing" or "liability matching" assets, on the one hand, and "return seeking" assets on the other. The former will be chosen on the basis of displaying as little volatility of historic returns as possible. With regard to the latter, higher levels of volatility will be tolerated, this being balanced by the expectation of compensating higher returns. While the actual labels "short term" and "long term" may not be used, this is equivalent to an investor having mentally divided their portfolio by investment time horizon, though we are here talking about a more complex decision process, where trade-offs of volatility, liability profile, correlation and internal resources and processes should all have been given due consideration too.

Whatever the case, commodity type assets would seem properly to belong not in the first of these categories, where volatility is definitely your enemy, but firmly in the second, where in many cases volatility could quite possibly be your friend.

There is one exception to this, and it is a very important one since it encompasses a whole separate approach to investment, and one which has many dedicated managers offering products and services bearing its name.

Global Tactical Asset Allocation (GTAA)

This is not a book on investment strategy, but we are considering alternative assets as a background to the whole business of asset allocation and so it is important to understand the difference between strategic and tactical asset allocation. Briefly, and perhaps over-simply, the former is long term while the latter is short term.

A strategic asset allocator will attempt to model the liabilities, both long term and short term, of an investor and then construct a portfolio which seems to offer the best compromise between matching the near term ones and having enough money when the time comes to be able to pay the long term ones. Generally speaking, the asset mix once having been chosen will not be interfered with except for periodic rebalancing to bring it back within its target parameters.

Incidentally, rebalancing is itself generally a benign process, since not only does it restore diversification but also forces the investor to buy something when it goes down and sell it when it goes up; surprisingly, in practice many investors do exactly the opposite. Please note that we are here talking about types of assets, what are generally called asset classes, rather than individual assets. Should you be holding a portfolio of individual shares (stocks) then this section is not advice to buy more of one automatically should it go down in price (a process known as "averaging down"). On the contrary, there may be very good reasons why it has gone done, and equally good reasons to sell your remaining holding before it goes down any further. We are here talking about a situation where you might be holding, say, an S&P500 tracker fund as a way of having exposure to US equities, and where the value of that tracker fund may have declined relative to your holdings in, say, real estate simply because US equities *as a whole* have dropped in price relative to real estate *as a whole*. Like it or not, it does seem to be the case that over long periods most asset classes move within broad (sometimes very broad, as with gold, for example) bands and that rebalancing will tend to force you to buy towards the bottom of the band and sell towards the top.

Tactical asset allocation is seen as much more exciting, which is why many investors around the world seek to practice it. Here, you might get together as a team on a Monday morning, or on the happening of some specific event which seems significant, and think about what asset classes seem over-valued or under-valued, or likely to be so in the near future. You will then seek to buy (or, more likely since this is essentially a hedge fund type approach, go long) the ones you like and seek to sell, or go short those you do not.

This is a deceptively simple description of what is a very complex approach, which blends into Global Macro, and can also make use of active currency strategies, as well as exposure to commodities by way of Managed Futures. It can be performed at a very simple level by means of ETFs, or executed in much more complex fashion with leverage, derivative positions and currency overlays. Whatever the case, it essentially involves taking short term bets at the level of asset classes or types (not individual assets).

Given its exciting nature and sexy acronym, it is small wonder that many investors around the world feel drawn to GTAA and try to adopt it as a strategy for at least part of their portfolio. Alas, reality soon re-asserts itself. Tactical asset allocation requires a very quick decision process (sometimes a matter of minutes) and a strong nerve, both things which are in short supply among the world's institutional investors. If it takes you a year to decide that this may be a good time to short the dollar, then, even if you were right when you started writing your first paper to Investment Committee you certainly are not any longer, since the opportunity will have long passed. If you can take the emotional stress of running a losing position for several months, then fine, but is there any guarantee that your committee will not pressure you (or even direct you) to close it out?

So, most investors who want to move in this direction take the decision sooner or later to appoint an external GTAA manager, though most do so, in common with all their alternative asset allocation decisions, in respect of such a small percentage of their portfolio that the time and effort required in appointing and monitoring the manager is out of all proportion to any positive impact which the GTAA exposure might have on their overall returns.

There is another point to be considered here. Some investors try to classify strictly every type of risk to which they are subject, and in what proportion of their portfolio each one is present; indeed, some are required to do so by their legal or regulatory environment. GTAA raises an insuperable problem here, since the GTAA manager cannot specify in advance what asset types they will consider, nor will the investor necessarily know from one week to the next in what they have invested. So, if you do have just such a rigidly demanding risk management system then you should consider very strongly whether GTAA is really an area you wish to get into.

The reason it is useful to mention GTAA here is that, as pointed out above, this might be seen as something of an exception to the principle that commodity type assets may not be suitable for short term investors. Within a GTAA portfolio, it may be precisely short term volatility upon which the manager is relying for their return, believing that it is about to move in their favour.

Subject only to this one exception, however, it seems reasonable to state as a principle that commodity type assets are not suitable for short term portfolios, since if one cannot choose the time of one's selling then one is always going to be at unacceptably high risk of short term downside in the market price.

An Alternative Way of Accessing Conventional Assets?

Before we leave this chapter on attempting to delineate exactly what we are talking about when we mention alternative assets, it is necessary to deal with an argument which was advanced in an earlier book[9] to the effect that alternative assets are simply an alternative way of accessing conventional investments, or "just different investment strategies within an existing asset class". Such a statement seems very difficult to accept.

---

[9] *The Handbook of Alternative Assets*, Mark Anson, John Wiley & Sons, New York, 2002.

If you buy a bar of gold, then surely you are doing so because you want a bar of gold? You might, for example, be buying it as the ultimate defensive investment, and intending to bury it in a biscuit tin in your back garden, intending to recover it on emerging from your personal bunker after a nuclear holocaust, as one Swiss banker of the writer's acquaintance was indeed known to do. To say that you are somehow trying to put yourself in the position of having bought something else entirely seems impossible to conceive.

Even if one were to take a less obvious example, could it really be said that by committing money to a limited partnership which intends to make seed stage venture capital investments in start-up companies in the US, one is somehow buying a proxy for the NASDAQ or the S&P? What about oil, or pork bellies, or infrastructure projects? What about silver, coffee or an office block in Mayfair? What other, conventional investments are these supposed to represent?

On the contrary, the reason people invest in alternative assets is precisely because they are "different", because they offer different return profiles (in some cases, even different types of return) and because they offer at least the possibility of uncorrelated returns.

So, as is clearly stated at the beginning of this chapter, there is indeed no universally accepted definition of "alternative assets", but they clearly must be different to something else, something "other", or the phrase would be a meaningless one altogether. To suggest, as the writer of the earlier book does, that the assets themselves are not alternatives, but sub-sets of mainstream, conventional asset classes, and that only the means of investors' access is "alternative", seems impossible to accept. Of what "existing asset class" is real estate "just a different investment strategy"? Or infrastructure projects? Or natural gas? Not to mention Stradivarius violins ...?

What We Will be Considering

Having made some sort of attempt at defining what we are talking about when we refer to alternative assets, it may be helpful to set out exactly what we are going to be talking about. It is acknowledged that the following may not be a perfect intellectual exercise in asset classification, but it does at least have the merit of being broadly in line with current investor thinking.

- Real estate
- Energy
- Private equity
- Hedge funds (but discussing active currency separately)

- Infrastructure
- Commodities
- Gold
- Active currency
- Other (including forestry)

SUMMARY

There is no universally agreed definition of "alternative assets", nor even any consensus as to which individual asset types may be so described.

For the purposes of this book, we will adopt the view that investment in anything other than either bonds or (quoted) equities will be seen by investors as "alternative". It is submitted that this fits reasonably well with prevailing investor beliefs, particularly outside North America.

An alternative view, that alternative assets simply represents an alternative way of accessing conventional assets, must be rejected.

Some alternative assets can be classified as "private assets". These are private equity, real estate and infrastructure when accessed through private vehicles such as limited partnerships.

Some alternative assets can be classified as commodity type assets. These share three common characteristics: (1) they are liquid, (2) their prices are quoted on public exchanges and (3) they take the form of or, as traded, represent physical assets which are used either as raw materials, means of production or a measure of intrinsic value.

Commodity type assets tend to be highly volatile, and the key concept of volatility will be examined further in the next chapter. Briefly, there are situations where volatility can be your friend rather than your enemy, but it is important to be able to differentiate between these!

For the purposes of this book, the alternative assets to be considered are: real estate, energy, private equity, hedge funds, infrastructure, commodities, gold, active currency and "other".

2
Investing in
Alternative Assets

Performing consultancy assignments for institutional investors around the world in Investment Strategy and Asset Allocation[1] puts one in a perfect position to gauge investor sentiment, appetite and, it must be said, prejudice. One thing has, however, become clear over the past few years. Whereas some are still demanding "why should we invest in alternative assets?", an encouraging number are now starting to ask instead "how should we invest in alternative assets?"

To the first question we shall address ourselves straightaway. Answering the second question is the main purpose of this book as a whole, which will examine each asset type in turn and hopefully provide not just some useful background but also guidance on specific investment issues. There is of course a third and vital question, namely "what are alternative assets?", which we have considered in the last chapter.

WHY SHOULD WE INVEST IN ALTERNATIVE ASSETS?

There are many who claim that the recent financial crisis[2] has changed the world of investment for ever, and that a completely new approach may now be required. We shall return to consider this view at the end of the chapter. For the moment, let us note a few points and move on.

It is true that the crisis highlighted various factors which had not previously been supposed to be particularly significant, of which the most obvious example would be counterparty risk. It also threw into prominence one issue the existence of which had never really been guessed at, though logically it might have been supposed to occur in certain circumstances, namely man-made correlation. Finally, it exposed yet another tendency, the existence of which *had* been realised by

---

[1] Which are not actually the same thing, contrary to much popular belief.
[2] The word "recent" is not intended to suggest that the financial crisis is over.

proponents of alternative assets (or, more properly, a multi asset class approach to investment strategy) but ignored by the traditionalists, namely the obvious link within a portfolio between greater levels of liquidity and greater levels of volatility.

These are all extremely important points with which the investment community is still struggling to come to terms, and we will consider each of them in turn. However, while this is not a book on financial theory, and nor does it pretend to be, we must also briefly describe the worldview of the traditional investor, since if we do not then we may find ourselves floundering with problems of definition and perspective.

Though the discussion of reality and perception has a long and honourable history, having first been raised by Aristotle and Plato, it has largely been ignored when considering the fundamentals of finance such as risk, return and so on. There are two possible approaches here. One would be to point out, as gently as possible, that many of the preconceptions which investors bring to work with them in the morning as a result of having studied traditional finance are just plain wrong, most notably the myth that all the material risk of an investment may be measured by the volatility of its historic returns, a myth indeed upon which the whole unsteady edifice of our financial system rests.

To do this, however, would require a whole book, not just one section of one chapter, and in any event this is not that book. So, this book will inhabit the Ptolemaic universe of normal distribution, volatility-as-risk, perfect markets and rational investors, a universe in which the future is a perfect mirror of the past, a universe moreover in which the possibility of cataclysmic events and the unpredictability of human behaviour can alike be ignored. The reason is simple; this is the universe which investors actually inhabit, and the one within which they make their investment decisions. Let us leave the finance of Galileo and Einstein for another book in some far distant time when financial dogma can more easily be questioned. The author hopes that you will grant him your indulgence, however, should, despite his best efforts, the curtain occasionally twitch and reveal a brief glimpse of reality as it is.

THE TRADITIONAL WORLDVIEW

Risk (Volatility)

The world of traditional finance decrees that the risk of any investment may be measured by the volatility of its historic returns, customarily expressed as one standard deviation.[3] Underlying this key belief are two assumptions: (1) that provided you have a large enough sample of historic returns available for analysis then normal distribution will always apply and (2) that past performance is a good guide to what is likely happen in the future.

The expected return on any investment should be directly proportionate to the level of risk which it exhibits; a high risk investment is capable of earning a high return, whereas a low risk investment is not, but then neither should it exhibit so significant a loss in bad times. In other words, the returns of a high risk investment are likely to occur within a broader range than those of a low risk investment; that, after all, is what volatility measures.

However, in contradiction of this basic belief that the relationship between risk and return should generally be represented by a straight line, traditional finance makes use of a mechanism known as the Sharpe Ratio.[4] This measures the level of return of an asset or asset class against its volatility. Specifically, it measures the level of *excess* return (the return in excess of the risk-free rate) over the standard deviation of the excess return. This of course requires agreement as to what the "risk-free" rate may be at any one time, which may vary according to where an investor is located and what sort of investments they may be required to make, or prohibited from making.

"Contradiction" because if the original belief held true and there was a direct relationship between volatility and return, then one would expect every investment to produce the same Sharpe Ratio result, and there would be no need to use the Ratio as an aid to investment decision making in the first place. It is probably, thus, more accurate to say that traditional finance expects there to be a direct link, but recognises that in practice this does not always happen. On the contrary, measured by annual returns some assets (private equity, for example) have consistently exhibited high returns and low volatility relative to, say, quoted equities.[5]

Thus, a high Sharpe Ratio, such as that enjoyed by private equity, is regarded as a good thing, while a low Sharpe Ratio, such as that currently exhibited by quoted equities, is regarded as a bad thing. This

---

[3]Which is the square root of the variance, which is in turn a measure of the average distance from the mean (average) of each observation. The square root is necessary because in order to eliminate the minus signs from the individual distances these are squared before calculating the variance. Don't worry if you don't understand this – the important thing is to know that the standard deviation is a measure of the "spread" of the individual observations.

[4]After its creator, Nobel prize-winner William F. Sharpe of Stanford University.

[5]See de Groot and Swinkels, Incorporating uncertainty about alternative assets in strategic pension fund asset allocation, *Journal of Pensions*, Vol 13, No. 1 and 2 (2008) which is in line with the writer's own calculations.

then becomes an important aid to decision making. If two investments seem to offer the same rate of return but one has a higher Sharpe Ratio then, all other things being equal, that is the one you would prefer.

Volatility is thus a key factor which we will be considering when looking at alternative assets and it will be seen to be a particular problem in some cases – oil being a good example.

It is fair to say that volatility is regarded as the ultimate bogeyman by traditional investors; after all, it is regarded as the same thing as "risk" and it seems logical to keep as much risk out of your portfolio as possible. Thus, any time you hear of people running a "risk model", what they actually mean is that they are running a "volatility model". This is a difficult but vital point to grasp for someone, such as a pension fund trustee or a business school student, coming to the business of finance and investment for the first time.

Actually, the assumption that volatility is your enemy is itself highly questionable. After all, without volatility you could probably never make any significant return. It seems more logical to say that if you are a short term investor (having short term and/or unpredictable liabilities), then volatility is indeed your enemy since you may be forced to sell an asset during one of its big down-swings. If, on the other hand, you have long term and/or predictable liabilities, then within reason you can choose the moment when you sell an asset, in which case volatility becomes your friend. This view, though it is not shared by the vast majority of the world's investors, will be developed a little later in this chapter.

Liquidity

"We must have liquidity" is a mantra chanted by most institutional investors around the world as they get up in the morning and go to bed at night. Another one "liquidity good, illiquidity bad", helps them through the stresses and strains of the working day. We will examine a little later just how justified this view may be, but for the moment let us content ourselves with being quite clear about what liquidity is.

Liquidity is the ability to turn assets into cash, instantly and in any circumstances, and so a "liquid" asset is one which is capable of being treated in this way. Note the stipulation "instantly and in any circumstances". An asset is either liquid or it is not. An asset cannot be a little bit liquid, just as a woman cannot be a little bit pregnant. This fact was brought into stark prominence during the dark, difficult days of September 2008.

Investors had previously sought out instruments such as US T-Bills[6] as their source of liquidity. Others, particularly if they were not US

---

[6]Treasury Bills – short term US Government bonds.

dollar investors, had used bonds issued by governments such as Britain, Germany and Japan. During the heady equity market returns of 2003–2006, however, many started to become dissatisfied with the very low returns which such instruments generated, and yearned for something a little more exciting. In trying to put this desire into action, they shifted the balance of their bond portfolios from high quality government "paper" to more lowly rated, and thus higher return, corporate "paper" issued by large companies in America and elsewhere.

Everything went swimmingly until Lehman Brothers filed for bankruptcy in September 2008, at which point the corporate bond market simply curled up and died for a while. Consequently, some investors, particularly in the US, found themselves in a situation which was quickly dubbed "Cash 22", in which they had assets which had high notional valuations, but were unable to generate cash at short notice in order, for example, to honour capital call notices issued by private equity funds.

Hopefully, this issued what is known in America as a "wake-up call" to investors regarding the true nature of liquidity and the rationale for holding liquid assets. Sadly, however, less than two years later investors were already starting to extol once again the virtues of corporate bonds.

In fact, as we will see shortly, the traditional approach to liquidity within investment portfolios is in any event badly flawed, but let us leave that to its proper time. For now, let us simply take in the fact that, just as traditional investors believe that they cannot have too little volatility in their portfolio, so they believe that they cannot have too much liquidity.

In summary, then, the traditional approach to investment will see a portfolio as producing whatever return can be earned by its constituents, defined by reference to the volatility of those returns, and containing so far as possible only liquid assets. There are a number of important consequences here for the way in which this prompts traditional investors to view alternative assets.

PROBLEMS POSED BY THE TRADITIONAL WORLD VIEW SO FAR AS ALTERNATIVE ASSETS ARE CONCERNED

The Tail Wags the Dog

The first problem is posed by the words "(investors) will see a portfolio as producing whatever return can be earned by its constituents". This may seem a very innocuous phrase which does nothing more than state a simple fact, but in fact it is much more sinister than it might at first appear. You see, traditional investors see returns as being driven by the portfolio, rather than the portfolio being driven by returns.

Instead of calculating their target rate of return and then choosing as the constituents of their portfolio that mix of assets which they feel is most likely to achieve that target return, they simply adopt some arbitrary mix of assets and then accept whatever return does in fact emerge. Rather than them controlling the portfolio, it controls them. The tail is wagging the dog.

There is a further complication here in that certain investors are forced by law or regulation into selecting from a very restricted choice of assets (and sometimes just one – usually domestic government bonds). However, even if we ignore these unfortunates, many investors, notably pension funds, actually select assets (or rather determinedly ignore certain asset classes altogether) on grounds which have nothing to do with investment fundamentals at all, but rather artificial accounting and actuarial calculations.

The Parallel Universe of Pension Funds

It is necessary to explain this briefly, since pension funds are responsible for such a large part of the world's investment capital. Ignoring the fact that a pension fund's liabilities must be paid not today but as they fall due, which can in some cases be many years in the future, they calculate a net present value of those liabilities (which is in any event necessarily a subjective exercise since it is dependent on the making of many assumptions, not least the correct discount rate to employ). They then set this figure against the current market value of their assets, and see their task primarily as managing the "risk" that these two figures might move relative to each other.

When explained to business school students, this produces blank stares of incomprehension. Clearly, however, pension fund trustees, consultants and regulators inhabit some parallel universe where the normal rules of logic do not apply. When taken to its *reductio ad absurdam*, this approach can result in a large part of the portfolio being dedicated to hedging "interest rate risk" by means of swaps, or as security for such swap positions.

Since such thinking is so difficult to penetrate, it may be useful to seek to explain it. If interest rates change then so does the appropriate discount rate and so (unless possibly the whole portfolio is held as fixed interest bonds, and yes there really are people who do that) "the liabilities will go up and down".

What the business school students spot immediately, of course, despite many of them having no mathematical background, is that the liabilities do not go up and down at all; only the net present value does. There again they also spot at once that the real "risk" to which a pension fund is subject is the possibility that one day they will not have enough money to meet a liability, not that one or both of two figures on their balance sheet may be different from one day to the next.

We could pursue this state of affairs still further and note that in many cases this approach is pursued by pension schemes that already have a large funding deficit, in which case any normal person would go to bed at night hoping desperately that the two figures *would* move relative to each other the next day, but let us not strain credulity too far.

Suffice it to say that, as will be seen even from this very brief account, that the mind-set of a pension fund investor, certainly outside North America, is far removed from anything one is likely to encounter in the world of pure investment management, and for this reason discussion of Alternative Assets is likely to prove difficult, except perhaps in respect of some small part of the portfolio which might have been carved out from the real business of managing "risk" and designated "return seeking". Here again, business school students tend to ask the obvious question: how can you have an investment that is *not* return-seeking?

Volatility as Risk

As we have already seen, the traditional approach to investing assumes that all the material risk of any investment can be measured by the volatility of its historic returns. It also believes that this number (for it is indeed a "number", the output of a mathematical calculation) is the one right answer, and is fixed regardless of the circumstances of the investor, since the risk attaches to the investment, not the investor, and must therefore be viewed objectively.

In order to measure the volatility of historic returns, first one needs historic returns data. Second, in order to measure the volatility itself these data need to show the returns earned in successive periods, whether years, quarters, months or whatever.[7] Such return data are thus known as "periodic". This causes problems in respect of alternative assets whose returns cannot validly be measured in periodic terms.

The example most commonly given is private equity, and particularly venture capital. Such is the level of uncertainty governing the extent, timing and type of any outcome[8] that any meaningful valuation

---

[7] In some situations, such as VaR analysis, even daily data may be used.

[8] Much research suggests that 50% of all early stage venture companies will fail to return their initial capital. See Fraser-Sampson, *Private Equity as an Asset Class (Second Edition)*, John Wiley & Sons, Chichester, 2010.

is impossible. While this is an extreme example, all other types of private equity funds share this characteristic to some extent or other, as do private real estate funds and private infrastructure funds, particularly of the primary variety. We will be examining all these asset types in due course, but for the moment let us accept that for the reasons just given they very sensibly take the view that the only really meaningful way to measure their returns is by way of an IRR based on the actual cash flows of the fund during its lifetime. There are also various ways in which these IRRs can be aggregated across each asset type as a whole for benchmarking purposes.

This is very bad news for these asset classes when they come to be considered by traditional investors, who discover that they cannot accommodate compound returns over time into their "risk model". Historically, rather than face up to the unpleasant truth that any risk model which cannot accommodate multiple asset classes is essentially not fit for purpose, many investors chose simply to shun the inconvenient asset classes in question. Incidentally, this was one reason (though not the main one – see below) why investors often sought exposure to alternative assets through quoted vehicles; a periodic return could be measured very easily here in exactly the same way as for any other quoted equity.

There is a further twist to this story, however. If you really want to, it is possible to measure the periodic returns of these asset types, though obviously any such attempt must be heavily valuation-based, which equally obviously introduces a strong subjective element unless one is simply going to take everything at cost. Thus, you *can* measure volatility if you really want to. If done, such analysis frequently shows that an asset such as private equity has produced relatively higher returns and lower volatility than, say, quoted equities, thus giving a much higher Sharpe Ratio. So deeply engrained, however, is the belief that there must be some direct relationship between "risk" and return that many investors, particularly pension funds, simply change either the input or output numbers arbitrarily to bring them into line with their own instinctive expectations.[9]

So it can be seen that the belief in some direct relationship between "risk" (volatility) and return is persistent and casts a long shadow, even to the extent of impelling investors and those who advise them to discard the results of their own beloved mathematical processes; a classic example of altering reality to fit one's beliefs, rather than the

[9] de Groot and Swinkels (2008) already cited suggests for example mistrusting these numbers and using the volatility of Emerging Markets as a proxy for "uncertainty" instead, or even asking pension trustees to express their own subjective assessment.

other way around. Here again, the contrast with business school students, who come to this issue with open minds, is striking. The latter will almost at once say "but it all depends what you mean by 'risk' and 'return', surely?" Quite.

Liquidity

This is the third of the problems which the traditional investor's worldview poses to Alternative Assets, and is by far the most powerful. Though John Maynard Keynes first denounced "the fetish of liquidity" as long ago as 1936[10] it remains alive and well, as the events of September 2008 demonstrated all too clearly. The traditional investor's obsession with liquidity was described a little earlier, and while one would expect this to pose problems for clearly illiquid asset classes such as real estate and private equity, it seems to affect others too.

Intellectual inconsistency seems to be one of the hallmarks of the traditional investor. For what could be more liquid than currency, which is after all money? Yet active currency rarely features in the list of portfolio candidates. Nor does physical gold, which is arguably more liquid still. Even if a particular currency ceased to have any perceived value then gold would still be capable of being turned instantly into some other currency since it has a well-recognised intrinsic value of its own. It is not for nothing that it is known as a currency without a country.

These two exceptions aside, all the Alternative Assets which we will be considering in this book are illiquid to some extent or other. At the illiquid end of the spectrum we find the "private" asset types such as private equity, private real estate and private infrastructure. At the other end of the scale would come commodities and energy, which are publicly traded, yet for practical purposes often come in the shape of derivative instruments which arguably cannot be regarded as truly liquid since they carry some small yet undeniable counterparty risk. Somewhere in the middle come the likes of hedge funds, which many investors prior to the crisis treated as being liquid, but found to their cost were nothing of the sort.[11]

So, if investors are going to impose a requirement that all the investments in their portfolio must be fully liquid, then this will greatly restrict the range of investments which they are able to consider, and

---

[10] *The General Theory of Employment, Interest and Money*, BN Publishing, London, 2008 but originally published in 1936.

[11] At least, not in abnormal market conditions, which is arguably exactly when you need liquidity the most.

certainly spell trouble for our efforts to interest them in alternatives in general. Fortunately, however, a gradual realisation is dawning that even within the confines of traditional finance theory (1) the traditionally perceived need for liquidity is misconceived and (2) that there are good reasons for holding illiquid assets. In addition, some aspects of liquidity were exposed by the crisis the existence of which had been hitherto unsuspected.

How Much Liquidity do You Really Need?

An investor's need for liquidity should be driven by the nature of their liabilities. After all, the purpose of liquidity is to be able to generate cash at a moment's notice, so if you are not likely to have any need for cash for the next few years then you do not need liquidity. To take an extreme example, suppose that the investor in question is a trust fund which has been established for a baby a few weeks after its birth and which is legally prevented by the terms of the trust deed from making any payments until the child is at least 21 years old. Clearly there will be no need for cash for many years, and therefore no need for liquidity.

On the other hand, if an insurance company is writing cover against risks such as fire, accident and terrorism then it is impossible to predict when liabilities will arise. It is quite possible that some terrible disaster could occur tomorrow which would result in a large and immediate need for cash. Here, liquidity clearly *is* necessary.

Unfortunately traditional investors seem unable to grasp this simple principle. If your liabilities are long term and/or predictable then you may actually need very little liquidity at all. If, by contrast, your liabilities are short term and/or unpredictable then you may need a great deal of liquidity. In short, liquidity is a tool, and like all tools it is designed to do a specific job, namely generating instant cash on demand. It is not an end in itself.

Yet this is exactly how most of the world's investors see it, not to mention regulatory bodies. The prevailing principle seems to be "as long as you've got liquidity then you're in good shape", but sadly this is not necessarily true. Indeed, as we will see below, it can in some cases be very damaging to have liquidity – at least, too much liquidity, more liquidity than you actually need.

In general, life insurance companies, pension funds, family offices, endowments, foundations and Sovereign Wealth Funds will be long term investors, while the likes of banks, non-life insurance companies and corporate treasury departments will be short term. Whatever label is attached to a particular investor, though, it is essential that they model their liabilities, find out just how much liquidity they need, and hold that amount but no more. No more, since from an investment point of view liquidity is actually a bad thing that should be avoided, not a good thing to be sought out.

The Illiquidity Premium

Question: Why does an investor consider holding illiquid assets within their portfolio?

Answer: Because they expect them to deliver a higher long term return than liquid assets.

This principle is well recognised even by traditional finance, which has dubbed it "the illiquidity premium". Since you are being asked to give something away (liquidity) then you are entitled to expect to be paid something to compensate you for what you have given away. That something is a higher return. So, the rationale for investing in illiquid asset types is that should a sensible investor have some part of their portfolio in respect of which they do not require short term liquidity (and this will be true of most investors if they analyse their situation honestly), then they should give up this unnecessary liquidity against the expectation of a higher long term return.

So, as David Swensen of the Yale Endowment points out,[12] having too much liquidity in your portfolio is expensive. It is costing you money in the shape of those extra returns which you should be enjoying, but on which you are losing out. By the way, Swensen puts his money where his mouth is; at any one time Yale are typically about two thirds illiquid.

To pursue this argument to its logical conclusion, if there were no criteria other than long term investment returns then you would not actually have *any* liquid assets in your portfolio at all. You would be entirely invested in the likes of private equity, real estate and so on. Of course there always *will* be other criteria in practice, but this can be a good way of getting the message across should you find yourself addressing a room full of traditional investors.

So, the principle of the illiquidity premium is well known. Unfortunately, many seem to believe that you can take some bits of traditional finance theory (the bits which suit your immediate purposes) and leave the other bits (the inconvenient bits which might force you to change your approach) behind. This approach of turning a blind eye to awkward problems is coming under ever more strain, too, since there

---

[12] Swensen, *Pioneering Portfolio Management, Second Edition*, Pocket Books, New York, 2009.

are some problems with liquidity which since the crisis have become just too obvious to ignore.

PROBLEMS WITH LIQUIDITY

Imagine the stock market as the sun sitting in the middle of the solar system. It exerts a powerful gravitational pull, which grows weaker the further away from the sun you are situated. We call this gravitational pull "beta". Beta is the extent to which the stock market will go up and down of its own accord and in the process drag up and down the individual stocks which comprise it. For example, should you hear on the news one evening that the Dow Jones index in New York closed up sharply on the day, then it is highly likely that almost all of the individual companies which make up the Dow Jones index also closed up. As the Americans say, "a rising tide lifts all boats".

So, if the FTSE 100 index in London were to be the sun, then all its 100 constituent company shares would be clustered around it in a very tight orbit. A little further out, but still strongly influenced by it, would be the other companies which make up the London Stock Exchange but which are not big enough to make it into the top 100. So too, incidentally would be various other major stock markets such as New York.

Certain asset classes, such as private equity and real estate have lingered towards the outer part of the solar system,[13] while certain assets, most notably gold, seem to have broken free of the sun's pull altogether and gone wandering off into space to pursue meandering courses of their own.

Again, this effect is well recognised. A financial model known as the Capital Asset Pricing Model (CAPM) was developed in the early 1950s by Harry Markowitz, for example, to measure the extent to which any individual share was affected by the beta of its own stock market, and this was developed by others such as Sharpe in the 1960s. There is an important point to note here, by the way. CAPM was developed to measure the relative volatility of any single stock within a portfolio of similar stocks, *not* to compare different asset types against each other.

What was not well recognised until the recent crisis was the extent to which stock market beta could dramatically (and, some would argue, artificially) affect both volatility and correlation. Since this is the first time we have encountered the concept of correlation, let us leave this point until last, not least because it happens to represent perhaps the strongest argument of all for investing in alternative assets.

---

[13]Measured on historic figures.

The Stock Market Goes Supernova

There are actually two gravitational pulls operating within a star, one inward and the other outward, and for the vast majority of a star's life the two hold each other perfectly in check. However, the outward pressure requires the constant expenditure of fuel and towards the end of a star's life the fuel begins to run out and the inward pressure takes command. It is almost as though this is what happened to stock markets around the world as we went through 2008; the force pulling everything towards and into them suddenly became very much greater.

This had very serious implications for those who had sought to capture exposure to illiquid alternative assets through a liquid vehicle, such as a publicly quoted company. One example, using notional figures but based on what actually happened to 3i, will serve to illustrate the point. 3i is to all intents and purposes a quoted, open-ended private equity fund, but it also just happens to be one of the constituents of the FTSE 100 index.

Let us assume that in early 2007 3i's net asset value was 100, and it was trading at a premium to net assets of 30%. In other words, its share price was 130. Incidentally, it should be noted both that many investors had sought exposure to private equity by investing in such vehicles, and that historic performance had in general been very satisfactory.

What happened during the crisis was that 3i reduced the value of its assets by about 18%.[14] So, assuming they had been 100 they had now declined to 82. However, 3i's share price had fallen 78% during the year to March 2009, and much more than that from the peak. So, let us assume that the share price would now be 22% of 130, which is less than 29, a 65% *discount* to net asset value. In other words, rather than going down relative to the value of its assets, it had been dragged down by stock market beta. Similar examples could be found in other types of alternative assets, most notably real estate.[15]

Liquidity and Volatility

This has the very obvious effect of greatly increasing the volatility of an investor's portfolio. Suppose that they had held the equivalent of 3i's assets but through a private (unquoted) vehicle such as a limited partnership. Based on the audited accounts, the investor would have suffered an annual loss of 18% (the fall in asset values). However,

---

[14] 3i Annual Report as at March 2009.
[15] There were other problems with this approach as well, which will be discussed in later chapters.

holding exactly the same assets through a quoted company would have cost the investor an annual loss of 78% (the fall in the share price).

In other words, what the events of 2008 showed us, by grossly magnifying the effects, was that the more liquidity you want in a portfolio then the more volatility you must be prepared to accept. The stated intention of seeking both high levels of liquidity and low levels of volatility is impossible. This is a bitter pill for traditional investors to have to swallow, and they are still struggling with how to digest it. After all, volatility is risk, and private equity had always been seen as much "higher risk" than investing on the stock market!

It is here that we can clearly see the result of a mistaken view of liquidity. Unless one actually needs to be able to turn the assets in question into cash at a moment's notice, then if volatility is a concern, one is arguably better off investing in an illiquid vehicle. Choosing the liquid option should not be a knee jerk reaction, but a considered decision. There are in fact benefits to illiquidity, not just in the expectation of higher long term returns but also in the possibility of acting as a damper on oscillating asset values.

Liquidity and Correlation

Volatility and correlation are often confused with each other, but in fact are very different. Volatility measures the extent to which any asset or market goes up and down over time. Whether individual or collective, though, it is only measuring what happens to one set of returns. If you want to measure the volatility of two different shares, you have to perform two separate calculations and arrive at two different answers.

Correlation looks at both shares, and measures the extent to which they go up and down to the same extent at the same time as each other. So, volatility measures how *one* thing behaves in isolation, whereas correlation measures how *two* things behave relative to each other. If both shares go up at the same time, that is positive correlation. If one share goes up while at the same time the other share goes down, that is negative correlation. If the two appear to zoom about in an entirely random way, without seeming to affect each other at all, that is zero correlation.

Obviously any time the stock market exerts a gravitational pull on assets, it is prompting them to behave in the same way as itself at the same time, just as in the 3i-based example above. For reasons we will explore in a moment, many investors are now seeking to limit the amount of stock market beta which they have within their portfolio. Investing in quoted vehicles which will tend to move up and down with the market is therefore a bad idea, since you are simply adding, not subtracting stock market beta. Again, this is a difficult message for traditional investors to absorb, since they have always assumed that liquidity is desirable as an end in itself. Yet, just as liquidity tends to increase volatility, so (at least in the case of stock market beta) it also seems to increase correlation. So, just why is the concept of correlation so important?

Extending the Efficient Frontier

The concept of the efficient frontier is again well recognised by traditional finance. It takes the form of a diagonal line, representing the best possible outcome of the relationship between "risk" (volatility) and return. If you think of all the portfolios in the world which generate a return of 4.3%, then somewhere there must be one that has the lowest standard deviation. That one sits on the efficient frontier, while all the others will sit beside it, stretching off into higher and higher standard deviations (remember that this is a measure of volatility and hence also of "risk"). Now think of all the portfolios in the world which have a standard deviation of 11%. There must be one of them which provides the highest possible return, and this one sits on the efficient frontier, with all the others sitting below it, at lower levels of return. So for any given level of return there will always be one portfolio which exhibits the lowest level of risk; and for any given level of risk there will always be one portfolio which gives the highest return.

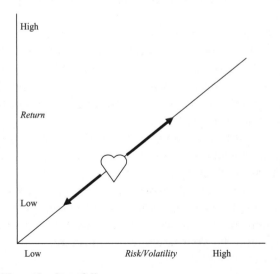

Figure 2.1   The optimal portfolio

A rational investor should always strive to achieve the optimal portfolio which sits on the Efficient Frontier, irrespective of their chosen level of risk or return. To do otherwise would be illogical. Either you would be taking extra risk for which you were not receiving any corresponding extra return ("unrewarded risk"), or you would be receiving a lower level of return than might otherwise be the case by selecting a different mix of assets without increasing the overall risk of your portfolio.

Note here that under this classical view of risk and return you can theoretically slide your optimal portfolio up and down the line. You can "de-risk" by selling highly volatile assets and replacing them with less volatile ones, provided you are prepared to accept a lower rate of return. Similarly, you can chase higher returns but only if you are prepared to accept higher levels of volatility.

During the 1960s, however, a subversive thought began to pervade the corridors of finance faculties. Suppose that it might be possible to extend the Efficient Frontier? Suppose that instead of moving up and to the right in search of higher returns, it might be possible to move straight upwards, or even up and to the left?

Traditional finance of course says this is impossible. Once you have arrived at the optimal asset mix within your portfolio then by definition this cannot be improved upon. Yes, you can go in search of higher returns, but only at the cost of incurring extra risk. Except that actually you can. Note here that we say "can". It will not happen in every case, but it can happen from time to time, and all sorts of considerations come into play, not least over what period you calculate your returns, how you calculate them and how frequently. Nonetheless it *can* happen.

A practical example is oil and natural gas, at which we look in more detail in the chapter on energy. Both individually are high volatility assets with very low Sharpe Ratios. Yet it is possible to create a blended historic portfolio of the two which shows both a higher return than either asset individually, and lower volatility. In other words, it *is* possible to extend the efficient frontier.

You can see just how exciting this is as a concept. If you can get it right then you can find a totally new asset to add to your portfolio, which will increase your returns at no extra cost (in terms of higher risk). Similarly, if you are already comfortably hitting your target rate of return, you might try to add a new asset which will help you still generate the same return, but with less risk, and thus a higher probability of continuing to hit your target return in future.

So how does it work?

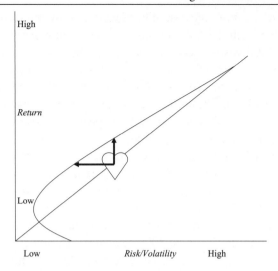

Figure 2.2   Extending the efficient frontier

Correlation

It works because the traditional view of finance only looks at two dimensions (risk and return) and ignores the third, which is correlation. Actually, as we have already noted, there is a fourth dimension as well – time – which using periodic rather than compound returns effectively ignores, but let that be. Correlation, it turns out, is really crucial.

When looking at new assets to add to a portfolio with a view to extending the efficient frontier, the two criteria for a successful candidate seem to be that it has (1) at least the same return potential as and (2) low correlation with what is sitting within the portfolio already. Hence what has become known as the search for uncorrelated returns. The oil and gas example, for instance, works because these two assets have historically exhibited very low correlation with each other.

We have seen that all quoted equity type assets seem to exhibit very high correlation as a result of stock market beta. This has two important consequences for alternative assets.

The first relates to good, old-fashioned diversification. Even if one ignores highfalutin finance theory, it is simple common sense to have a diversified portfolio rather than being horribly exposed to the risk of just one asset type (common sense, though, which has been ignored by many investors). Just as holding a sufficient number of individual stocks will diversify away the risk of any one individual stock, so the same holds true of a portfolio of different asset types. In the former case, you may be able to diversify the risk of holding one individual stock but you will still be left with the risk of holding equities in general.

Traditionally investors have sought to diversify their equity risk by holding equities from different countries, but this is frankly foolish. The S&P and FTSE indices in the US and the UK respectively have historically exhibited about 90% correlation. Thus, you are not removing any stock market beta from your portfolio. All you are doing is adding unnecessary and unrewarded US dollar risk.

For, just as with liquidity and volatility, investors have not really grasped the essential truth. Diversification is not about buying something different. It is about buying something which is likely to behave differently within your portfolio. In fact, in direct contrast to the traditional approach, which might have a 20% allocation to something labelled "US equities" and a 30% allocation to something labelled "fixed income", it matters not at all what something is called, but only how it will behave. Some Infrastructure projects, for example, have much the same investment characteristics as a government bond.

So in order to achieve any real diversification, one is forced to step outside the world of bonds and equities into the more complex world of alternative assets. It simply is not possible to achieve satisfactory diversification in any other way. Nor is it enough to dabble a toe in the water by means of some very small (3%?) allocation. Each allocation to a particular asset type must be meaningful, which almost certainly means at least 10% and ideally quite a lot more. The Yale Model famously features roughly equal allocations to four or five different asset types. An allocation of 10% is most unlikely to have any significant impact on the portfolio as a whole. In addition, investors tend not to take small allocations seriously, failing to give them the time, money and resources which they demand in order to be pursued successfully.

Similarly, in any quest to extend the efficient frontier, an investor is quickly forced to look beyond their traditional back garden. Quoted equities will fail the low correlation test, while most bonds will fail the potential return test, and those that may not are likely to carry very high levels of default risk. So, just as in the search for diversification, the investor has no option but to consider alternative assets. As already noted, one proven example of the ability to extend the efficient frontier will be demonstrated in the chapter on energy.

In fact, most of the alternative assets described in this book have historically demonstrated low correlation with quoted equities,[16]

---

[16] See Fraser-Sampson, Multi Asset Class Investment Strategy, John Wiley & Sons, Chichester, 2006.

although care needs to be taken here. First, most of the work which has been done, and certainly that in the author's own 2006 book (see footnote), has focused on UK performance figures, particularly for things like Real Estate, for which there were at that no time no reliable data available in other countries. However, it seems unlikely that similar patterns of correlation will occur in every country, and so care should be taken to analyse local domestic data wherever possible. There is at least a strong belief, for example, that in certain Asian markets there may be very high correlation between real estate and quoted equities.

Second, measuring correlation for a period ending in 2007 and then again for a period ending in 2008 demonstrated some dramatic differences, with certain asset classes, notably private equity and real estate, showing suddenly higher numbers. It seems undeniable that during 2008 quoted equities, in falling, dragged the returns of a lot of other asset types down with them, the only exceptions appearing to be gold and active currency.[17] There were those who pointed to this as evidence of a structural shift in financial markets, or even of belief in uncorrelated returns having been nothing more than a myth.

Almost certainly, neither of these claims are true. What happened at times during 2008 was panic selling of everything except T-Bill type instruments in a frenzied flight to liquidity. If everything is being sold at the same time, then it is little wonder that the price of everything should head downwards at the same time. This combines with the supernova effect which we noted earlier to create what the author has referred to in speeches and interviews as "man-made correlation".

As for basic belief in uncorrelated returns, this should for the moment remain unshaken; although final judgement must be reserved for a few years to see whether the pattern of 2008 might be repeated. Even if it were, however, the point bears repeating that had your portfolio contained physical gold and active currency, then at least two of your four or five asset types would have shown positive returns.

ACTIVE AND PASSIVE INVESTING –
BETA AND ALPHA

The existence of both beta and alpha returns in respect of many asset types opens up the intriguing question of the rival claims of passive and active investing. Note the word "many". There are some asset types, most notably private equity, where no recognised beta exists, and an investor therefore has no alternative but to adopt an active (alpha-seeking) approach. Briefly, a passive investor is happy to accept

---

[17] As measured by the Deutsche Bank active currency index.

the beta return, the return of the market or asset type as a whole, whereas an active investor seeks to go one better by choosing the best performing assets or managers.

By way of example, if an investor was seeking coverage of UK quoted equities, then the passive investor would be happy to buy a fund which tracked the FTSE 100 index, while the passive investor would seek to "stock pick" the shares of those companies which they thought likely to out-perform the market, or hire a manager to do this for them.

So there is an important difference between a passive investment manager and an active investment manager. The passive manager has no choice as to which investments to select. Their obligation is to match the beta return with as little "tracking error" as possible, hence the description of funds which do this as "tracker" funds. Thus, in our chosen example, the passive manager would simply check which companies currently made up the FTSE index, and in what proportions, and then simply reproduce ("replicate") that mix within their own portfolio. The active manager, on the other hand, would be free to choose from within the index, even to the extent of excluding some companies altogether, since their objective would be not to match the index performance but to exceed it. For this reason, alpha can often be referred to as "manager performance".

It is only fair to note that most of the world's investors display something close to an obsession with active investment, which can even extend to the world of bonds, surely one of the most extreme examples of investor irrationality. One does not hold bonds as an investment, but to match certain liabilities, or perhaps as a hedge against inflation. One is not seeking an investment type return, a real return after inflation, since bonds cannot be relied upon to produce this anyway. Why, then, risk not achieving even the risk-free rate of return by seeking alpha?

There are two things which need to be understood about alpha. First, there is no guarantee that it will be higher than beta, but only that it will be different; it is quite possible that it may be lower. Second, alpha is much more expensive than beta, since active managers charge higher fees than passive managers. Thus, it is actually more likely that an active manager will under-perform beta since they must first earn back the higher fee. Indeed, as Sharpe pointed out some years ago,[18] if one assumes investment, or at least quoted equities investment, to be a zero sum game, then it is a logical impossibility for any active manager consistently to out-perform on a "net of fees" basis.[19] Strangely, while Sharpe's famous ratio constitutes Holy Writ for investors and their

[18] Sharpe, The Arithmetic of Active Management, *The Financial Analysts' Journal*, Vol 47, No 1, 1991.
[19] See the chapter on active currency for a discussion of the "zero sum game" concept.

advisers, his compelling arguments against active management have been widely ignored.

A full discussion of active versus passive investment lies well beyond the scope of this book, and may ultimately come down to the matter of individual temperament. In the author's view, the basic problem here is that, as we have seen, most investors do not actually know what their target rate of return is, or should be, and thus have no way of determining (even if the question were actually to occur to them in the first place) whether they can happily accept the beta return, or need to go off chasing alpha.

It is submitted that in accessing any asset type for possible inclusion within a portfolio, the first question should be whether a beta return can be identified, and whether that return, at least when measured historically, appears likely at least to match one's target rate of return. If it does not, then it seems more logical to reject it in favour of some other asset type whose beta returns appear more promising, rather than importing extra risk into one's portfolio by hitching the success or failure of your investment programme to the fortunes of alpha-seeking managers.

There is an important qualification to the phrase "at least when measured historically", since this book is rightly critical of those who believe that the past is a good guide to the future. This procedure should be carried out intelligently. Where there are obvious indications that structural change may have occurred within certain asset types, markets or investment thinking or practice, then we cannot blindly adopt historical data; a good example of this occurs in the chapter on private equity. However, at least as a starting point for strategic discussion, historical data are all we have.

Caution should also be exercised not just in respect of the actual data, but in the way in which is the data are treated, in particular in the way in which returns are calculated. Periodic returns such as annual returns, and in particular "annualised" (average) returns can greatly distort the true picture over time, since they ignore the time value of money. Compound returns (IRRs) should *always* be run, even if only as a sanity check. Should there be a significant discrepancy between the two approaches, an intelligent investor will sit down and think about just what such a difference may be illustrating.

In identifying a beta return, there are some important questions to be asked. Is it "representative"? In other words, does it give a proper picture of the performance of a particular market or asset type? Is it "investable"? In other words, can it be replicated within a fund or portfolio, or is there some other way of investing in it, perhaps by way of synthetic (derivative) exposure?

If the first question cannot be answered in the affirmative then it raises serious questions about the validity of using it as any sort of indication of likely performance. If the second cannot be answered in the affirmative then passive investing will not be possible and an investor will, thus, be forced to accept manager risk, which extra risk will logically require an expectation of extra return to compensate for it.

For these reasons, we will find ourselves considering, in respect of each alternative asset, what measures of beta return are available and to what extent these may be said to be both representative and investable. We will see that commodities, for example, seem to raise a fundamental problem of acceptable return levels, while Hedge Funds indices raise problems both of "representation" and "investability".

THE RATIONALE FOR ALTERNATIVE ASSETS

Hopefully the harsh experience of the financial crisis will have finally brought home the message that one cannot simply hold bonds and equities in one's portfolio.

Bonds, at least of the blue chip government variety, are not an "investment". They cannot produce any sort of investment return. Even the belief that they provide an automatic hedge against inflation is incorrect. There have been periods, for example, when the real return on UK government bonds has been negative for a decade or more. This expectation also ignores taxation. If you are a tax-payer, then bonds can never provide protection against inflation. Holding bonds in your portfolio is best thought of as driving your car with the handbrake on.

If you are, say, 120% funded relative to your liabilities, whatever form they might take, and you are comfortable that the various assumptions you have made will remain valid for ever, then perhaps you might hold bonds and sleep easily. In any other circumstances, holding bonds is a very dangerous thing to do, as they will make it progressively more difficult, as one year succeeds another, that you will *ever* be in a position to meet your liabilities. To achieve this requires the earning of some level of true investment return, an excess return after the combined effects of inflation and taxation. This is why investors hold equities.

With return comes risk, however, and let us assume for the sake of argument that this may be expressed by volatility, for this is after all what traditional investors believe and so it seems only fair to apply their own beliefs to their own portfolios. In so doing, the illogicality of their position becomes apparent at once. For if you believe that volatility is a bad thing, why would you want to burden yourself with one huge bucket of risk which, when it produces strongly negative returns, is going dramatically to reduce the value of your whole portfolio? Surely any rational investor would prefer to have four or five small buckets of risk, all of which will hopefully produce different levels of return at the same time?

Diversification away from equities – true diversification, that is – is impossible without involving at least some of the asset types which we will be considering in this book. This poses considerable challenges, since levels of knowledge about them are currently very low, and investors are understandably nervous of venturing into what seems such complex and exotic territory for the first time. As we have just demonstrated, however, they no longer have a choice.

SUMMARY

The traditional investor's view of the world envisages that the risk of any investment may be expressed by the volatility of its historic return, customarily expressed as one standard deviation. Implicit in this view are the assumptions (1) that normal distribution will always apply and (2) that the past is a good guide to the future.

Volatility ("risk") is seen as a bad thing to be avoided, since it expresses uncertainty of outcome. Traditional investors therefore strive to have as little volatility as possible within their portfolio consistent with their chosen level of return.

A sense of the potential "risk adjusted" return of any asset or asset type can be gained from the Sharpe Ratio, which expresses the excess return relative to the standard deviation of the excess return.

It follows that for any chosen level of risk (volatility) there will be an optimal portfolio which delivers the highest possible level of return. Similarly, for any chosen level of return there will be an optimal portfolio which exhibits the lowest possible degree of risk.

The traditional investor is obsessed with the need for liquidity, and will seek to have as much of it as possible in their portfolio, for example, in the shape of quoted equities and/or restricting their exposure to illiquid asset types to that which is available through quoted vehicles.

Unfortunately, experience has shown that the effect of stock market beta (the gravitational pull of stock market returns) will tend to produce volatility. This creates a paradox for the traditional investor, who now has two contradictory and mutually incompatible desires.

The investor also faces a choice between passive and active investment in each asset area. Passive investing seeks to track the beta return, while active investing chases alpha, which should logically be different, though not necessarily higher. Sharpe argues strongly in favour of passive investing where possible. Most investors are unable to resolve this issue, however, as they have never ascertained what their target rate of investment return is, or should be.

The traditional view of investment tends to ignore correlation, the extent to which two assets will behave similarly or differently to each other at the same time. This is a bad mistake, since true diversification is impossible without low correlation. In some circumstances, low correlation also makes it possible to "extend the efficient frontier", producing a portfolio which offers a higher level of return for the same level of risk, or a lower level of risk for the same return.

For both these reasons, exposure to alternative assets is impossible to avoid. The challenge facing investors, therefore, is to gain knowledge of the intricacies of these asset types and confidence in deploying them within a truly diversified portfolio.

3
Real Estate

The terms "real estate" and "property" are used synonymously to describe this asset class, the former being of American derivation and the latter British. As with most investment terms, the American version is increasingly being adopted around the world, and will for the most part be used in this book. It is in any event more strictly accurate since "property", in addition to having some meanings that have nothing to do with ownership of assets at all, covers two main types of assets. "Real property" is restricted to freehold interests in land, while "personal property" covers everything else, including property held on lease, no matter how long the term.

Let us dive straight into these terms, since they are important. A freehold interest represents absolute ownership of property or, more properly, land. Out of any freehold interest can be created a lease for a term of (usually) years. Out of this lease can be created a sub-lease which must be shorter, even if only by one day, than the superior lease. Out of this sub-lease can be created a sub-sub-lease, and so on. The difference is that the freeholder is and remains the owner of the land, while any leaseholder, no matter how long their interest, has only the right to occupy and use the land. Should a leaseholder commit any serious or persistent breach, then the freeholder will usually have the right, subject to certain procedural requirements, to bring the lease to an end, a process known as "forfeiture".

In Islamic law jurisdictions, the situation has been slightly less clear-cut, partly because the prime document of reference is the Holy Koran, and different judges can, and do, interpret the same passage in different ways, partly because, unlike under Anglo-Saxon legal systems, precedent is merely persuasive, not binding. After the fall of Constantinople in 1453, we know that the system of Islamic law introduced by the victorious Mehmed II did not recognise individual ownership of land on any sort of freehold basis. However, it could be argued that Mehmed's code was actually in advance of the West. In England at the same time, for example, all land belonged ultimately to the crown, whereas under the Ottomans it at least belonged to the state treasury, rather than to the ruler personally.

Yet Islamic law has always included the concept of "ijara", which any Western lawyer would recognise instantly as a lease, and in any event this is becoming something of a redundant issue as Islamic countries increasingly adopt Western-style property laws in order to facilitate modern real estate transactions and development; the Dubai freehold law of 2006 would be a good example. Of more current importance is that certain Islamic countries still do not recognise the principle of a mortgage, or of equitable interests.

A mortgage is a legal charge over property by way of security, usually requiring registration in some public records office, not, as is commonly believed, the loan which it secures. For this reason the borrower is called the mortgagor (the person who grants the mortgage), not the mortgagee (the person to whom it is granted). Islamic lawyers seek to arrive at the same practical result by different means. Usually the bank will actually buy the property from the vendor and then re-sell it to the purchaser at a higher price, since Islamic (Sharia) law prohibits the taking of interest.

The non-recognition of equitable interests represents a rather trickier matter. Ownership of property is actually broken into two under Western systems: legal and equitable. Usually both types of ownership sit simultaneously with the same person, but they can be split. The legal owner has the right to be registered as the owner of the property and to enter into any transactions concerning it, including its sale or mortgage. However, the equitable owner is the beneficial owner, the one who has the right actually to receive the proceeds of its sale. The most obvious example of this is where someone holds property in trust: the trustee will be the legal owner, while the beneficiary will be the equitable owner.

One important consequence of this is that an equitable interest can be bought and sold in its own right, subject to any contractual limitations, leaving the legal ownership in the same hands. Another is that there is a whole class of remedies available under Anglo-Saxon legal systems which depend on the recognition of equitable interests: these would include, for example, restitution, tracing and constructive trusts. In practice this problem is usually avoided by having the relevant documentation subject to, say, English law and the jurisdiction of the English courts, though this does in turn raise the issue of being able to enforce any English judgment in the country in question.

There is just one more attribute of Real Estate to note before we move on, and that is the concept of privity of estate. We have all heard of privity of contract, the notion that only a party to a contract may sue upon it; thus, if someone buys you a washing machine as a present and it proves defective, it is that person who must sue the shop who sold it to them, not you. With both freehold and leasehold property, it is different. The current owner of any interest takes legal responsibility for any acts committed or omitted by their predecessors. Thus, it is not unusual to find a tenant (lessee) at the end of their lease term being sued for dilapidations (damage to the property during the term of the lease beyond what may be considered fair wear and tear) which were actually caused by a previous tenant. For this reason, an indemnity is commonly taken on the assignment of any interest.

It is these four characteristics – the right to grant binding legal security over many property interests, the right to grant inferior or shorter interests to third parties, the division of ownership into legal and equitable, and the fact that rights and obligations "run with the land" – which set real estate apart from other asset classes and which facilitate a wide range of property transactions. Furthermore, the complexity of property interests and transactions continues to grow and develop, as we will see when we look at the exciting new area of synthetic exposure to real estate.

REAL ESTATE BETA

Thinking back to our discussion of beta returns in Chapter 2, it may at first sight seem that no property market beta could possibly exist. After all, if it did then it would have to encompass, or at least represent, a slice of the return that could be made on every individual building within a given area (whether country, region or whatever), and such a concept is difficult to envisage. Even if this were possible, then it would also have to be investable, and this seems equally hard to imagine. In fact, as we will see, this is almost true but not quite.

Let us deal with the first point first. The surprising truth is that until very recently, with the honourable exception of the UK, there were no reliable property indices available around the world, not even in the United States. "Reliable" in the sense of covering the whole market, and being designed to represent the actual performance of the market, rather than merely being prepared for client advisory purposes. Even where indices existed, they were not uniform, either in the type of property which they represented (commercial, residential, etc.), the type of return which they covered (capital gain, rental yield or total return), or in their methodology (valuation based, transaction based, etc.). This is now changing as IPD, the UK index provider, is rolling out their product on a global basis: but most of their non-UK indices are as yet still very young, and will take some time to reach the levels of maturity, sophistication and reliability of the flagship product in the UK.

So, in the UK there is, and has been for many years, an index which is acceptably representative of the whole market, but this is not yet true of any other market in the world. Real estate insiders reckon that Canada and France (at least for office buildings) are probably closest behind the UK in the journey towards a true beta return measure, but other countries may take much longer to achieve this. In the UK, for example, the index began in 1981 and is estimated to cover 61% of total market value, whereas in Japan it began only in 2003 and covers just 17% of the market.[1]

For the record, the IPD index methodology is uniform around the world, and is based on valuations submitted quarterly by independent valuers retained by investors, including funds. A property must be revalued at least once a year to remain in the index. It also takes into account rental yields, and is therefore a total return index.

The IPD index is not truly "investable" in the sense that it cannot be replicated, and thus neither can a tracker fund portfolio be constructed. However, as we will see when we come to consider synthetic exposure later in this chapter, it can be the subject of various derivative instruments, and thus it is possible to invest for a beta return, but with two important short term limitations.

The first has already been mentioned; at present, beta-seeking investors are effectively limited to the UK.[2] The second is that thus far the volume of the market, though growing steadily, is still fairly limited. According to IPD data, by the end of 2009 there were on average about 100 UK derivative trades being executed each quarter, at an average value of about £10 million. Thus, for really large investors this is not really a realistic option (as yet).

It follows then, as we move to discuss the different ways of obtaining exposure to real estate, that all of them except synthetic coverage deal with alpha returns, not beta (at least, not real estate beta!).

REAL ESTATE EXPOSURE

Investors can access real estate directly (by buying land and buildings) or in one of three indirect ways: quoted, unquoted and synthetic. Quoted and unquoted can themselves each be divided. In addition, gridlines representing the type and location of property may be overlaid on all of these four avenues to produce an even more complex picture. Let us consider these various areas in turn.

---

[1] All figures from RBS as at January 2009.
[2] Very small markets exist for France and Germany, but none elsewhere – not even Canada or the United States.

Direct

The most traditional method of investing in real estate is simply to go out and buy the stuff. There are references to investing in property to be found in the Old Testament, and with the exception of gold it is probably the oldest surviving[3] asset class for investment purposes. Certainly by the Middle Ages it was widespread. Eleanor of Castile, for example, was publicly portrayed as a much-loved consort to Edward I of England. It is to her that various English places owe the "Cross" at the end of their names to signify that they were the locations of Eleanor Crosses built to commemorate the passage of her cortège, the best known of which is Charing Cross in London. In reality, she was hated by the population in consequence of a lifetime of rapacious property acquisition, often facilitated by the surprisingly modern practice of buying up somebody's debts and then foreclosing on their property.

The Direct approach has the benefit of certainty and, some would argue, simplicity although "straightforwardness" would probably be a better word; you know that you own a particular office block rather than an interest in some pooled vehicle. You can have your surveyors and valuers check the building out. You can negotiate, with your lawyers, exactly the terms on which you wish to buy it. You can decide how much to borrow as part of the purchase price. Furthermore, since investment undeniably operates on a largely psychological basis on many occasions, let us also note that a certain type of investor derives emotional comfort from the knowledge that they own an identifiable single building; these are often referred to as "real asset" investors.

It is also subject to various disadvantages. For a start, bricks and mortar are illiquid and to some investors this is an important drawback. The importance may well be mistaken, but it is real nonetheless. So, anyone obsessed with liquidity is not going to favour the direct option.

It takes time. In fact, it can take a lot of time (maybe three years or more) to build a portfolio if one wishes to do so at one's leisure, able to pick and choose between what is on offer. For investors who are looking to hit their target asset allocations quickly, this can seem like a long wait.

Finally, for anyone other than a very large investor indeed it is almost impossible to arrive at a diversified portfolio. Even ignoring geographic diversification, since most investors are strangely reluctant to invest outside their own country, some institutional investors may be so small

---

[3] Slaves and ivory having fallen by the wayside.

that they can afford to buy only two or three buildings. These may all be office blocks in a particular city, thus failing to give coverage across different sectors. Even worse, this fails to diversify away the risk of holding any one particular building. For example, rental yield forms an important part of property returns, and a "void" (a period when the building is remaining empty, without a tenant) can hurt you badly if it takes away a third or even half of your rental income.[4] Thus, it is only truly large investors (typically Sovereign Wealth Funds and the largest pension funds) for whom direct real estate is really a viable option.

Quoted

Investors can access real estate through two main different types of quoted vehicles: shares in property companies and REITs. As will shortly be seen, there other types of investment vehicle, such as unit trust and OEIC type structures, which might technically be considered "quoted", in that prices for their units are publicly quoted, but which fall to be considered under "unquoted" as they are not exchange traded.

This is a valid approach, since it is this very quality which bestows the main perceived advantage of quoted vehicles, namely liquidity. For those who seek exposure to illiquid assets and yet crave the fetish of liquidity, such an approach seems an ideal compromise. As we have already noted elsewhere, this belief is mistaken. Yet, like all beliefs which have hardened into dogma, it is likely long to persist.

Quoted (1): Property Companies

Traditionally, many investors have sought to access real estate by buying shares (stocks) in property companies. As became tragically clear during the financial crisis which began to unfold in mid-2007, but had actually been apparent for some time,[5] this approach has two major flaws.

The first is that what you are buying is not a proxy for land but, at least in large part, an operating business which is subject to all the usual business risks. British Land, for example, which forms the largest holding in some "property" ETFs, is much more than a property portfolio. They carry out major development projects, participate in joint

---

[4] Voids will occur naturally even in well-managed portfolios and with high quality tenants, since the building will need periodic refurbishment; also, rent-free periods are often agreed at the commencement of commercial leases to allow for tenants' own works to take place.

[5] See for example the writer's own *Multi Asset Class Investment Strategy*, already cited, at page 188. This passage was written in 2005.

ventures, and also run a fund management business, all of which form part of what is represented by a share in the company.

The second is that what you are actually buying is an equity (a share or stock), and equities are perceived and treated very differently by investors than are, say, real estate assets.

For one thing, investors are bound to look at the valuation of a particular equity at least partly in terms of its earnings, and in the case of a company like British Land that will be their group operating earnings, not the rental stream from their property portfolio. They may also look at the share at least partly in terms of its dividend yield (indeed, some funds look at nothing else), and this is a function both of the level of operating income and management's dividend policy, which can change from one year to the next.

For another, large property companies such as British Land form part of an equity index: the FTSE 100 in this case. This means that any time somebody buys the index (for example, by replicating the FTSE constituents within a tracker portfolio) they must necessarily buy British Land, and equally when they sell the index they must sell British Land. These purchases and sales will obviously drive the share price up and down; it is well known, for example, that whenever a company drops out of the index it suffers an immediate further fall in its share price as all the index funds automatically sell their holdings. All these things happen automatically by virtue of being part of the index. It is pure beta, and has no connection at all with an analyst's view of the company and its management. Still less does it have anything to do with the total return on UK real estate.

It is an important point which appears in other places within this book, but which bears repeating as so many investors seem to have trouble grasping it. Anybody attempting to access any alternative asset type in this way is falling at the first hurdle in the search for uncorrelated returns. Indeed, all they are doing is importing hefty chunks of stock market beta straight back into their portfolio.

Quoted (2): REITS

Real Estate Investment Trusts came surprisingly late to some markets. Having been around since 1960 in the US, it took nearly 50 years for them to be introduced into the supposedly sophisticated London market. Less surprisingly, it was the dreaded UK Treasury who were the party-poopers for many years, fearing that worst catastrophe of all – a small drop in tax revenues.

The basic concept of a REIT is impeccable. Investors subscribe money to an investment vehicle, which then goes out and buys real estate to the same value. Thus, a share in the REIT becomes a participating interest in a portfolio of tangible properties. The practice, unfortunately, has proved rather different, particularly in the UK.

A fact was deliberately withheld from the reader in the last section. British Land is itself a REIT. That it was able to qualify, given its various business activities, demonstrates instantly what has gone wrong. The very thing which investors should want to *ex*clude – operating business exposure – has instead been *in*cluded, thus opening up the can of worms which is outlined above. The fact that a REIT can sit within the FTSE 100 index simply compounds the problem.

Small wonder, then, that research by a leading specialist investment firm in London,[6] shows that a back-tested REIT portfolio would have significantly out-performed the IPD index until about the middle of 2007, but has very significantly under-performed since about the middle of 2008. A proxy for direct real estate exposure they are not. Indeed, over the four years from the beginning of 2006 their cumulative return is only about half that of the UK property index.[7] As with other alternative asset types, it seems that quoted vehicles will always trade at either a premium or discount to asset value, depending on market sentiment.

Quoted (3): ETFs

A word of explanation is due at this point on ETFs, since they are examined as means of accessing other alternative asset types in this book. Unfortunately, as with Infrastructure, for example, "property" or "real estate" exchange traded funds are simply stock market sector funds. They will hold shares in the sort of quoted companies we have just been talking about; replicating whatever sector index is being tracked. They are not a proxy for holding real estate assets, nor do they pretend to be (as REITs do). They are simply a unitised form of exposure to the sort of stock market beta which is described above, but this time limited to property companies rather than across the stock market as a whole.

Unquoted (1): Unlisted Property Funds

We must be careful with our terminology here, since we are going to be considering private real estate separately, and such vehicles could technically also be described as unlisted property funds. This first section is designed to deal with funds such as PUTs (Property Unit

---

[6]inProp Capital, data to December 2009.
[7]Figures and workings from inProp Capital as before.

Trusts) in the UK, or their equivalents around the world. They share the characteristic of operating on a capital redemption structure similar to the way in which most hedge funds are now constructed. Units in the fund, whatever they might be called in different countries, are not publicly traded on an exchange (though private transfers can and do take place on a secondary basis), but are issued and redeemed by the fund manager.

That brings us to an important issue, which has bedevilled such funds in the same way as it has hedge funds in recent years (though less dramatically, since in the case of hedge funds high levels of gearing have made the problem even more acute).

Any fund vehicle which involves the ability for investors to redeem their capital is prey to potential disaster if everyone tries to redeem at once, as happened during the abnormal market conditions of 2008 during the famous "flight to liquidity". It is rather like a fire breaking out in a theatre and the panic-stricken audience stampeding for the exits. Many are likely to be trampled underfoot, whereas perhaps none might have been burned to death during an orderly evacuation if sang-froid had been preserved.

The explanation as to just how harmful this can be lies in that phrase "flight to liquidity". Unfortunately, most investors cling tightly to the concept of liquidity like a weak swimmer hanging onto the ladder of a swimming pool. They venture away from it only with the greatest reluctance, and at the first sign of trouble they lunge desperately for it again. Once they get it into their heads that danger threatens, then the mob is quite likely to crush anyone who gets in its way. When they see something as liquid, or potentially liquid, just because it has a redemption facility then that is one button which they can and do press unthinkingly. "Unthinkingly" because what they have invested in is in reality a pool of illiquid assets. Cash can only be generated for mass redemptions by selling assets, and who would want to sell assets on a fire sale basis in poor market conditions? In fairness, as pointed out above, PUT type vehicles have not suffered from this phenomenon nearly as much as hedge funds have but, as discussed in an earlier chapter, the mere possibility of its occurrence has emerged as a major consideration for investors when choosing their method of access; one now hears it referred to at conferences as "co-investor risk".

There are rival schools of thought here. The fund manager would doubtless argue that it is illogical for investors to redeem, since real estate is an illiquid, long term asset class and they have presumably chosen it in the first place because they are long term investors who can afford to sacrifice some short term liquidity. The investor would contend that, even if this were so, logically in poor market conditions it will be easier to sell high quality assets rather than mediocre ones, and so these are likely to be sold first to satisfy redemptions. Therefore, a rational investor should always tend to redeem too hastily rather than too slowly, since if they do not they risk (1) increasingly severe lockups being imposed, (2) a fund with dwindling cash and (3) a fund with a steadily falling quality of portfolio assets.

There is a danger of getting drawn too deeply into what is a contentious area, and arguably only of peripheral importance to real estate as a whole. However, the fact remains that if you are a long term investor then this is a far from ideal way of accessing and holding the asset class, since your objective of long term return will be constantly under threat from possible random, emotionally driven actions by third parties, particularly in abnormal conditions, which is exactly when you would choose *not* to sell the underlying assets if you held them directly. This is what we discussed earlier as the "private fund factor".

It might be thought that timing, in the sense of putting money to work in the first place, would not be nearly such a big issue with indirect vehicles as it is with direct investment. This is nearly true, but not quite. First, if you are buying an office block then the due diligence which you must carry out is relatively straightforward; a mix of technical property matters and legal issues. Investing in a fund, however, carries a heavy and complex burden of due diligence, as well as both qualitative and quantitative assessment of the team, market, track record and investment model. Even for a sophisticated, well-resourced investor, this process could easily take six months from start to finish. Second, if you are unlucky enough to be trying to put money to work when "it's a bad time for fundraising" then you could in any event have to wait quite some time for quality fund products to become available, and even then not be able to satisfy your appetite in full. The only option then is to try to pick some interests up in the secondary market from people who would otherwise be looking to redeem.

Finally, one must mention the vexed question of fees. PUT type vehicles are undeniably a very expensive way in which to access the real estate market. There will always be a 'spread' between the prices quoted for issuing new units, and redeeming existing ones. In the alternative, or in addition, there may be fees imposed on both events. The total 'round trip' costs (the cost of first entering and then leaving the fund) can be as high as 5%. Bear in mind that these fees are in addition to the management fee and the costs to fund of executing property transactions. In fairness, some other methods, such as private real estate, also carry a high fee and cost burden but, even so, the true levels of costs involved in a PUT type vehicle are often not properly appreciated by investors.

Unquoted (2): Private Real Estate

Yet again we find ourselves grappling with terminology. What we are about to discuss is often referred to as private equity real estate, or PERE[8] for short. This is a most pernicious tendency, and should you ever hear anybody utter these words you will be doing the world of investment a great favour by persuading them to take a long walk on a short pier in shark infested waters. This asset type has nothing to do with private equity at all, save only that it uses the same sort of fund structure. It is therefore something of a mystery why anybody should ever seek to suggest otherwise. It is rather like saying that a parrot is essentially the same thing as a monkey because they both have two legs and live in the jungle. These funds are staffed by property professionals and invest in buildings, not companies. They are real estate, not private equity.

You will remember that this was one of three "private" asset types which were identified in an earlier chapter: private equity and Infrastructure being the other two. In order to qualify for the "private" epithet one must satisfy two conditions: (1) the underlying investment assets must be illiquid and (2) the fund vehicle must be a limited partnership type structure. Private real estate is therefore distinguished from PUT type exposure not by the type of assets in which it invests, but by the way in which investors are prepared for their capital to be treated.

The key differences between the two are set out in Table 3.1.

We have already examined in an earlier chapter the newly emergent arguments in favour of private funds in the wake of the recent financial crisis. Since there is no need to rehearse these again, let us focus on exactly how private real estate works.

Table 3.1 Key differences between (1) PUTs and OEICs and (2) private real estate

	PUTs/OEICs	Private Real Estate
Fund vehicle	Unit trust or investment company	Limited partnership
Open/closed ended	Open	Closed
Capital payable	Up front	As and when needed
Sale proceeds	Reinvested	Distributed or recycled
Return measurement	NAV	IRR
Capital redeemable	Yes	No
Gearing	Usually prohibited or limited*	Usually unlimited

*For example, the Hermes Property Unit Trust can borrow up to 30% of its asset value.

---

[8] Sometimes also PERA.

As with private equity, private real estate vehicles are typically officially of ten years duration, but effectively of 12, since there will usually be two opportunities for the manager (General Partner) to extend for one year at a time. Thus, just as with private equity, investors should not venture into this asset type unless they are comfortable with the concept of long term investing in illiquid assets.

Money will be drawn down from investors (Limited Partners) as required to pay for new investments. There will usually be an official five year investment period, after which money can no longer be drawn down for new property purchases, though in practice the manager will be aiming to be fully invested after three years, at which time they will go out and raise a new fund.

Private real estate has long been an accepted way of making property investments in the US, and has grown particularly since about 2001, but until very recently opportunities for investors in Europe have been scarce. Things are changing, however, and there are now a number of both established and new players from which to choose. For example, in 2009, though this was the worst year for fundraising since 2004 (by capital raised, and since 2003 by number of funds) both Blackstone and Orion each raised their third European funds, totalling about $4.5 billion combined.[9]

To put the size of this asset type in context, 2009, though a relatively bad year, saw just over $42 billion raised worldwide; the peak was, perhaps surprisingly, in 2008 when $133 billion was committed to new funds. However, it is true to say that Europe and other regions still have relatively little coverage compared to the US. So, private real estate is one area in which one can comfortably predict a steady, and perhaps rapid, increase in capacity.

The investment approaches of private real estate funds can be broken down into five broad categories: Core Plus, Value Added, Opportunistic, Distressed and Debt.

Core Plus is strictly speaking a slightly enhanced version of another strategy called (appropriately) Core, but the latter is little used and is now generally reckoned to have been subsumed within Core Plus. Core funds would invest only in the very highest grade buildings (generally referred to as Class A property) and use very little gearing. In other words, they would be seen as low risk/low reward. Perhaps because of the private equity type fees being charged, this approach seems now to be regarded as inappropriate (or at least unexciting) for private vehicles.

---

[9] All figures in this section are from Preqin, unless stated otherwise. The writer gratefully acknowledges the contribution which Preqin have made to making industry data available across the whole range of private asset types.

Core Plus funds will venture a little further down the quality chain, but usually only if there is some specific reason why a building is lowly rated, and some identifiable "fix" which will pull it back quickly to prestige status. They will be prepared to use slightly more gearing too, but still usually limited to no more than about 50% Loan to Value.

Value Added involves acquiring buildings the value of which can be enhanced in some way, most usually by what is called "development gain", for example by buying a house and obtaining planning permission to convert it into apartments. Another obvious possibility is physical enhancement, perhaps where the building has become dilapidated as a result of the current owner being unwilling or unable to spend money on it. Value Added is seen as a medium risk/medium reward strategy.

Opportunistic funds are sometimes referred to as high yield funds within the sector, since they chase the highest returns of all, and accept correspondingly higher levels of risk in the process. For example, they will use higher gearing (anything up to about 70%), and will invest across a broad range of real estate assets including buying land and participating in development projects. They will also be prepared to buy real estate debt, and indeed many see the genesis of these funds having been the sell-off of non-performing assets by the Resolution Trust Company[10] following the Savings and Loans crisis in the US (in the late 1980s, culminating in a credit crunch and banking upset in 1991, at which time the "junk bond" market also collapsed following the failure of Drexel Burnham and the imprisonment of Michael Milken).

Distressed funds will aggressively target both properties and the loans which are secured on them, in many cases looking to acquire both at the same time. For example, many are talking of the opportunities represented currently in the US by the government prompted sell-off of toxic assets. Ideally, the "distress" should apply to the seller rather than to the asset being acquired, but the professionals within these funds are highly skilled financial engineers, and will often also have specific insolvency and restructuring skills and experience.

Debt funds are often the real estate arm of an established debt investor. A good example would be Apollo, perhaps the most famous debt investor of all, who set up a real estate operation in 2008, and in December 2009 launched a fund to invest solely in US CMBS (Commercial Mortgage Backed Securities) debt. Obviously different

---

[10] A rescue fund set up by the US Government.

debt funds will have different investment models and risk/reward profiles.

According to a recent survey by Preqin, it is Opportunistic and Value Added funds which are overwhelmingly the most popular, suggesting that investors see private real estate as an opportunity to chase high returns, and this is reflected in the amounts actually raised for each strategy in 2009. These two strategies accounted for 74% of fund-raising, with Core Plus coming in at just 3%.

Given the various limitations of the other means of access to real estate assets which we have examined so far, it would seem that private real estate funds offer the best investment route, certainly if one of your objectives in allocating money to real estate is to achieve a source of return which is lowly correlated with quoted equities. This would, however, be subject to various caveats: (1) you must be comfortable with the idea of sacrificing liquidity and tying up your money over a period of several years, (2) you must be prepared either to buy in or outsource the expertise necessary to choose the best managers, since no beta is available, and (3) you must be able to stomach what seem at first sight to be very large fee and profit share (carried interest) arrangements. As with private equity, you must focus on the net return to investors, *after* the deduction of all fees, costs and carried interest.

Another aspect to bear in mind is that private real estate funds customarily use leverage by way of debt, just as Buyout funds do in the world of private equity. In other words, a private real estate fund is not putting an investor in the same position as if they held property assets in general, but in the same position as if they held a geared equity interest in a small number of specific properties. This can be both good and bad.

Good, if the properties are well chosen, reasonably priced and the amounts of leverage sensible, since wherever one has leverage then one must necessarily also have some extra element of risk. Bad when one or more of these elements goes wrong, in which case the results can be dire indeed. Morgan Stanley Real Estate Fund VI, claiming at $8 billion to be the largest private real estate fund ever, began investing in the summer of 2007, when property prices in many markets, including London, were at their peak. The IPD UK property index has since recorded about a 22% loss, yet the fund, because of its geared positions, has written down its assets by about 67%.[11]

Perhaps in due course un-geared funds may be offered as an alternative, in much the same way that private equity investors who are nervous of leverage can choose to invest in development, growth or

---

[11] *Daily Telegraph,* 15 April 2010.

venture capital rather than buyout. Doubtless some would argue that this could be difficult given the private equity type fee structures of these funds, which need high returns to justify them, these high returns in turn requiring leverage to help create them.

However, it is as yet a little early to be making a final judgement on this matter, since there still remains one type of real estate investment to consider, and it is perhaps the most exciting of all.

SYNTHETIC

Real estate investors have been enthusiastically predicting the advent of property derivatives for some years now. After all, wherever an index exists then it is possible to write derivative instruments based upon it. For quite a long time, however, nothing much happened. There were a few structured products, but these were not available in any great value or volume, and were thought by many to be prohibitively expensive (sometimes costing as much as 3% a year) and thus not offering acceptable levels of net return.

These early instruments were usually either notes or swaps. A Property Index Note (PIN) was designed to replicate the cash flows of actually holding property, complete with quarterly payments representing notional rent. A swap was usually a Total Return Swap, under which the investor paid the issuer a fixed interest rate (usually expressed as LIBOR plus a margin) and either paid or received in return the difference between this and the actual property return as measured by the index. These suffered from two main disadvantages.

One disadvantage has already been noted above. Usually the margin above LIBOR was so great that on any "risk adjusted" view few investors were attracted to try their luck. The other was in fact a far greater risk, but one which lurked largely unnoticed in the background until late 2007, and only came fully into prominence with the collapse of Lehman Brothers in September 2008. These were all contractual instruments, and therefore dependent entirely on the ability of the other party to the contract (the counterparty) to make any required payment on the due date. Until Lehman Brothers filed for bankruptcy, the risk of any bank actually going bust was felt by many to be so minimal that it could safely be ignored. After September 2008, it was realised that this was in fact a major issue. The disappearance of the various counterparty positions which Lehman represented sent shock waves through every sector of the financial world, from hedge funds right through to capital guaranteed bonds which had sold to retail investors.

In early 2009 Eurex, which now claims to be the world's largest derivative exchange, began listing property derivatives based around the IPD index. These new instruments have two essential differences compared to the "old" derivatives which we have just been discussing.

The first is that they are real futures contracts. The purchase price is based on a notional figure of 100 plus whatever price the market is currently putting on the expected performance of the index. At the end of the period, one party must pay to the other the difference between this and the actual index movement. Thus, if you want to track property beta as closely as possible, then this would seem in theory to be the ideal way to do it.

The second is more important: these instruments are exchange traded, rather than being traded on an OTC (Over the Counter) basis as were the "old" derivatives. The exchange guarantees that every instrument will be duly settled, and takes margin payments from anyone who trades on the exchange to help secure this guarantee. In this way, counterparty risk is effectively eliminated, or, more accurately, reduced to such a minimal level that now it probably *can* be safely ignored.

As we saw earlier in the chapter, this market is currently largely confined to UK property beta, although there are fledgling markets in respect of France and Germany. For the US, there are currently no exchange traded products available at all which approximate real estate beta.

This statement can be qualified slightly. There are some exchange traded futures offered by CME Group. However, the problem here is with the non-availability of any universal index. These futures are based around the S&P/Case-Schiller Home Price index which, as the name suggests, tracks only residential property, and is not a total return index. Some private "counterparty risk" old-style instruments have been written, but these are largely based on the NCREIF[12] index which, while it is a total return index, only covers a very small percentage of the total US market. It is to be hoped that exchange traded futures based around the new IPD US index will in due course make proper beta exposure possible.

A word too about rental swaps. Historically these have been available only when issued against a particular property or property portfolio. The property owner may want the certainty of a fixed rate of return to match a fixed rate of loan interest, or perhaps be in need of a lump sum payment to meet short term cash flow needs, and so sells to an investor the right to receive the actual rental return over the life of the swap. Obviously the availability of property owners wishing to enter

---

[12]National Council of Real Estate Investment Fiduciaries.

into such arrangements has in turn limited the availability of such swaps.

However, there seems no reason in future, as market volumes of derivatives grow, that universal rental swaps should not be offered in exactly the same way as the existing total return swaps. After all, IPD can break out for its data subscribers the total return into its constituent parts of rental and capital value, so why should not three types of future be offered instead of one? It seems hard to believe that such a development will not occur.

Indeed, there are many who believe not only that increasingly for real estate the future is synthetic, but that one day soon it may be possible to adopt what they are calling "a hedge fund approach", under which there would be no need at all to enter into substantive transactions in respect of real assets. Instead of buying property one could buy a futures contract based on the property index. Instead of lending money into real estate transactions one could buy a credit default swap and an interest rate swap based on a portfolio of such loans. Banks looking to hedge or otherwise de-risk their property loan books should be happy to sell such futures, just as property owners looking to hedge their debt servicing exposure should be happy to sell rental swaps.

There may be a "chicken and egg" quality to all this, however, at least in the UK, where such developments have been predicted for some time but have, thus far, largely failed to materialise. Some point the finger at the banks,[13] claiming that while US banks are largely insulated in terms of their existing real estate loans by means of hedging the CMBS index,[14] UK banks have failed to follow suit.

Consider for a moment the position of a bank which may be pondering the health of its property loan book. One obvious danger is that property values may fall, resulting in LTV (Loan to Value) covenants being breached. This has a significance beyond the individual loan or loans in question. As well as being saddled with the problem of dealing with loans in default, the bank will be forced by banking regulations to move those loans from one part of its balance sheet to another. Thus, this is not just bad news for the loans in question but also for the bank as a whole. In the extreme case of a major crash in property values then this may impinge on a lender's credit rating, or even lead to it failing, as happened during the Asian crisis, which began in 1997.[15]

---

[13] See for example an article in *Estates Gazette*, March 2010 by Markus Wolfensberger.

[14] Which covers recent Commercial Mortgage Backed Securities issues, and can be shorted through a total return swap.

[15] As happened to Finance One, previously the largest financial lender in Thailand.

What could be more sensible, then, than banks with active property loan books effectively to short the property market itself? This way, should property values fall then they would make money on their derivatives exposure, while if property prices rose then the price of the futures contract would represent a sum paid to reduce risk. This would be a classic "hedge"; paying a sum of money to a counterparty in return for them effectively assuming some of your risk. Indeed, it seems such an obvious step for banks to take that it is a matter of some surprise that they have not, just as it was a matter of considerable surprise that they did not seek to short the CDO market in 2007.

While the reasons for the latter omission remain obscure, one of the reasons given by banks for failing to utilise property derivatives is apparently that the market is too small to be useful.[16] This smacks more of an excuse than a reason. Many investors give the same reason for not seeking to use the derivatives market to access real estate beta. It therefore seems logical that if extra supply was made available (by the banks) then demand would follow (from investors).

In the meantime, the size of the available market remains a significant practical limitation for any moderately large investor. Suppose, for example, that one had even $10 billion of assets and decided to put 20% of this into real estate. This would represent about half the total value of contracts executed in 2009 – clearly not a practical option. However, it is only fair to point out that 2009 was a very quiet year; the 2008 total was three times greater.

Supporters of the synthetic approach point to the growth of other types of derivative markets in support of their view that within a reasonable time the property futures market will reach similar proportions. One issue here is undoubtedly the current reluctance of investors around the world actually to venture into the market, which seems strange given that, provided the futures contract is held to maturity, it appears to be the only way of tracking exactly real estate beta. One can only conclude that the siren call of alpha returns is currently too strong to be resisted.

Note that "real assets", as opposed to real estate, also comprise forestry and (some would argue) oil and gas royalties.[17] By reason partly of space and partly of definition, forestry is dealt with in the chapter on other alternative assets. Oil and gas royalties are dealt with in the chapter on energy.

---

[16] Wolfensberger, already cited.
[17] More recently, some investors have also been buying agricultural land as a sort of commodity-related asset.

SUMMARY

Real estate is an illiquid asset class of long standing – perhaps the oldest of all save only for gold.

Real estate can be a strong source of uncorrelated return relative to quoted equities, though care should be taken to measure this across local markets, as correlation levels can vary largely.

Real estate is characterised by certain qualities which set it apart from other asset types, including the ability to grant legal charges, the ability to create subordinate leasehold interests, the separation (in many jurisdictions) of legal and equitable ownership, and privity of estate, under which obligations run with the land rather than being merely personal.

Real estate beta is properly available only in the UK at present, based around the IPD index (and even here there are limitations of market size), though it seems inevitable that this will change gradually.

Access may be direct, indirect or synthetic. Indirect exposure may be through either quoted or unquoted vehicles.

Direct exposure allows an investor to choose their own portfolio of property assets, but is time-consuming and, except in the case of a very large investor, it is almost impossible to achieve a properly diversified portfolio.

Quoted vehicles may be split into (1) property companies and (2) real estate investment trusts (REITs). Neither offers a good proxy for actual real estate exposure, seeming to move more with stock market beta than with underlying property values. Often considerable exposure to operating business risk is involved.

Unquoted vehicles may be split into (1) unit trust and Open Ended Investment Company (OEIC) type vehicles and (2) private real estate, operating through limited partnership type structures. The former are subject to various limitations, not least that a stampede of capital redemptions can work to the detriment of true long term investors. The latter utilise the same fund structure as private equity funds. In both cases (but particularly in the case of private real estate) there can be big differences between gross and net returns, and investors need to be sure they have calculated their true return after all fees and costs.

Synthetic exposure is believed by some to represent the future of real estate investing. A new breed of exchange traded derivatives has effectively removed the issue of counterparty risk. However, coverage is currently restricted to the UK, and take-up by both banks and investors has thus far proved disappointing.

4
Energy

A global market for energy, in the form of coal, developed during the nineteenth century, with prices being quoted both spot and forward in coaling stations around the world. Various coal futures contracts are still traded today. For example, there is the Central Appalachians contract, which is based on physical delivery by barge on the Ohio and Big Sandy rivers. However, these are today a very small part of the overall energy market.

Steam power not only made possible the railway revolution, but also changed forever the shape of the shipping industry and international trade. Welsh anthracite became highly prized and spawned a vast mining industry in the valleys of South Wales. America picked a quarrel with Spain and went to war to grab a chain of bunkering points for a new "blue water" navy: Guam and the Philippines, when combined with Hawaii, offered the prospect of free passage right across the Pacific.

Then the British navy, at that time by far the largest in the world, made the strategic decision to switch to oil, and Britain's rivals had to follow suit. The word "bunkering" stuck though. Even now, supplies of fuel oil for ships are referred to as "bunkers" and there are many specialist bunkers experts among the world's oil traders. For oil, which underpins both industry and transport around the world, enjoys one of the busiest of the world's great trading markets. In addition to the bunkering market, there are specialist sectors looking after aviation fuel, heating oil, gasoline (petrol) and various forms of petro-chemicals, as well as a related market in natural gas, which we will be examining separately.

The main oil market however has two main variants, or at least two main reference points relative to which other things are priced. These are Brent Crude, the oil produced from offshore platforms in the North Sea, and its US equivalent US Light Sweet Crude, also known as West Texas Intermediate. These two products are made available by means of both futures and options contracts and we will be examining how investors might make use of these instruments, as well as swaps. Dubai crude and Asian Tapis are also used as benchmarks, but with more limited derivative exposure available. So, at any one time there will be a range of prices displayed, both spot and forward (though individual contracts may be priced at either a discount or premium to these benchmarks).

SPOT TRADING

Spot trading, however, is strictly for those who have no problem with handling physical cargoes of oil. Indeed, much spot trading takes place between members of the oil refining industry in order to regulate a steady flow through their manufacturing process. If they suddenly find themselves with too much oil (even taking into account their storage capacity) then they will offer the excess on the open market. If, on the other hand, they find themselves with too little then they can buy some of somebody else's excess supply. When a general interruption, or even the threat of a general interruption, to supply becomes evident then very violent swings can occur in the spot price. Both the first Gulf War and the more recent conflict in Iraq, for example, sparked huge increases. Terrorist risk, with its attendant threat to oil platforms or, even more damagingly, pipelines, is thus a major factor in the oil market.

Spot trading is fine, then, if you can happily afford to buy or sell whole cargoes of oil being transported by super-tankers, and many of the world's leading oil and petro-chemical companies do exactly this, but unless you have the means of taking delivery of it, and either processing it or consuming it, then it is of little use to an investor. This is in direct contrast to gold, for example, where many investors are happy, indeed eager, to take physical possession of the asset, either directly or indirectly.

Spot pricing is obviously very important as a knock-on factor in futures pricing, particularly where the futures contract or option is very shortly to expire. In some countries, such as the UK, spread betting on oil prices has also become common, particularly among ordinary retail investors. Just one of the spread betting companies in London (IG Index) recently reported that they take over 30 000 individual bets on oil a year, with an underlying market exposure in excess of £1 billion.

It is thus worth considering the various factors which can impact spot pricing, since this will in turn influence the pricing of derivative contracts. We have already referred to day to day imbalances in supply and demand among the refining community, war and terrorism, but there are various others.

Incidentally, US crude oil inventory figures are published on a weekly basis by the Energy Information Administration, and these are seized upon eagerly by economists and oil industry analysts alike for what they may reveal about short term supply and demand.

INFLUENCES ON PRICING

Untapped Reserves

Supply and demand do not move in a straight line, or even a curve, but strictly speaking are stepped, at least in theory.[1] This is because there are various reserves of oil still untapped around the world which only become economically viable to extract at relatively high levels of pricing: $70 a barrel is frequently mentioned. This could be because they are in deep ocean, or in difficult terrain, or just of low density, quantity or quality.[2] However, the proviso "in theory" is a necessary one since these supplies cannot be brought on stream overnight. On the contrary, one will usually be talking about a long and complex project which could take months or even years of discussion before a decision can even be reached, let alone implementation begun, and if by that time the price has dropped back below the magic number then the whole idea will be mothballed once more. So, it may be that the idea of this untapped supply works as a factor rather than the supply itself, but a factor it certainly is, if only in keynote addresses at energy conferences.

The (US) Strategic Petroleum Reserve

America maintains an emergency stockpile of nearly 600 million barrels of oil in huge underground silos around the Gulf of Mexico. This is presumably so that in the event of war disrupting supplies, US refineries would still be able to produce fuel for both civilian transport and military purposes. This amount remains constant, and so strictly speaking does not impact spot pricing, but were the Federal Government ever to decide for some reason that it was no longer necessary then it would obviously flood the market (as the British Government did when it decided to sell its gold reserves, having cannily broadcast news of its intentions in advance).

Production and Growth in Oil Hungry Economies

There are certain countries in the world which have a huge demand for oil, and are thus big importers of it. A prime example would be China, which is second only to the US as a consumer of oil, and which is

---

[1] For the International (privately owned) Oil Companies, higher prices can actually push production volumes lower. This may seem counter-intuitive, but is driven by complicated proportionate costs provisions in many production sharing contracts.

[2] This is particularly true of "unconventional" oil such as tar sands and oil shale – see below.

believed to import around 8.2 million barrels per day;[3] to put that in context, Abu Dhabi, which produces the bulk of the UAE's oil, only pumps about 2.5 million barrels per day.

When manufacturing production, evidenced by GDP growth, is rampant in such an economy, it acts as a very significant stimulant on global demand, and thus an upward pressure on prices. Similarly, when industrial output slows so demand for oil will fall. However, even here one must be careful about predicting direct cause and effect because China manages its oil reserves very intelligently, buying heavily when prices are low and stockpiling for periods of more expensive pricing. Thus, while this is undoubtedly a factor, the existence, or at least the potential for, these buffer stocks will have a smoothing effect in the short term.

Weather

Weather can affect both the supply and demand side of the oil equation. When a large oil consumer, such as the US, experiences severe winter weather then demand can increase dramatically since many US homes are heated by oil, some power stations are powered by oil, and oil is also used for start-up purposes in coal-fired power stations. Given that the US is the world's biggest consumer of oil, such an obsession with American weather patterns, particularly on the Eastern seaboard, is understandable among oil traders.

The other reason that the weather is particularly important in this area is that most of America's off-shore drilling platforms are in the Gulf of Mexico, and these can be closed down, or even destroyed, during severe hurricanes. Hurricane Katrina (the one which flooded New Orleans in 2005) accounted for about 20 such production platforms.

Political Factors

During the Yom Kippur war of 1973 The Organisation of Petroleum Exporting Countries (OPEC), whose then membership was drawn almost exclusively from the Arab world, imposed dramatic price increases which sparked history's first recorded oil crisis, with motorists around the world queuing for petrol. Many observers blamed the oil crisis for the stock market crash which quickly followed.

With the discovery and development of fresh oil reserves, most notably in Alaska, Russia and the North Sea, OPEC's power and influ-

---

[3] IEA: China is expected to have accounted for about one third of global oil demand in 2010.

ence has diminished, and its official role now is to attempt to "stabilise" oil prices, which it tries to do by persuading its members to regulate supply, with Saudi Arabia acting as the global swing producer within OPEC to make this balancing act work. However, the economic considerations of individual oil-producing countries now play almost as important a role. Where oil production is under direct or indirect government control, then they will naturally try to restrict production when prices are low, and boost it when prices are high, but again this can be stated only as a general principle rather than a universal rule, since it depends on the country's willingness, and ability, to use its Sovereign Wealth Fund as a piggy bank to fund current expenditure, and for how long.

While this book was being written, the full scale of the BP tragedy in the Gulf of Mexico began to become apparent. Press coverage has, rightly, focussed on the appalling scale of the environmental damage, but there will be a political and economic price to pay as well. It is already becoming apparent that the Obama administration, understandably, will almost certainly halt the granting of any further offshore drilling licences until tough new production and inspection regulations are put in place, and it seems inconceivable that other countries will not follow suit.

Terrorism

Oil installations are frighteningly vulnerable to terrorist attack. Pipelines, for example, are almost impossible to defend along their entire length. There is constant speculation, about what would happen were a bomb to be placed somewhere on one of the major pipelines which crosses various parts of the former Soviet Union. Certainly major disruption to supply would occur.

Similarly, terrorists routinely occupy and hold to ransom offshore rigs off the coast of Nigeria, which has caused the oil "majors" at various times to close down these production facilities as being just too dangerous to ask people to work on.

Its reliance on oil remains the global economy's choke point and, sadly, many terrorist movements are led by intelligent people. It seems reasonable to assume, therefore, that the risk of terrorist attack on oil related facilities is likely to increase in the future rather than decrease.

The US Dollar

It may seem strange to treat the US Dollar as one of the determinants of the price of oil. After all, oil is denominated in dollars – and that is exactly the point. If you are not a US dollar investor, if your liabilities are not in dollars but in some other currency, then the current exchange rate of the US dollar against your currency will be one of the mathematical factors which determines how much it is actually costing you to buy it. Of course, as a matter of strict financial theory this is not a factor influencing the price, but rather currency risk attached to the asset. In practice, however, it is an element in your own pricing equation, not just for oil but for many other asset types as well, and one that is often overlooked by investors. What you choose to do about it, if anything, is up to you, but it is important at least to recognise that it exists, and to discuss how to handle it.

Just how long oil remains a dollar denominated asset, at least exclusively, is, however, open to considerable doubt. Russia, one of the three biggest oil producers in the world, has for some time been accepting payment in roubles, and recently three other producers (Iran, Iraq and Venezuela) have been happy to quote prices in Euros, Iran also having publicly mooted the possibility of pricing all their oil in roubles "to try to free the world of dollar slavery".[4]

We will have to see how all this plays out, but one important point should be understood. The intrinsic value of a barrel of oil must always be the same at any given moment of any given day on a global basis; the fact that it may be quoted in different currencies cannot change that. Thus, any price quoted in a currency other than dollars must be being based on the underlying dollar price since, like it or not, this is currently the ultimate expression and validation of that value. Were it to be otherwise, then arbitrage opportunities would open up whereby one could buy oil in one currency and immediately sell it in another, or vice versa.

All of which has led to considerable uncertainty over, for example, the true long term value of the rouble which has consistently been a major component of both hedge fund and active currency trades over the last few years, and means that options on oil are often being used as part of a pairs trade, or an even more complicated series of trades, involving different currencies.

Needless to say, if either the rouble or the Euro does succeed in dethroning the dollar as the default pricing mechanism for oil, then this would have serious implications for the American currency. It may be priced against gold, at least nominally, but it is as the measure of a barrel of oil that it carries the most practical weight in the modern global economy. Given the volatility of both its rival currencies in recent years, it seems likely to keep its mantle for the time being, but

---

[4]Press Release from the Euro-Arab Mashreq Gas Co-Operation Centre, 21 February 2008.

were things to pan out differently a major weakening of American economic power and influence might ensue. It would, for example, almost certainly provide the impetus for some other currencies, such as the United Arab Emirates dirham, to de-couple themselves from the dollar. So, let us make no mistake; what may seem like posturing and empty rhetoric about what currency oil should be priced in is actually global power politics at its most naked and potentially explosive.

ACCESSING OIL AS AN INVESTMENT

We have seen already that physical ownership of oil is simply not a practical course for investors to adopt. Until recently, the remaining options were limited to only two real alternatives: (1) indirect exposure to oil by investing in the shares of oil companies and (2) synthetic exposure to oil through futures or options contracts.

Investing in the Shares of Oil Companies

This approach used to be widespread, not just in oil but also, as we will be considering separately, in areas such as property, infrastructure and commodities. This issue is referred to in a number of chapters, but this may be a convenient moment to consider it in more detail.

The problem is that it simply does not work, although to be fair it probably took the recent financial crisis to demonstrate just how far it fell short of any acceptable level of compromise. For example, at the time of writing (February 2010), the one year return on BP shares is 13.26%, while the comparable figure for Brent Crude is 54.7%. Quite a difference! Nor could we have done any better by trying to spread our coverage across the sector as a whole rather than just stock-picking BP; the relevant one year FTSE sector return is 8.85%, so in fact we would have done even worse.[5]

There are two main reasons for this, the first of which has been made much more obvious by the stock market turmoil which began in mid-2007.

As we have seen, according to classical investment theory, shares carry two types of risk (using "risk" in its artificial, traditional sense of "volatility"): systemic risk and specific risk. The first is that volatility which is represented by the stock market itself going up and down, and dragging its constituent shares with it. In addition to systemic risk, this can be referred to as market risk, market beta or just beta. The second is the extent to which this one share might itself move up and down

---

[5] All figures from www.digitallook.com.

independently – under its own power, so to speak. This may be referred to as specific risk, or alpha.

The existence of systemic risk means that any share which is listed on a stock exchange will move to some extent (even if only a very small one) in response to the movement of the market as a whole. What the recent upheaval demonstrated was that this market beta can turn out to be a much more powerful force than we had previously realised, and that even shares which represent some underlying assets, such as office blocks or private equity investments, will tend to move up and, particularly, down in line with the market rather than necessarily with the valuation of the underlying assets. As we have already seen, a prime example would be 3i, a UK public company which is really just a huge quoted private equity fund. Going into 2007 it was trading at a premium to net asset value, yet by early 2009 it was trading at a very significant discount to NAV, despite having written down its assets in the meantime.

There is a tool which purports to measure the specific risk of holding an individual share rather than the market as a whole, and it expresses this as a ratio of the market beta. Put another way, the outcome shows the extent to which the individual share is likely to be dragged up and down by the market. It is called the Capital Asset Pricing Model, and works on the principle of "volatility as risk" which we have already met.

It is not important that you should know how the model works, but much more so that you understand the concept behind it; and if you are content with this then please simply skip the following paragraph. For the mathematically minded, the formula is

$$\frac{E(Ri) - Rf}{\beta} = E(Rm) - Rf$$

Which can be re-stated for $E(Ri)$ as

$$E(Ri) = Rf + \beta(E(Rm) - Rf)$$

Where

$E(Ri)$ is the expected return on the single asset (share)
Rf is. the risk-free rate
$E(Rm)$ is the expected market return

And Beta is a calculated value calculated as

$$\frac{CoVar(Ri, Rm)}{Var(Rm)}$$

Sorry about that, for the rest of you. The concept is actually very simple. The model, or at least that part of it which calculates Beta, is simply looking at two things: the extent to which the market as a whole goes up and down, and the extent to which the individual share goes up and down relative to the market's own movement. It then expresses this as a ratio of the market beta, which is always presumed to be one, because if you had the market as a whole on both the top and the bottom of your calculation you would be comparing something with itself, and anything divided by itself is one. A score close to one means that the share will move broadly in line with the stock market. Lower than one and it will move by a lesser amount. Higher than one and it will move by more.

BP has a beta of 0.88 which means it will move broadly in line with the market,[6] but within a tighter dispersion: if the market goes up or down by 10% then the BP share should go up or down by 8.8%. Another way of expressing this is that over the long term BP has been highly correlated with the FTSE index – 88% correlated. Brent Crude over more than 20 years has a correlation of only about 10% with the FTSE index. Thus, we see that the one year figures are no aberration. Not only would we not have replicated anything like the oil price by investing in BP over a one year period, but by persisting for over 20 years we would have had no success whatever; we would have matched the performance of the London Stock Exchange pretty closely, but we would not in any way have put ourselves in the same position as we would have been in had we been able to hold oil over the same period.

So, any attempt to replicate exposure to oil by investing in the shares of oil companies simply does not work. Worse, it is likely to lead to even more stock market beta in your portfolio, whereas by investing in alternative assets you are presumably attempting to achieve exactly the opposite.

Synthetic Exposure

Note the proviso "had we been able to hold oil over the same period". This, until recently, was where the problems arose.

Let us suppose that we want to obtain synthetic exposure to oil. In other words, we want to put ourselves in the same position, by using derivative instruments, as if we had bought some physical oil and could hold on to it indefinitely in some notional storage tank somewhere.

---

[6]Note that CAPM, like all traditional finance, assumes that the past is a perfect guide to the future and, in particular, that the possibility of low probability but high impact events such as the BP incident in the Gulf of Mexico in 2010 can safely be ignored.

Today, there are various ways in which we might seek to do this, since both futures and options contracts[7] are available several years out, but traditionally it was not so easy, since most options contracts were relatively short term affairs, and on expiry had to be renewed or continued. This came at a price, which was often referred to as a contango payment. Unfortunately this is a very confusing use of this term,[8] since it also, and more importantly, refers to a particular state of a futures market, as we will see elsewhere, but let us simply note that this carrying charge (for that is effectively what it is) could and did "eat index investors' lunch".[9] It was not uncommon to hear at investment conferences that in some circumstances perhaps as much as the first 10% of annual return could be eaten away in this way. Unsurprisingly, many investors took the view that this was so unattractive a prospect, and/or so complicated an arrangement to have to manage, that they took the decision to ignore oil as a potential portfolio asset.

That is not to say that there are not still complications. In fact there are various issues which most investors do not even stop to think about.

For a start, we cannot actually put ourselves in the same position we would be in if we were to buy oil and hold it since, as we have seen, this would entail taking physical delivery. Thus, the only way we can manufacture synthetic exposure to oil is by using the underlying futures contract(s). However, no investor in their right mind would want naked exposure to a futures contract, since they can give rise in some circumstances to unlimited losses.

There are various ways around this conundrum. Some investors might choose to buy and sell matching futures contracts at the same time, which is fine but likely to lead to very limited returns unless you can leverage your position greatly with debt, and if you do this you are obviously then opening up your position to all sorts of other risk, such as the lender asking for their money back at the least convenient moment.

Others might choose to buy options based on the underlying futures contract. This gets away from the possible unlimited loss issue, but only at the expense of opening up others. Options which expire out of the money lose you the original cost of the options contract and then have to be replaced with new contracts – the "carrying cost" problem we referred to earlier – and if they are in the money then they rely for

---

[7]Derivative instruments in general are more fully explored in the chapter on hedge funds.

[8]The expression "negative roll yield", which we meet elsewhere in this book is unfortunately just as obscure.

[9]Brad Zigler, "Seeking Alpha" www.seekingalpha.com 17 December 2007.

their execution on the ability of the contractual counterparty to perform. Prior to 2008 nobody gave very much thought to counterparty risk, but since the collapse of Lehman Brothers it has become a key question in investment manager due diligence and risk analysis.

So, we must concede that whatever solution we adopt to the practical problems of investing in oil is going to be a compromise and, as with all compromises, will never offer a perfect answer, never give us everything we want, and always carry inherent trade-offs. It is, however, increasingly the opinion of many of the world's investors that a new generation of commodity based Exchange Traded Funds (ETFs) do in fact offer an acceptable approach.

Oil ETFs

Commodity based ETFs fall into two distinct categories. Those which operate by means of physical ownership of the underlying assets (the original, pure ETF model), of which physical gold ETFs are probably the best example, and those which do not. These others operate by way of synthetic exposure, and oil ETFs fall firmly into this latter category. They are thus subject to all the possible limitations set out above. Recently, however, a new methodology has appeared which is exciting, but as yet little appreciated.

These ETFs operate by way of return swaps. These have long been used in mainstream financial circles. Suppose that investor A has future liabilities to meet which are index linked to the rate of inflation. Investor A may well decide to try to match these liabilities by buying index linked bonds in the same currency – but what if such bonds are simply not available in the market, or not available in sufficient quantity? Investor A may be aware of another investor, investor B who already has in their portfolio exactly the bond that A would like to buy. Suppose that B does not want to sell the bond, because they want to hold it long term. They may however be willing, for a limited period and at a price, to put A into the same position as if they actually held B's index linked bond. Provided they can agree on an appropriate price, A will agree to pay B a fixed rate of interest for the duration of the contract period, while B will pay A the actual interest paid by the index-linked bond, whatever it may be. Such contracts are routinely used by pension funds, for example.

There are two different ways in which return swaps may be used in oil ETFs. The first involves a financial counterparty, such as a bank, and has no physical connection to oil whatever. The second involves an industrial counterparty, typically an oil company, and operates by reference to a specific quantity of real oil.

The financial variety involves a bank essentially accepting a bet from you on the price of oil at a future date. If the price declines in the meantime, then on the due date you have to pay them the difference. If, on the other hand, the price rises, then they pay you the difference. The beauty of this is its simplicity. Its disadvantage is that banks are not known for their altruism or philanthropy, and so such products come at a price. The absolute minimum price that a bank will charge is about 0.75% (75 basis points), and can be much higher; for example, one such product based around a UK property index carried a 3% annual fee.

The other disadvantage is of course counterparty risk, as mentioned above. Before the financial crisis this issue would hardly have appeared on anyone's radar screen, but these days a proper spread of counterparty risk is quite rightly seen as essential (which raises problems in this instance as there are only a limited number of banks around the world willing to offer these instruments).

The second type of return swap involves an oil company, whether a producer or refiner, and (at least nominally) a real amount of oil. Here a producer who wishes to lock in a particular price for cash flow reasons will agree to pay a bank the market price on the due date for some oil, in return for fixed payments in the meantime.[10] The producer's risk is that the price rises in the meantime, resulting in a balancing payment having to be made to the bank. If the price falls, they keep the fixed payments and have effectively made a profit. This process continues throughout the life of the swap, some of which may last for years.

Similarly, a refiner may wish to lock in the maximum price that they have to pay, by doing the opposite of this. They will agree to pay fixed payments to the bank, but will receive the market price on the due date. Their risk is that the price falls in the meantime, in which case they will effectively have paid too much for the oil. If the price rises, they will receive a balancing payment from the bank.

In each case, the industrial partner is buying a different type of certainty, and is willing to pay a price for it. In swaps of this second type the bank can actively participate as a counterparty, perhaps looking to match a financial swap into which it has already entered with an investor, or can stand in the middle of two matching swap contracts, one each with a producer and a refiner.

So, as stated above, a swap based ETF is not an ideal solution, but only in the sense that the "ideal" solution would be a perfect proxy for holding physical oil, whereas this approach still involves counterparty

---

[10]This is known as a "Fixed and Floating" swap.

risk, but most investors seem happy to accept it as the best available of getting some oil exposure into their portfolio.

Incidentally, the first type of swap exposure can also be obtained by way of a Contract For Difference (CFD), which is really the same as the situation we looked at when we described a return swap involving a financial party, such as a bank. The only dissimilarities are:

- a swap is technically a private contractual arrangement between two parties, whereas many CFDs can be traded in a limited way on an OTC (Over The Counter) basis;[11]
- a CFD does not usually have a fixed expiry date, but can be closed at any time. However, it must be closed out by daily settlement to the extent of (1) the required margin and (2) the carrying cost, which will usually be expressed by reference to some interest rate benchmark such as LIBOR.

BIO-FUELS

One of the attractions often touted for oil as an investment is its finite nature; there is only so much oil in the world, and there is never going to be any more. Yes, we may not yet have found every last reserve (there are persistent rumours about the Falkland Islands, for example), and we may be aware of reserves which are not as yet commercially exploitable, but the total amount is fixed and cannot increase.

Oil is a diminishing resource, being pumped out of the ground at a rate of nearly 90 million barrels a day. Much speculation has centred around the moment of "peak oil", the time when peak oil production is reached, with production thereafter gradually tailing off towards a forlorn dry sucking sound. In fact, the situation is more serious than that. Global demand for oil is continuing to rise, so the decline, when it comes, could be quite rapid.

A London based research body[12] reported in February 2010 that peak oil would be reached by 2015, with the growing possibility of shortages, insecurity of supply, and economic and political disruption thereafter. The CEO of Petrobras, the Brazilian oil company, had a few weeks earlier given an even more alarmist view, claiming that 2010, not 2015, was likely to be recognised in retrospect as the time of peak oil, and that from then onwards the equivalent of one new Saudi Arabia

---

[11] A very limited number of CFDs are fully exchange tradeable in Australia, and one might expect this trend to spread, particularly given the apparent intention of the US government to make all derivative instruments effectively exchange tradeable, or have them issued by a recognised clearing house which would take upon itself the counterparty risk.

[12] UK Industry Taskforce on Peak Oil and Energy Security.

would be required every two years in order to maintain equilibrium. For the record, other senior oil industry executives[13] have also recently stated their belief that oil production has already reached its peak plateau.

In fact, this theory, though it may hold true with respect to conventional oil in specific countries, such as Russia, is now being questioned. Note the reference to "conventional oil". The reason that the "peak oil" school are being challenged by other industry experts is that there exist a whole range of other sources of oil, including tar sands, oil shale and heavy oil, known collectively as "unconventional oil". As reserves of conventional oil declines, so these other observers argue, prices will be driven higher, at which point exploitation of unconventional oil, though expensive, becomes economically viable, meaning that oil reserves will in fact last much longer than the peak oil theorists are projecting.

However, if, despite the counter-arguments, many people believe that global reserves of oil are finite and declining, why has the whole field of bio-fuels not come under close scrutiny? Well, the short answer is that it has, but thus far has not been able to come up with any commercially viable alternative that can be applied on a large scale.

Yes, given the relatively simple chemistry involved, trees and a wide range of agricultural products can be turned into ethanol (which has for many years formed a major part of the fuel used in Grand Prix motor racing), and cooking oil, even used cooking oil, can be turned into diesel fuel. The problems are scale and cost.

For a bio-fuel plant to produce a lot of fuel requires a lot of whatever substance(s) it is going to use as its raw material. There is a heavy cost to procuring and transporting this (which is why most bio-fuel plants today are very small and situated next to a source of supply, such as next to a lumber mill, working on wood chippings). Even where the process is subsidised, as, for example, the production of ethanol from corn has been in the US, it is highly inefficient. Some believe that producing the energy equivalent of ten barrels of oil in this way may consume as many as eight barrels in the process.

So, this is not currently a viable alternative, not even industrially, and thus certainly not for investors, though various specialist "alternative energy" funds do operate, and we must continue to hope for one or more technological breakthroughs which may transform the situation. Fuel cells, for example, were much hyped at one time, but have thus far failed to deliver anything approaching a total solution, although research continues in a number of exciting areas.

---

[13]Such as Christophe de Margerie of Total.

NATURAL GAS

Gas, for which an active trading market has existed since about 1994, used to be viewed as some sort of poor relation to oil. This was always a little hard to understand. From an industrial point of view, demand for natural gas is said to be growing twice as quickly as that for oil. It is particularly popular as a fuel source for power stations, since gas turbine generating plants can be built more quickly and cheaply than nuclear plants and with a lot less political unease.

Gas is much cleaner burning than either oil or coal, in terms of both carbon and greenhouse gas emissions. Already one fifth of the world's electricity is produced from gas, and that proportion looks set to climb steadily. In 2010 the CEO of Exxon said at a conference in Houston that he now saw natural gas as the future for his company, not oil.[14]

The other growth area is as a fuel source for vehicles. Both utilities and public bodies are under pressure to switch their vehicle fleets away from petrol or diesel engines, and gas is currently seen as the most practical solution, given the relatively short range and long charging time of electric vehicles. For example, in the US early in 2009 AT&T announced a $565 million programme to acquire 15 000 gas powered vehicles, and many cities around the world are said to be urging bus operators to take the same path.

Natural gas actually has a much longer history than many might suppose. According to Confucius, the Chinese were using natural gas, transported by a bamboo pipeline, to heat water to make salt as early as 500 BC. Six hundred years later the king of Persia had a royal kitchen built around a continuous flame provided by lighting a natural gas spring. By 1800, cities such as London were using piped gas to light homes and streets, though this was industrially manufactured coal gas, rather than the natural variety.

Gas as an investment can be accessed in exactly the same way as oil. In particular, there are various ETFs available, including some which are leveraged, and some which run a permanent short position. Thus, there is no reason in principle why investors should not be just as ready to include gas in their asset allocation plans as oil.

Why both? Well, there is an intriguing possibility here. The returns of gas and oil seem to be very lowly correlated against each other; in other words they do not seem to go up and down at the same time as each other and, indeed, if anything rather the opposite. In five out of the last 14 years, the annual return of one has been negative while the

---

[14]CERA, March 2010.

other has been positive, and very nearly so in one further year. In fact, their correlation from 1994 to the end of 2009 can be calculated at about −12%.

We have to be careful here, as we are using returns which are measured from one year end to the next, and so both correlation and volatility may be very different if measured, say, monthly or even weekly. Let us note this point and move on, though.

In principle, lowly correlated assets are the holy grail of asset allocation, or at least they are if you believe in the idea of extending the efficient frontier. Simply put, this states that it is possible, by adding lowly correlated assets to a portfolio, to create a new portfolio which may have both a higher rate of return, and a lower or similar level of "risk" (expressed as volatility). This flies in the face of traditional finance theory, which generally assumes that there is a fixed relationship between risk and return, and that you can only have one at the price of also accepting more of the other. This may be a convenient moment to demonstrate that the traditional view is mistaken, and that it is indeed possible in some circumstances to extend the Efficient Frontier.

If you look at Table 4.1, you will see that both oil and gas are hugely volatile asset classes. Even measured on a year-end basis, both their return ranges have a standard deviation in excess of 40%. Consequently their Sharpe Ratios, which show the relationship between their excess return and its standard deviation, are very low, signalling that these are relatively unattractive assets on a volatility adjusted basis. The FTSE Total Return index, for example, has a Sharpe Ratio which is nearly twice as high as that of oil, and four times as high as that of gas.

However, let us see what happens if we now construct a notional portfolio of 70% oil and 30% gas, and hold it throughout the period from when gas prices began to be available in 1994. See how the new combined portfolio shows both a significantly higher average return and yet lower volatility. The comparable FTSE figures are shown for comparative purposes.

Table 4.1   Oil and gas return characteristics

	Oil	Gas
Average annual return (%)	12.02	7.24
Standard deviation (%)	43.03	40.42
Sharpe Ratio	0.21	0.10

Note: Oil measured as Brent Crude from 1986. Gas measured from 1994. Sharpe Ratio calculated using a risk free rate of 3%.

Table 4.2   Oil and gas: effect of creating a blended portfolio

	Oil	Gas	Combined	FTSE
Average annual return (%)	12.02	7.24	15.45	9.46
Standard deviation (%)	43.03	40.42	33.87	16.34
Sharpe Ratio	0.21	0.10	0.40	0.40

Note: All figures calculated as before. Combined portfolio calculated as 70% oil and 30% gas.

You will see that holding a combined portfolio gives a much better result – a perfect argument in favour of a properly diversified portfolio. Yet how many investors would have thought that they could "diversify" their portfolio by holding two different types of energy asset (though they seem very happy to do so by adding different types of equity product)? There is a valuable lesson here: diversification is not about investing in something "different"; it is about investing in something which is likely to behave differently.

Of course, it could be argued that all we are doing here is to play around with historical performance figures, and yes, that is correct. Yet historic figures are all we have, at least as a starting point, and we are not trying to argue that this would have been exactly *the* right portfolio to hold over the given period, but only that it would have been *a* good one, and one, moreover, which almost certainly nobody would have ever considered.

So, yes, they are just historic figures, but they do show for the record that investors might have been much better off holding a blend of energy assets from 1994 onwards than investing on the London Stock Exchange, even assuming re-investment of dividends.

OIL AND GAS ROYALTIES

There is one other way of investing in oil and gas, and that is to buy a piece of the income streams which they produce. This sort of investment has been around for quite a long time. It is said to have been the brainchild of the legendary oilman T. Boone Pickens[15] in the late 1970s. Whether this is true or not, he was certainly prominent in the early days of royalty investing.

The theory is simple. An investment vehicle pays a fixed amount up front to purchase the right to receive a stream of production royalties

---

[15]Who, incidentally, is yet another senior industry figure who believes that "peak oil" has already occurred.

in the future. Thus, at least in cash flow terms, it is analogous to buying a bond or some other income producing instrument. The oil producer is able to pull forward the moment at which they receive the bulk of the income on their production, and so boost their working capital for things like prospecting for and developing new reserves, but there is a price for this. The price is that the agreed present value of the future royalties is pitched at such a level that the investors will enjoy a healthy yield on their initial investment.

Within a few years, institutional investors such as university endowments were participating in these ventures, drawn by the high yield nature of the returns. They continue to do so to this day, and in fact oil and gas royalties have remained a predominantly American asset class, perhaps partly because the whole way in which such investments were structured was expressly designed to be tax effective under US (and others under Canadian) law, so that the investment vehicle itself was not taxed but was treated as a tax transparent ("look-through") entity, with its individual investors being assessed for tax instead on their own personal percentage of the income, subject to their own individual tax circumstances. In this way, tax exempt investors such as college endowments could enjoy full flow-through of the royalty income without suffering any tax leakage which they may not be able to reclaim.

It should come as no surprise to learn that limited partnerships were frequently used for these purposes, since these have always been the look-through vehicle *par excellence*, at least under American law. However, from the very beginning royalty trusts were also used. These were able to achieve the same favourable tax treatment as limited partnerships provided certain conditions were fulfilled (the main one being that effectively all available earning had to be distributed as dividends). However, it currently seems as though Canadian royalty trusts ("Canroys") are likely to lose this favourable tax treatment in the near future.

The main difference between royalty trusts and limited partnerships is that the former are typically quoted, and thus are at least technically liquid, rather than being private vehicles. A difference between Canadian and American royalty trusts is that the latter are set up specifically to acquire one particular set of royalty streams, sometimes even specifically from just one oil field, whereas Canadian ones can purchase new royalty assets as they go along, if they wish. Thus, American trusts must sooner or later cease to have any income and get wound up, since one royalty stream cannot last forever, while Canadian trusts can operate as "evergreens", constantly renewing their assets if they wish, and running an ongoing investment business.

Unfortunately there is no publicly available data on how royalty trusts and partnerships have performed. However, the fact that investors continue to find space in their portfolios for them suggests strongly that they have performed at least in line with expectations. There is also some hearsay evidence that as they, like bonds, will tend to go up when interest rates go down, and vice versa, then they can provide some negatively correlated counterweight to quoted equities, but it must be stressed that this idea cannot scientifically be tested.

The advantages of holding interests in royalty streams are obvious from a cash-flow point of view, provided that you can bring your individual circumstances within the situation required for tax transparency; there are some circumstances, for example, in which non US resident investors can suffer withholding tax on income arising from investment partnerships, at least unless they are prepared to undergo lengthy and tortuous filing procedures.

The disadvantages of holding them from an investment strategy point of view will hopefully also be obvious. Yes, theoretically you are gaining some underlying exposure to oil or gas, but only in the form of an income stream. If we ignore what an investment is called, and focus instead on what it is and how it behaves, this situation seems much closer to buying a bond than to buying an oil futures contract, or some related derivative instrument. The latter gives you exposure, for better or worse, to the future price of oil, whereas the former just gives you a running yield, an income stream. If you were to buy a corporate bond issued by an oil company, would you not be in a very similar position, apart perhaps from the tax treatment of the income? The only real difference is that in the case of a corporate bond there may be significant default risk, whereas with a royalty vehicle the income stream is generally paid into a separate trust account. However, any such increase in perceived risk could easily be accommodated by lower pricing, and thus a higher return.

There is no intention here to be unduly negative about royalty trusts and partnerships. They have for many years performed a valuable service for investors and will continue to do so for many more years yet, but it is important to understand what they are and what they are not.

They are a valuable source of potentially high yield income in a tax-effective manner. They are not any real proxy for holding physical oil or gas. Apart from anything else, income of this nature tends to be relatively predictable, whereas holding gas or oil, or some synthetic equivalent of it, can be hugely volatile, with every possibility of either a very significant loss or a very significant gain. This certainty of outcome is undoubtedly one of the main attractions of a royalty trust or partnership. This possibility of dramatic upside is undoubtedly the main attraction of exposure to the asset itself. Neither can provide what the other has to offer.

ENERGY AS AN INVESTMENT

We have looked at the main ways in which investors can gain access to energy assets, and hopefully you have been persuaded that they merit at least serious consideration as portfolio components. The main element to bear in mind is their extreme volatility. These are absolutely not suitable assets for short term investors, and for these purposes "short term" would include anyone who might for any reason be forced to sell at a time that is not of their choosing. When dealing with volatile asset types, the imperative is to be able to choose when to sell; provided that you can fulfil this condition then volatility can be your friend, not your enemy.

This chapter would not be complete without a reference to electricity and carbon trading. Electricity trading has grown rapidly since deregulation in terms of numbers of transactions, but is still predominantly an industrial market in which few investors play (at least as yet). The main difference of electricity is that it is an energy source which cannot be stored, save in very limited circumstances, but must be consumed at once. Thus, in setting a price for a futures contract, one is setting a price to be agreed for future production and consumption, without any buffering or impact of stockpiles. The other, related problem is that because electricity has to be generated as required, it is very easy for producers, should they wish and should they be allowed to, to manipulate pricing by cutting generator output. Indeed, many blame deregulation for the economic disaster which befell the State of California in 2001 when they decided to sell off some of their generating facilities to out-of-state entities in the touching belief that the resulting "free market" would result in fairer (lower) pricing.

As for carbon emissions, there is an active market particularly under the European ETS.[16] However, it is small as yet, and it remains to be seen to what extent such trading will spread more widely, though some hedge funds have been established specifically for these purposes. Probably neither electricity nor carbon trading could currently be recommended as significant portfolio components, though they do deserve to be kept on the watch list.

---

[16]Emissions Trading System, which uses Emissions Trading Units (ETUs).

SUMMARY

An active global market for coal was established in the nineteenth century. While coal futures still exist, the overwhelming bulk of energy trading today takes place in oil and gas.

Physical ownership of oil is not a realistic option for investors. Their remaining choices are between (1) owning the shares of oil companies, (2) some form of synthetic exposure or (3) pooled synthetic exposure through ETFs.

Owning the shares of oil companies is not a good proxy for owning oil, as they will be heavily subject to stock market beta and thus have relatively little correlation with the price of oil.

Synthetic exposure can come at a significant price, particularly when futures markets are in abnormal ("contango") conditions, and also carries counterparty risk.

Most investors now accept ETFs as offering an acceptable compromise between investors' ideal requirements and what is practical given market reality.

Another recognised form of investment is to take an interest in royalty streams, either through a trust or partnership. These have been attractive cash-flow investments, but do not offer a valid proxy for the physical ownership of oil or gas.

Gas and oil are uncorrelated assets and seem to offer the possibility of both increasing returns and reducing volatility when held together, at least when historic data is analysed.

Non-US dollar investors should remember that both gas and oil are denominated in US dollars (though this proposition is increasingly coming under threat) and the implications of this should be fully discussed when deciding whether, and how, to access energy as an asset class. In particular, the use of some sort of currency overlay should be given serious consideration.

5
Private Equity

Private equity and hedge funds are alike widely misunderstood and often the butt of a great deal of prejudice. As in so many situations, prejudice is often born of lack of knowledge. In private equity, this ignorance even extends to a basic lack of understanding of what "private equity" actually is.

When conducting consultancy for clients on investment strategy, one will actually come across people, experienced investors or financial professionals from other backgrounds, who when private equity is mentioned will say something like "you mean illiquid, leveraged equity, don't you?" and then sit back and smile in a superior sort of way. These are usually people who also believe that private equity is really just a rather riskier proxy for holding quoted equities, and that they can simulate a private equity return by holding a quoted equity portfolio and adding leverage to it. This is particularly disappointing since there has been firm evidence available since 2006 that this does not work, and when quoted equity returns turn negative can work out very badly indeed;[1] the same research established that such a leveraged return was no match for even a capital weighted average private equity fund return, let alone the upper quartile.

It may be instructive, then, to set out a general definition of private equity, and then list the (very) different investment approaches which make up the asset type in general.

PRIVATE EQUITY – DEFINITION AND TYPES

For once, the name really does say it all. Private equity is about making investments usually structured as equity or equity related instruments in unquoted (private) companies. While this definition is no longer quite as watertight as it once was, it still holds generally true, since the only exceptions to it are very small in number: (1) when buying a public company (but even here the objective is usually to take the company private, hence the descriptions "Public to Private", "P2P" or "Take Private") and (2) inserting a convertible debt instrument into a public company (known as a "PIPE", standing for Private Instrument

---

[1] See *Multi Asset Class Investment Strategy*, already cited, in particular pages 124–129.

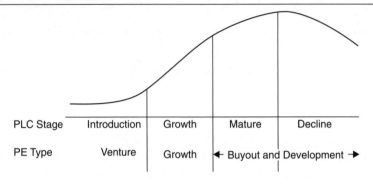

PLC Stage	Introduction	Growth	Mature	Decline
PE Type	Venture	Growth	◄ Buyout and Development ►	

Figure 5.1 Private Equity and the Product Life Cycle

in Public Equity). How small in number? Probably no more than one in every thousand transactions around the world.

There are four main types of private equity investment in companies: buyout, development capital, growth capital and venture capital. In addition, there is a fifth, mezzanine, which feeds on buyout transaction and therefore could not exist in its own right.

It may be convenient to think of the four main types of Private Equity as targeting companies at different stages of the Product (or service) Life Cycle. As will be seen, venture capital finances start-up and early stage companies, growth capital facilitates the sort of intensive business development which is essential in order to succeed in high growth markets, while buyout and development capital are appropriate for well established companies in mature, or even declining, industries.

Buyout

Characteristics

This is where the confusion really occurs, in that people believe that buyout, and indeed even one small part of the buyout industry, and "private equity" are one and the same, ignoring the fact that these funds represent only about 6% by number of the global population of private equity funds as a whole.

Buyout is characterised by two things which really set it apart from other types of private equity, so much so, in fact, that it is probably legitimate to question whether private equity really qualifies as one single asset class any more, with buyout transactions and funds, particularly the very largest examples (usually called mega-buyout), perhaps now constituting their own separate asset type. Fortunately, as pointed out elsewhere in this book, it probably does not matter what an asset is called, but only how it behaves, so we do not need to concern ourselves with this point further.

The first thing which sets buyout apart is that it takes majority stakes in companies. Indeed, it will usually seek a controlling interest of 100% or close to it;[2] all other forms of private equity take minority interests. For this reason, buyout is sometimes referred to as "control investing". The main reason for this is not necessarily a desire to be totally in control of the company's management (though that obviously confers a great advantage), but to facilitate through tax consolidation[3] the off-setting of operating earnings against the interest payable on debt which is taken out to help finance the buyout, which leads us into buyout's second distinguishing characteristic.

Buyout is the only form of private equity which uses acquisition debt, often referred to as "leverage" or "gearing". For that reason, all buyouts are in fact LBOs (leveraged buyouts), though this phrase is best avoided since it seems to have acquired a special sense of refer-ring to very large buyouts. As noted in the last paragraph, this sort of financial engineering depends on the availability of fairly sophisticated tax legislation, and this is available as yet only in a small number of countries; fortunately, they include most of the world's main financial centres.

Because of the need to service acquisition debt, buyout firms are ideally looking for companies which have strong positive cash flows. The idea of them targeting struggling and/or loss-making businesses is largely a myth for this reason. Distress and turnaround deals do get done, but mostly by specialist firms who operate in this area, and they are often debt rather than equity based. Classic buyout targets success-ful businesses where there may yet be potential for squeezing out some extra value.

Drivers

There are three drivers of buyout returns, representing the three ways in which value can be added to a buyout transaction. These are earnings growth, multiple expansion and debt.

---

[2] In practice, the company's management will be encouraged to take shares too. These are often referred to as "sweet equity" since they may be bought at a lower price than those of the buyout fund making the investment. However, for structuring reasons, these will usually be taken at the level of a new holding company, specially set up for the purpose.

[3] In many countries (particularly in Asia) this sort of group accounting for tax purposes is not available, and this is one of the most likely reasons why buyout activity may not be present in that country.

"Earnings" really splits into three, though in practice this is usually treated as just one category, not least because detailed financial data is usually unavailable. In reality, though, this can be a function either of (1) improving the company's cash flow by better management of working capital, (2) growing the company's sales or (3) improving the company's margins.

"Multiple expansion" refers to the possibility of selling the company on a higher multiple of earnings (or cash flow) than that which was used for valuation purposes when buying it. At least in the realm of mega-buyout, this has not been a realistic option for some time.

"Debt" refers to the possibility of paying off some of the acquisition debt during the period of ownership, thus effectively increasing the equity value on a dollar for dollar basis. The effect of debt is of course much more subtle and complex than this in reality, and to get a proper measure of this we would have to model the performance of the investment first on an unleveraged basis and then a leveraged one. However, at this point mathematical difficulties arise which render this all but impossible, at least without making certain arithmetic concessions, and so the more simplistic approach is commonly adopted.[4]

History and Development

It is important to understand that the nature of the buyout industry has changed dramatically since the glory days of the early 1990s where (particularly in Europe) it earned very high returns. For buyout has been very much a victim of its own success.

Very good returns in the early and mid 1990s, particularly in Europe, pulled increasingly large amounts of money into the industry, after the customary five to ten years which it seems to take most investors to spot an opportunity, so that from 2000 global fundraising increased greatly, and positively exploded from 2005 onwards, with average buyout fund sizes moving towards $1 billion. This, it should be stressed, was the *average*, with certain leading firms routinely raising more than $10 billion.

There are only two ways in which a private equity manager of any type can accommodate more fund capital: either do more deals, or do bigger deals. The former is difficult since it would clearly require more staff, and skilled private equity professionals take several years to train. So it was that, at least in the world of mega-buyout ($1 billion or more fund size), the nature of buyouts changed quite rapidly. Whereas in the

---

[4] See *Private Equity as an Asset Class* (Second Edition), John Wiley & Sons, Chichester, 2010, at page 92 for an explanation of Foucault's "three bodies" problem.

early 1990s (at least in Europe – the US buyout market developed earlier) target companies were often privately owned and relatively small, by the mid "zeros" they were much bigger, and consequently either public companies or subsidiaries of public companies. Deal-sourcing methodology also changed. Around 15 to 20 years ago, vendors could be approached proactively and a period of exclusivity agreed. Today, all deals now go through some form of controlled auction run by an investment bank.

In other words, the buyout market has transitioned from an imperfect market to a perfect one – bad news for investors, since it is market imperfections that usually offer the best chance of superior returns. From 2005 onwards a massive buyout bubble was created, driven partly by much larger fund sizes and partly by the sudden availability of "cov-lite" acquisition debt, as bankers fought with each other for the attractive arrangement fess that would drive their own personal annual bonuses. Even without the financial crisis and resultant credit crunch, buyout returns would have gone through a period of doldrums as highly priced deals slowly worked their way through the system. In the aftermath of the crisis, what would have been disappointing returns threaten to turn disastrous, with the very real possibility of the equity value of many buyouts being reduced to zero, and the companies being taken over by the banks.

It should be stressed that these comments apply overwhelmingly to mega-buyout, and that many smaller, "mid-market" buyout firms may emerge from the post-crisis period bloodied but unbowed, since the excesses of over-pricing and over-valuing were much less pronounced away from the blast furnace of public market multiples and cov-lite lending. Logically, therefore, investors should be turning towards small buyout firms and away from their big brothers, but there is little sign of this actually happening; indeed, as at the time of writing (May 2010), $10 billion buyout funds are once again being raised and/or announced. Sadly, therefore, it appears that as with US venture (see below), the necessary lessons have not been learned. Whatever the case, those who invest in mega-buyout funds are clearly going to have to accept much lower returns in the future than might once have been the case.

DEVELOPMENT CAPITAL

Characteristics

Development capital also targets mature, established companies, but takes a minority stake rather than a controlling position, and this essential difference from buyout transactions carries two important implications.

First, because what might be loosely termed "tax consolidation" is not available, it is not advantageous to use acquisition debt, and therefore this is very rarely found. The only way in which some element of leverage may be introduced is through the use by the private equity investor of loan stock (or loan notes, depending on which side of the Atlantic you inhabit), the interest on which is tax deductible. These will carry conversion rights known as "kickers" to place the investor in essentially the same position as if they held equity in the first place.

Second, the development capital firm must consider its position as a minority shareholder. There are two important issues here: protecting one's ability to exit from the company even though a minority shareholder, and protecting oneself from adverse management decisions in the meantime.

Minority Shareholder Protection

As we will shortly see, private equity returns are driven entirely by cash flows. Unless and until one is able to realise an equity position for cash, it counts for little in the eyes of any experienced fund investor. It is thus essential that in any position in which one is a minority shareholder, one is able to force an exit after a certain period (say three years or so) has elapsed. So, this consideration also weighs heavily in growth capital and venture capital, since they are also forms of minority investing, but it is much more pressing in the case of development capital; with both growth and venture, the company will normally be growing quickly and thus even if one takes a slightly longer ride there should be a correspondingly higher return at the end of the day by way of compensation. In the case of development capital, any discounted cash flow based valuation will tend to peak after about three years and thereafter decline, perhaps very rapidly. Exit protection is therefore essential.

A detailed discussion of private equity terms lies beyond the scope of this book,[5] but suffice it to say that you should expect a development capital investor to take some or all of the following:

- **Tag-along** gives the PE investor the right to force the majority shareholders to sell the minority stake alongside theirs in the event of them negotiating a sale.
- **Drag-along** is the opposite, giving the minority shareholder the right to negotiate a sale of the whole company, and to force the majority shareholders to sell their shares alongside the minority stake.

---

[5]But see Fraser-Sampson, *Private Equity as an Asset Class* (Second Edition), already cited.

- **Shoot-out** gives either side the right to name a price on certain dates, with the other shareholders then being forced to decide whether to buy or sell at that price.
- **Sell back** gives the minority shareholder a put option, usually based on some pre-agreed valuation formula, which might involve an earn-out.
- **Buy out** is exactly the same thing in reverse, i.e. with a call option instead of a put option.

The position during the period of minority ownership is dealt with by negative control, so called because it effectively gives the minority shareholder a right of veto over certain key management decisions. These would include the sale and purchase of business assets, bank lending, payment of dividends and salary levels.

Deal Types

Development capital transactions are traditionally divided into "money in" deals and "money out" deals, though in practice most are a hybrid of the two. In money in deals, the capital invested goes straight into the company in return for the issue of new shares, and will be used for whatever specific purpose has been agreed, which might be the opening of a new facility, entering a new market or paying down debt to recapitalise the business. In money out deals, the money goes not to the company in return for new shares, but to an existing shareholder who wishes to "cash out", against a transfer of some or all of their shares.

Development capital tends to be the first type of private equity activity to take root in a country, and so the world's emerging private equity markets (Asia, South America and Eastern Europe) feature it quite heavily, particularly since (as shown above) buyout activity will often not be possible in these markets for legal reasons.

Growth Capital

Like development capital, growth capital is minority stake investing, and the legal issues surrounding it, particularly as regards deal structuring, are very similar. For this reason many people confuse the two forms, but they are very different in their intent by virtue of the type of company which each targets. Whereas development capital is aimed, like buyout, at mature, established companies, growth capital is concerned with those which may still be relatively young, and (this is the important point) operate within markets which are experiencing very high rates of growth. Extreme examples of this occur during the introduction of new technology, such as video player and mobile phone type devices, but less obvious ones can be the growth of specialist consultancy following a government regulatory initiative, and even care related services for an ageing population.

It follows that when assessing a growth capital manager, investors should focus their enquiries and analysis on the manager's ability to grow sales. The fact that earnings (profits) may not grow proportionately should not be a cause for alarm; indeed, it is quite common for the earnings of a growth company to go down rather than up following a private equity investment. For this reason, many growth capital managers have reverted to a multiple of turnover as a valuation metric, a measure which would ordinarily seem very old-fashioned.

As pointed out above, the same considerations as regards minority protection will apply to growth capital as to development capital; however, so long as there is continuing growth potential within the company, then there is less urgency about this than would be the case with a business operating within a mature market.

VENTURE CAPITAL

Regarded by many as the most exciting form of private equity, this deals with the financing of early stage and start-up companies, understandably recognised and encouraged in the US as hugely valuable and desirable from a socio-economic point of view. A study originally sponsored by the NVCA[6] showed that even by 2000 venture backed companies had already created 8 million new jobs directly (roughly one for every \$36 000 of investment) and 27 million indirectly. Annual venture capital investment was equivalent to 1% of corporate America's capital expenditure, yet venture backed companies were responsible for 14% of American GDP. Less understandably, this point has never been grasped by European governments, either at national or Federal level, who, far from encouraging venture capital activity, go out of their way to deter it by excessive regulation and hostile tax regimes.

This difference of attitude towards venture capital at government level is mirrored by investors. In the US, venture capital has tended to be the private equity investment of choice, with investors being pushed towards mega-buyout by a combination of the sheer scale of the capital which they need to put to work, and the difficulty of accessing the best venture capital funds given the level of competition. In Europe, it is mega-buyout to which investors have turned, and when they do commit money to venture funds, these tend to be for investment in America,

---

[6]The lack of a country designation is a bit of a give-away here. National (US) Venture Capital Association.

not Europe. Consequently US venture is in general over-capitalised, with consequent upward pressure on valuations and downward pressure on returns, while European venture is dramatically under-capitalised to the extent that its very survival as an asset type must be in doubt.

Venture capital is different from other types of private equity in that they typically represent just one outflow, when the initial investment is made. With venture, investment takes place in a series of funding "rounds" over time (usually several years), with each round increasing in both size and value provided that the company remains on track. New investors will be introduced into some or all of these subsequent rounds, so that a venture capital manager has the option as to where they invest the bulk of their fund capital, and this is the first way in which we can differentiate different approaches to venture capital: by stage. There are three generally recognised stages of investment: early and/or seed, mid, and late.

These are easy to name but less easy to define. Early stage probably encompasses the first two funding rounds of a company's life, and at this stage the business will probably not have any customers. They may not even have finally settled on the exact nature of their product, nor fully developed it. Mid stage companies will tend to have worked through these issues and this is probably the most critical stage of a company's development since it is at mid stage that what some term the "rocket fuel" round occurs, which is intended to propel the company forwards very quickly indeed, so it is vital that it is first pointed in the right direction! Late stage companies will be those that now have established customers (though no profits, as they will still be spending heavily on expansion) and are building towards an exit planned either as a trade sale or IPO (flotation). For this reason, Late stage rounds are sometimes known as "pre-IPO funding".

The other way in which venture capital activity can be delineated is by the broad type of technology which the fund targets. Again, there are three: life science, information technology (IT) and telecommunications ("telecoms"). These are the three categories into which venture deals have traditionally been grouped, and there is thus a strong disincentive to change them since many large databases around the world would need to go back to the beginning of venture activity and start all over again.

This raises some obvious problems. Where, for example, does one put either cleantech or gaming, both of which are rapidly growing areas? Also, it is growing increasingly difficult in many cases to decide whether a business should be classified as IT or telecoms. For this reason, these two categories are often lumped together and described simply as "technology" or "tech".

Venture Returns and Home Runs

At the individual company level, venture returns are very binary. Studies suggest that roughly half of all venture companies will fail to return their capital, but that a very small number of big winners, known as "home runs", generate a very large proportion of total gains.[7] However, at the level of a single venture fund, which will typically invest in 20–30 companies, the capital risk is significantly reduced, while a properly diversified portfolio of funds will reduce the capital risk still further.

Like buyout, though, venture capital, at least in America, which dominates the global venture market by amount of capital, has been very much a victim of its own success. During the mid to late 1990s a small handful of the very best US venture firms (dubbed by the author "The Golden Circle", a term which has stuck) enjoyed spectacular returns. While it must be stressed that the returns of the industry as a whole were more pedestrian, these Golden Circle returns, and the publicity which they generated, drew a huge amount of new capital into venture capital which, combined with a technology and "dot com" bubble, created a cyclone of rapidly rising valuations, instant fortunes and highly blown reputations.

As we all know, this artificial utopia exploded in 2001, and since then venture returns, at least if measured by cash exits, have slumped. It is only fair to record that some, even some among the Golden Circle, have questioned whether the basic venture model itself may now be broken, particularly in view of the fact that fundraising has returned to mid-bubble levels, even without the proven returns which sustained it last time around.

Probably the best that can be said about venture capital, at least in the United States, is that "the jury is still out" as to whether returns can ever scale anything like the heights which they did in the mid 1990s. It is perhaps more likely that we may have entered a new age of much more modest returns, which will be permanently damped down by weight of investor capital. As at 2010, it was necessary to go back to 1998 for the year of birth of even the upper quartile US venture fund which had returned its paid-in capital. Was this just a "lost decade" of venture returns, a blip (albeit a very long one) in an otherwise consistently successful industry track record, or did it herald a stark new reality?

The answer to this question will emerge in due course, but one important consideration is that the best venture capital opportunities for

---

[7]See *Private Equity as an Asset Class*, already cited.

investors may well no longer lie in the US. This is a vital point to grasp for anyone contemplating accessing private equity through a fund of funds, since it is precisely these US venture funds, together with mega-buyout funds, which they traditionally target.

MEZZANINE

Mezzanine funds are complementary to buyout funds, providing the "mezzanine" layer of debt for individual buyouts. In Europe, mezzanine, taking the form of convertible debt instruments, tends to be the most common element of "junior debt" (so called because the conventional bank debt has the right to be paid back first in the event of any default or liquidation). In the US, bonds are more usual, particularly in "mega" transactions.

Mezzanine funds may typically be expected to provide a return to investors that is somewhere in between a corporate debt rate and a buyout fund return. They tend to perform well when debt is expensive and/or difficult to obtain, and to languish when the opposite is the case.

QUOTED PRIVATE EQUITY

Traditionally, as has already been outlined, "the fetish of liquidity" has driven many investors to seek to access even illiquid assets in a way which delivers liquidity (or, in some cases, apparent liquidity), and private equity is no exception. As we have already seen through an earlier example, there have for many years been quoted investment vehicles[8] on the London Stock Exchange, the most prominent of which is 3i (effectively a quoted private equity fund), but it has also been possible to invest in quoted funds of funds, such as Standard Life and Pantheon.

It is necessary here to draw a distinction between two different situations. In the first, an investor decides to access private equity through private fund vehicles, which we will examine in the next section. However, as we will see, the way in which these operate can leave large amounts of cash lying around uninvested at any one time. In this situation the investor, though committed to the idea of a programme of private funds, uses quoted private equity as a sort of money box, somewhere to park uninvested capital that will hopefully still earn some sort of private equity return.

In the second, the investor eschews private funds altogether for whatever reason and seeks exposure solely through quoted private equity.

---

[8]Traditionally known as PEITs ("Peets") as they were initially structured as investment trusts.

This might be driven for example by regulatory requirements forbidding an investor from holding illiquid assets, or those which cannot be marked to market. More often, sadly, it is driven by the sort of mistaken ideas about investment strategy which have already been outlined in a previous chapter.

There have been times when such an approach would have worked very well. Between 2004 and early 2007, for example, their performance (which is usually stated to exclude 3i, since the latter is part of the FTSE 100 index, which is used for comparative purposes) was dramatically better than that of quoted equities. Direct comparisons with private funds cannot be made, since returns are measured on different bases, but any investor would have been well satisfied with the results; $100 invested in mid-2003 would have peaked at about $240 in early 2007.[9] Impressive as they are, these figures should be analysed further, whereupon it emerges that this bull run was driven primarily by price, not asset value. In other words, what happened during this period was that the shares of these quoted vehicles were trading at a progressively higher premium to the net asset value (NAV) of the underlying portfolio. Put another way, one can argue that investor sentiment provided the major impetus for the bull run.

Investor sentiment is a double edged sword, however. When it turned negative in 2007, it proved to exercise an even more powerful effect in the opposite direction. We have already seen what happened specifically to 3i. If we now look at the other quoted vehicles excluding 3i, we see an even more dramatic picture. By the beginning of 2009 that market price of $240 had declined to only just above $50, representing a five year 50% loss even before considering the effects of inflation. NAV, however, was still about $130.

To be fair, nobody had predicted this and probably nobody *could* have predicted it. While everyone appreciated that as a matter of financial theory the price of any quoted vehicle such as 3i should always move to some extent in line with stock market beta, nobody had ever imagined that in abnormal market conditions such as prevailed at different times in 2007 and 2008 the results would be so extreme. Hopefully investors are now both sadder and wiser. We now know that seeking liquidity in respect of illiquid assets is likely to lead to greater volatility of periodic returns, not less, the exact opposite of investor expectations.

If ever we needed confirmation of the need for uncorrelated returns (and of the difficulty of obtaining them), surely the events of 2008 provided it. Traditional ways of looking at investment portfolios are wrong. Correlation (or lack of it) should be a far more pressing concern

---

[9]LPEQ / Morningstar.

for investors than volatility, and the more exposure one has to quoted markets then the less possible it will be to find low correlation. If one's exposure is to one particular quoted market, of course, then the task becomes all but impossible. Quoted private equity may provide liquidity, but one of the primary motives for investing in alternative assets is to seek uncorrelated returns, and here quoted private equity can be clearly seen to have fallen at the first hurdle. When the sun explodes, it is best to be as far away from it as possible.

For the sake of completeness, it should be noted that another form of quoted private equity revolves around the use of various private equity indices, which can be made "investable" by the use of ETF[10] type vehicles. All these represent, however, are different baskets of quoted private equity vehicles, and so one is really no better off than investing in 3i except that one has a more diversified portfolio.

In truth, quoted private equity can never provide a true proxy for investing in private funds, since the former may at different times be cash rich, and the return which they provide at these times may thus include a significant element of cash return, particularly should prevailing interest rates be high. Private funds, as we will see, specifically exclude a cash return since they do not hold uninvested capital.

These various stumbling blocks combine to cast very substantial doubts over the wisdom of investing in quoted private equity, at least if one's objective is to achieve a proxy for actual private equity exposure which is lowly correlated to public equity markets. Given the very significant extra volatility to which they are subject, even the attractiveness of using them to "park" capital which has been allocated to private equity but is as yet uninvested has now been seriously thrown into question – yet another lesson which should be drawn from the events of 2008.

PRIVATE EQUITY FUNDS

Private equity funds are generally structured as limited partnerships, hence managers are known as "GPs" (General Partners) while investors are known as "LPs" (Limited Partners).[11] So prevalent has this terminology become that it is frequently used by other asset types, such as hedge funds, even where the legal structure of the vehicle is not a limited partnership at all.

---

[10]Exchange traded funds.

[11]There are some countries in the world where this is not possible, either because the limited partnership is not recognised as a legal vehicle, or because the concept of tax transparency upon which it rests has not yet been introduced. In India, for example, Private Equity funds are routinely structured as trusts, with an offshore beneficiary entity in Mauritius.

The idea behind a limited partnership is that there may be any number of passive investors. In return for agreeing to take no part in the decision making process the law confers limited liability upon them; in other words, they cannot be liable for any debts of the partnership (though in practice, a private equity fund, unlike, say, a hedge fund, will never have any) beyond the amount of the capital which they have committed to the partnership. There must, however, be at least one General Partner who actually runs the business (in this case, taking the investment and divestment decisions), and who will have unlimited liability.[12]

Limited partnerships confer three distinct advantages on private equity investing:

1. They allow the free movement of cash flows both in (by way of "drawdowns" or "capital calls") and out (by way of "distributions") of the fund as investments are bought and realised.
2. They allow for various legal requirements surrounding US pension funds (known as "ERISA"[13]) to be quite easily satisfied, US pension funds being a major contributor of private equity fund capital.
3. They are tax transparent,[14] allowing LPs to be taxed on capital gains in their own jurisdiction. This is clearly a major issue for those investors who are tax exempt in their own jurisdiction, whether wholly or partly.

Since partnerships are creatures of contract, it is open to the partners to agree any terms they like. What follows should, therefore, be taken as a brief summary of those terms which are commonly encountered.

Private equity funds are usually expressed to run for ten years, but with the GP having the right to extend the fund's life twice, for one year each time. Further extensions will require the consent of some proportion of the LPs. The legal documents will give the GP five years within which to invest[15] the fund's capital, though in practice they will aim to do this within the first three years, beginning to raise a successor fund around the end of year two so as to have a new flow of capital ready to come on stream at the end of year three. Each GP will therefore be managing multiple funds, raised about three years apart and denominated by Roman numerals.

---

[12]In practice, this is avoided by the use of a limited liability GP vehicle, such as a limited company.
[13]Employee Retirement Income Security Act.
[14]At least in those countries which recognise this concept.
[15]Or, in the case of venture funds, "invest or reserve", in other words taking into account money which is earmarked for the later funding rounds of portfolio companies.

The main feature which sets private equity funds apart from all others[16] is that the investors do not pay their money into the fund up front on day one. Instead they enter into a "commitment" (a legally binding promise) to pay the money as and when the GP asks for it, either for the purposes of making investments or paying fees and costs. Similarly, as the GP realises investments, that money will straight away be distributed back to the LPs. A private equity fund may accordingly be thought of as being rather like a water-pipe, existing only to facilitate the two-way flow of water (money), both upwards and downwards.

Thus, there is always a difference between committed capital (the amount pledged), drawdown capital (the amount so far called from the LP), and, in turn, invested capital (the amount which has actually gone into portfolio companies, as opposed to paying fees and costs). These differences, arising from the way in which private equity funds work, have important implications for the way in which private equity returns are made, measured, and analysed (see below).

GPs are rewarded for their efforts in two different ways – management fee and carried interest – and this model has been copied by the likes of hedge funds and private real estate. Management fee (usually between 1.5% and 2% depending on the size of the fund) bites on *committed* capital, and thus will be disproportionately large in the early years of the fund, when relatively little capital has been invested. Carried interest, or "carry", is typically calculated as 20% of the gains made on investments, though there are various ways in which this can actually be measured and paid in practice, which may take into account the losses made on unsuccessful investments, money drawndown for fees and costs, or even a certain preferred return to which the LPs are entitled before any carry becomes payable at all.

PRIVATE EQUITY RETURNS

The first and most important point to understand about private equity returns is that they cannot be measured by traditional periodic methodology, such as annual returns. In fact, there is a strong argument that annual returns are not a good measure of any asset type's returns, since they ignore cash flows and the time value of money, and that private equity is simply an extreme example of this.

By way of illustration, let us consider what would happen were you to analyse the annual return of a private equity fund at an early stage of its life. Since a significant part of the money going into the fund would be being used not to make investments but to pay fees and costs,

---

[16]Save only private real estate and private infrastructure.

the return would necessarily be negative, since the NAV at the end of the year would be less than the amount of capital paid in. Similarly, in the later years of the fund, as exits are realised at a profit and the proceeds returned to LPs, or perhaps some portfolios are revalued upwards based on offers made for them, or market comparables, the return would necessarily be positive. Yet neither would be a valid measure of whether this fund represented a good investment or not. For that, one must look at its performance over its whole life.

Of course, you might argue that you could measure the annual return for each year and then "annualise" it (take the average) just as you would for, say, a mutual fund. Why would this be inappropriate? Because it would ignore the time value of money. An annualised return assumes that the impact of every year is equally important, whereas the reality is that for every extra year that one has to wait to receive a cash flow, its present value diminishes. In other words, a rational investor, if asked to wait an extra year to receive money from an investment, would require a higher future amount. Annualised returns ignore this.

Thus periodic, or average periodic returns are not a valid measure where either (1) an investment exhibits positive and negative cash flows at different stages of its life or (2) where an investment provides no cash flows at all, but only a lump sum payback at the end of its life. Would it be fair, for example, to measure buying and holding gold for ten years in the same way as buying and holding quoted equities for ten years? Yes, in each case there will be a capital gain or loss, but quoted equities will provide you with dividends every year, whereas gold will not. If you *are* going to measure them in the same way, then surely the only valid way to do so would be by way of a compound return, which takes these differences of cash flows and timing into account?

THE J-CURVE, IRRS AND MULTIPLES

Let us consider the way in which the cash flows of a private equity fund occur.[17]

Figure 5.2 shows both the net annual cash flows of a typical private equity fund and the cumulative position at the end of each year. Note the shape: this is commonly referred to as the J-Curve.[18] Every private

---

[17]This figure is reproduced by kind permission of the publishers from *Private Equity as an Asset Class*, already cited.

[18]Though technically the J-Curve represents the (similar) pattern which is obtained by measuring the cumulative IRR of the fund at the end of each year.

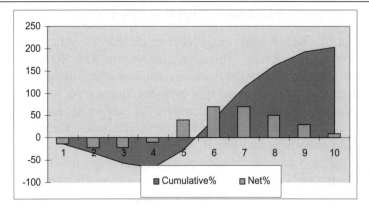

Figure 5.2   PE fund cash flow pattern

equity fund will have a J-Curve, though the shape of this may be different according to the type of investment (buyout, venture, etc.). While the overall pattern of the cash flows as a whole can be predicted, or at least expected, the individual underlying investment cash flows cannot. Indeed, they are entirely unpredictable as regards both their timing and their amount.

It is for this reason that it is customary to measure private equity fund returns by means of their IRR (internal rate of return). Do not worry if you have not come across this mechanism before; it can be easily measured by spreadsheets,[19] the only requirement being that the first cash flow in the series should be negative (which in the case of a private equity fund it always will be). It is simply a measure of the compound return to an investor of a series of cash flows over time.[20]

Another way in which fund performance can be assessed is by means of a simple money multiple, of which there are several varieties, each of which is useful for illustrating a particular point and/or at a different stage of a fund's life. It is important to have regard to both IRRs and multiples in order to arrive at a true and fair picture. For example, an investment which is held for a short period, say less than a year, can deliver a very impressive IRR without greatly increasing an LP's capital. An investment which is held for six or seven years, by contrast, might well need to generate a very significant amount of capital gain in order to deliver an IRR even half as (apparently) good.

---

[19]The Excel™ function is "=IRR (range, guess)". For "range" simply cut and paste the cells containing the relevant cashflows. "Guess" is optional and can be omitted.

[20]As a matter of financial theory, it is the discount rate which, when applied to a series of cash flows, produces a Net Present Value of zero.

VINTAGE YEAR RETURNS

The year in which a fund comes into existence is its vintage year – its year of birth, if you will.[21] Private equity returns, both IRR and multiple, are listed in the various industry databases by vintage year, and sub-divided broadly by geography and investment type.

In this way one can validly compare the performance of one fund against another, or at least against all other similar funds, since if they are all of the same type and began investing at the same time then they should logically all be at the same place on their respective J-Curves.

In any form of investment, diversification is an essential requirement. With private equity, diversification by time, that is exposure to each and every available vintage year, is perhaps even more important than diversification by geography and investment type. Investors should therefore look to plan their fund programme over time, committing their allocation over several years. In this way the disappointing returns of any one vintage year can be diversified away.

FUNDS, FUNDS OF FUNDS AND SECONDARIES

The way in which an LP chooses to access private equity funds will be in one or more of three ways, the mix being determined partly by the amounts of capital involved, and partly by the level of sophistication within the investing organisation.

An LP may choose to bring together an in-house team to make their own fund picks, building a portfolio of private equity funds over the years. Others choose to invest with a fund of funds manager, partly because the latter can reasonably be expected to display a greater level of expertise in fund and GP selection, partly because it represents a way of outsourcing the (considerable) management and administrative processes which a private equity fund programme requires.

Mention should be made of secondary investing, which is performed alike by LPs, funds of funds and specialist secondary funds. While it is true that private equity funds are illiquid investment vehicles, a thriving secondary market provides practical liquidity, at least for mature (largely invested) funds, and in particular for buyout funds, where the level of uncertainty of outcome is obviously much less than is the case with venture capital. Incidentally, this is one way in which an LP may seek to balance their exposure across different vintage years, by buying or selling in the secondary market as appropriate.

---

[21] Though, confusingly, this is referred to as "closing", whereas "opening" might be a more accurate description.

A word of caution should be entered at this point, however. Private equity is a long term investment class, and a commitment to a private equity fund should on no account be made with a view to doing anything other than remaining an LP for the life of the fund. For one thing, there can be no guarantee that a particular LP interest may be sellable at any particular time. For another, LP interests routinely change hands at a discount to their real value; how else could secondary investors make money …?

CONCLUDING THOUGHTS ON PRIVATE EQUITY

Private equity has traditionally offered an opportunity for very superior returns, consistently out-performing every other asset class, even on a capital weighted average[22] basis. However, there is considerable uncertainty as to how returns from vintage years 2005 onwards are likely to perform, and it would be dangerous, and almost certainly wrong, to assume that historic track record is here any valid guide to the future. On the contrary, the onset of the financial crisis in mid-2007 propelled all forms of private equity investment, but most notably mega-buyout, into what may come to be recognised as a critical period of structural change. Certainly it is a period which poses significant challenges for GPs across all investment types, and unless and until (1) the exit market stabilises and (2) financial markets, both debt and equity, return to anything like "normality" (whatever that may prove to be), it is impossible to come to any sensible conclusions as to the possible range of future private equity returns.

Certainly they will be lower, across the board, than in the 1990s – bad news for those who invest by gazing into their rear view mirrors – but just how much lower it is currently impossible to predict. Instinctively, however, it feels right that away from mega-buyout they should still out-perform public equity markets on a long term basis, and even within mega-buyout it may be possible for a very small number of skilled managers to continue to produce satisfactory returns (but almost certainly only if they are prepared to eschew public-to-private transactions, the investment rationale for which had always seemed tenuous, even before the crisis).

There are two things for investors to bear in mind. First, private equity is a classically illiquid form of investment. This means that where an investor is prepared to give up short term liquidity in the expectation of higher long term returns then private equity will always be a prime candidate for a significant allocation. Also, as we have seen,

---

[22]Probably the fairest indicator of the performance of the industry as a whole.

contrary to conventional wisdom, it has been shown that investing in illiquid assets actually reduces, rather than increases, "risk" (in its traditional sense of volatility).

Second, is the potential for private equity as a source of lowly correlated return. This is a slightly difficult discussion, however. As we have already seen, annual returns (which are required to calculate correlation), though available, are not a valid measure of private equity performance and, thus, this will always be a somewhat artificial calculation. For what it is worth, though, the results of such calculations suggest about 60%, which is certainly a higher level than one would normally target.

Apart from the obvious broad objection about the return measure itself, there are two other points to bear in mind, both of which must be dealt with on a conceptual level since there is no publicly available data to analyse.

First, since 2001, even more so since 2005, and particularly in Europe, an increasingly larger proportion of total private equity capital has been made up by mega-buyout funds. Logically, one would expect these to show high correlation with public equity markets since they will tend to exit their investments when quoted markets are strong, and have to write down their investments when public markets are weak. Thus, it is entirely possible that the annual return figures (which, sadly and inexplicably are only available for the global market as a whole) mask a situation in which mega-buyout has very high correlation with the stock market, while everything else, and particularly growth and venture capital, have very low correlation.

The second is the way in which private equity returns operate and again a distinction must be drawn between mega-buyout and the rest. Away from the media glare of these very large transactions, GPs struggle to keep their asset valuations as close to cost as possible (and in the case of venture this will always be the case, at least so far as the cost of the last funding round is concerned); after all, nobody wants to get a reputation for over-cooking their performance figures, something which exiting below book value would imply. This means that when an investment is exited there will normally be uplift in value. In accounting terms, that gain would show up in the annual accounts and thus have to be taken into account when calculating the annual return. It will thus have the effect of artificially increasing correlation since (1) PE funds will have more exits when public markets are strong and (2) it will appear as if all the gain has been made in the year of exit, rather than gradually during the life of the investment.

The whole question of the possible correlation of private equity returns must therefore be treated with great care and careful consideration. Certainly one cannot just look at the headline figures (unless of course you have decided only to invest in mega-buyout which, surprisingly, some people have done). The author's instinct is that it would be most unwise, in correlation terms, to carry both a large allocation to mega-buyout and a large allocation to quoted equity markets alongside each other in the same portfolio, but that a properly balanced and diversified private equity fund programme would be a very different matter.

Certainly given its excellent performance in the past, this is not an asset type that can be ignored. However, perhaps more so than any other alternative asset, it is one where investment should not be undertaken unless and until one has taken the time and effort required to learn all the intricacies of what is a very complex area. Recognition that there is more to "private equity" than mega-buyout might perhaps be a convenient starting point.

SUMMARY

"Private equity" covers a wide range of investment activity, of which buyout is only one strand and mega-buyout (which many investors believe to constitute "private equity") but one sub-strand. Other strands include development capital, growth capital, venture capital, mezzanine and secondary investing.

Buyout takes controlling interests in established companies and makes use of acquisition debt. Thus, all buyouts are leveraged transactions. All other private equity transactions (perhaps 90% of the total by number) are **not** leveraged.

Development capital takes minority stakes in established companies.

Growth capital takes minority stakes in companies in very high growth markets.

Venture capital takes minority stakes in start-up and early stage businesses.

Mezzanine is a very specialist area, providing convertible debt financing for buyouts.

Secondary investing involves buying existing interests in private equity funds.

Private equity funds are typically structured as limited partnerships. Thus, investors are known as LPs (Limited Partners) and managers are known as GPs (General Partners). They are closed end vehicles, typically lasting initially for ten years but with the possibility of at least two one year extensions. They differ from most other types of investment funds in that money is not paid into the fund up front, but gradually over time as the GP asks for it.

Private equity produced very high returns in the 1990s – consistently higher, in fact, than any other asset class. However, the size and nature of many areas of private equity investing (notably US venture and mega-buyout, particularly in Europe) have changed dramatically, and it seems almost certain that similar levels of return will be unattainable in the future. Exactly what future returns will look like is currently a matter of conjecture.

Private equity is a tried and tested institutional asset class, and is a strong candidate for a large allocation within any portfolio. However, perhaps more so than with any other type of investment, a thorough understanding of all private equity types and an intelligent approach to constructing a fund investment programme are essential. It is strongly advised that no allocation should be made unless and until these requirements can be satisfied.

6
Hedge Funds

INTRODUCTION

Perhaps no asset class is so little understood as hedge funds. Yes, private equity is seen as very mysterious, and most people do not realise that there are other forms of private equity than mega-buyout, but at least there is a basic understanding of what they actually *do*. They take stakes in private companies (though, as we have seen, that basic definition is now coming under threat). Very few investors, though, have any idea what hedge funds actually do.

Other basic questions follow close behind. What are they? How do they operate? What sort of investment approaches do they pursue?

These questions are not nearly as easy to answer as one would wish. For a start, there is great debate and confusion about what actually constitutes a "hedge fund". In fact, there is a deliberate ambiguity in the very first few words of this chapter. Are hedge funds really an asset class at all? If they are, then there must be certain basic similarities which run through them all. After all, an asset class suggests a collection of investments which are somehow homogeneous. Hedge funds, by contrast, display a baffling breadth of investment approaches. So much so, in fact, that most observers now agree that they are not really an asset class, in the true sense, at all. For example, we will be looking separately at active currency as an asset class in its own right, whereas many would class it (or at least the different strategies which currency managers employ) as a branch of the hedge fund genre. To muddy the waters further, the use of hedge fund type techniques is now being advocated in other asset classes, such as real estate.

So, right from the outset, let us be clear that in discussing hedge funds one will often be generalising, and that there will always be at least a small number of hedge funds which do not necessarily fit exactly what we are saying. If this were a book about hedge funds, rather than alternative assets, it would be fascinating to go into all the complex ramifications. Within the confines of a single chapter, generalisations are all that is possible. Hopefully any readers who actually work in the hedge fund industry will understand this, and forgive the occasional lack of specific discussion.

USE OF DERIVATIVE INSTRUMENTS

Much of the confusion as to what hedge funds might be arises from the word "hedge", for we think we know what hedging is, and actually this is not what hedge funds do at all. The confusion is entirely understandable, since the word "hedge" has a perfectly normal meaning in investment circles, and is here used out of context. In fact, some of the world's leading investors, such as the Yale Endowment, refer to them simply as "absolute return" funds, yet this in turn introduces even more confusion, since this term too can be used in a number of subtly different ways.

Let us consider first what we mean by hedging. This is a perfectly normal activity which is used by investors and businesses around the world on a daily basis. Let us ignore its use by those who want to reduce uncertainty in the price they will pay or receive for something which they use or produce in their business, and the related field of foreign currency exposure. Let us focus instead on its use by institutional investors. Perhaps a slightly silly example might illustrate the point.

Suppose that an investor is running a share portfolio and has been set a target rate of return to achieve during the calendar year of 10%. It is now the end of September and the investor has already made 11% for the year to date. If his figure is still no less than 10% at the end of December, he will get a large bonus. If it is less than that, he will not. What is he to do?

Well, one possibility might be to cash out his position. He can bank the starting capital and the 10% gain, thus guaranteeing that at the end of the year his performance bonus will be paid, and he could use the small amount left over to buy an option on the stock market. He could buy a call option, so that if the market continues to go up he will take some part of it (though not as much as he would have done if he stayed fully invested), but if it goes down all he will have lost will be the price of the option, which he can do without anyway. Instead of cashing out his position, however, he might decide to buy a put option. The value of his portfolio is now protected should the market suddenly fall, since his profit on the put option will off-set his loss on the share portfolio.

This investor has just hedged his position. He had a portfolio of shares being traded on a stock market, and he took out an option position (a "hedge") on the same market to protect that portfolio from any possible downside. For equities, this is most commonly done with options, but in other markets and situations may require more complex instruments such as credit derivatives or interest rate swaps.

So, a mainstream investor uses these instruments to hedge an underlying position of some kind. A business may do the same thing. A farmer who is growing a crop of wheat which is due to be harvested in August may decide, for example, to buy an August put option for the same quantity of wheat that he hopes to produce. The strike price of the option is likely to be less than he is hoping for ideally, but that difference represents the cost that he is willing to pay for certainty. Should there be a bad harvest, and the price of wheat shoot up, then he will lose out. He is more concerned to limit his downside, though. Should there be a bumper harvest and the price of wheat go down, he can sell his option and the money he makes should compensate him for what he would otherwise lose on selling the wheat. This is in fact exactly how options and futures markets originated, and why they are largely concentrated in Chicago, since this was the traditional trading post and exit port for much of America's agricultural produce.

The difference with a hedge fund type investor is that there is no underlying position, whether of shares, wheat or anything else. "Why tie up all my capital in the market", a hedge fund manager might ask, "when I can get the same amount of market exposure by buying an option for a fraction of the price?" So, if he thinks the stock market is likely to go up then instead of buying $100 million of shares he will buy a call option over $100 million of shares, which is likely to cost him much less, say $10 million for the sake of example. If the market goes up, he will make exactly the same gain that he would have made by buying the shares, but the advantage is that he will have had the use of the remaining $90 million for other purposes in the meantime. Thus, even if he has simply invested that cash in the money market he will be better off by the amount of the interest which it will have earned. "What could possibly be wrong with that?", the hedge fund manager would argue. "Surely it represents a more efficient use of capital?"

The answer to which is "it all depends". It all depends on the alternative use to which you put the remaining 90% of your money. If indeed you simply place it on the money market then in principle this is indeed a more efficient use of your capital. There are two things to consider, however, both of which may have a significant bearing on the issue.

First, what happens if the market goes down, at least in the short to medium term, rather than up? Options only run for a limited period and if the market goes down then a call option will become worthless (since it would require its holder to buy the market above its present level) and will expire. A fresh sum will then be required to buy a new option to cover the next period. If you had bought shares instead, you would be nursing a paper loss on your portfolio, but assuming that the market does indeed go up sooner or later, you would not have to lay out this extra cash. This is sometimes called the contango effect (though this is itself confusing, since the word is also used in a different sense) and we will be considering it further when examining other asset classes.

Second, there is that question of the alternative use of your capital. Suppose that you were certain that the market was going to go up and desperate not to lose out on the opportunity. Might you not be tempted to use the remaining $90 million as the purchase price of nine further options, so that now when the market goes up you will make ten times the gain you would have earned simply by buying the shares. The problem is, of course, that there is no "when" in the world of finance, but only "if". Should the market go down instead of up, then all ten of your options would expire out of the money, you would have blown all your capital, and your hedge fund would go bust.

It is not suggested, incidentally, that there is any hedge fund out there that has actually done this, or would contemplate such a high risk approach. It is simply an extreme hypothetical example, chosen to illustrate a point.

LEVERAGE

It must be the case, though, that if even some of the remaining capital is used for any purpose other than accumulating a risk free return then you will have effectively leveraged your position. This was, incidentally, something that was overlooked by a lot of investors who went into "portable alpha" schemes, many of which used some variant of this device. Similarly there was much talk before mid-2007 (but none since) of so-called "90/110" or even "80/120" funds, which were designed to capture 110% or 120% of the market return while being only 90% or 80% invested in the market. This is a classic example of the search for extra return necessitating the adoption of the extra risk which the leverage represents.

All hedge funds leverage their positions in this way, although this is not necessarily as alarming as it might at first sound since, as we will see, each position will often be largely balanced against another contrary or complementary one.

In addition to this, however, is the very real leverage provided by the use of debt. In pre-credit crunch days this was provided by the prime brokerage market.

As the name suggests, a prime broker provides a hedge fund with both dealing and custody services. It is much more than this, however. Prime brokers are all part of a banking organisation, and so also were able in the run up to the crisis to provide them with debt – lots of it. When Carlyle Capital Corporation went bust, for example, they had about 33 times gearing. In fairness to them, though, it should be pointed out that many others, at least according to rumour, had very much more – well in excess of 100 times.

An obvious objection to hedge fund activity might be that to bring such high levels of gearing to bear on what are already effectively leveraged positions because of the use of derivative instruments could be regarded as highly irresponsible. Again though, it must be remembered that many hedge fund approaches involve the setting up of two or more trades in conjunction with each other which are designed to be at least partially off-setting. Thus, provided normal market conditions prevailed, the overall risk was often perceived as small. What the hedge fund industry could not have predicted was a prolonged period of abnormal market conditions (of which September 2008 was probably the most extreme example) when both pricing mechanisms and liquidity collapsed.

However, some at least had seen the risk. In the early part of 2007 the Bank of England issued a brief report on the hedge fund industry, dealing in particular with the collapse of Amaranth in 2006, an event which had sent shock waves through investors around the world. The Bank pointed out:

> *Amaranth's failure occurred at a time when market conditions were generally benign. In more adverse circumstances, fire sales of assets could have been more dangerous and the impact wider.*[1]

In retrospect, this was of course a statement rich in dramatic irony, since this is exactly what transpired shortly thereafter, and on a massive scale.

Yet, how did such large exposures of debt build up? This was in part a combination of rising markets and investor expectations. In a rising market, a long only manager will make good returns. If a hedge fund is taking some contrary positions (i.e. is long/short) then it should logically perform less well than the market. There are only two ways to address this problem. One is to become long only yourself (which many hedge funds effectively did). The other is to leverage your returns by the use of debt.

A cynic might argue that this whole cycle was essentially fee-driven. The hedge funds had persuaded investors to pay them private equity-like levels of fees and carried interest. Most hedge fund strategies, though, were extremely unlikely to deliver anything like long term private equity returns. Indeed, as we have just seen, in rising equity markets many were unlikely to out-perform even a conventional long only manager, since many of their strategies were as much about reducing risk

---

[1] Bank of England Financial Stability Report April 2007.

(or, at least, volatility) as increasing return. So, in order to earn the sort of superior returns which might justify their high fees, they asked their prime brokers for significant amounts of debt, which the prime brokers were happy to provide as they could charge the hedge funds some fees of their own.

Again, in fairness to the hedge fund industry, we should note that none of this was seen as a problem at the time, that not all hedge funds use leverage anyway, and that they were pretty open, at least with their own investors, as to how much leverage they were using. The fact (or at least the strong suspicion) that many investors put money into things which they did not understand can hardly be laid at the door of the hedge fund community.

SOME COMMON ELEMENTS

It may be helpful to set out various elements that many hedge funds have in common. Let us bear in mind, however, that we are using "common" in the sense of "frequently occurring"; there is no uniformity.

Legal Structure

The development of hedge funds took place entirely within the US investment management community, and different forms of legal structure were adopted for "onshore" and "offshore" funds, the idea being that the former would have US resident investors while the latter catered for non-US investors, though this distinction has gradually broken down. Onshore funds were traditionally structured as limited partnerships, since these are tax-effective for the great majority of American investors, while offshore funds were structured as companies (corporations), usually based in a tax-friendly environment such as Bermuda or the Cayman Islands.

Today, non-US funds are often found in some sort of OEIC (open ended investment company) format, and those which intend to market themselves in various countries within the European Union will also usually be compliant with the UCITS[2] directives, and thus may also be referred to as "UCITS funds".

In what may be seen as a logical extension of these developments, many hedge funds will now also be quoted, at least nominally, in somewhere like Ireland or Luxembourg, and some cater to retail investors.

---

[2]Undertakings for Collective Investments in Transferable Securities.

It is still common, at least in the US, to find investors operating both onshore and offshore funds through a brokerage account and a master fund, sometimes referred to as a "master-feeder" structure.

There is an echo of this at the fund of funds level, where managed accounts are becoming increasingly popular compared to what may be seen in some quarters as the relative inflexibility and expense of a stand-alone fund structure.

Type of Trades

We will look shortly at the different types of investment strategies employed by hedge funds, but if we focus on the level of individual transactions, then in many cases they trade in very similar ways.

First, as we have already seen, they favour investment in derivative positions rather than the underlying instrument, whatever it may be.

Second, they will often be matching[3] two or more of those positions against each other. We will see a specific example of this when we look at market neutral funds. However, there are many others. For example, one approach is to match a position in the ordinary shares (common stock) of a company against an option on an instrument which can convert into those same shares. Another approach may see matches being made which at first sight may have little to do with each other, perhaps US dollar futures against oil price futures, for example.

Third, many hedge funds carry out a great many trades every day, perhaps even every hour. This is particularly true of investment strategies which rely on program trading models. These use pre-set buy and sell limits as trading triggers, usually operating on the interplay between different types of collective investment measures. Special dedicated computers perform this analysis and, at least in London, many of them have been given the names of Hollywood film stars by their analysts.

Lack of Transparency

It follows from this that it ranges from very difficult to impossible for any investor to know exactly what their hedge fund is actually investing in on a day to day basis. Incidentally, this is a major argument in favour of using a fund of funds approach rather than investing directly in individual hedge funds (sometimes referred to as "multi manager" as

---

[3]Be aware that "matching" can also be used in a different sense, namely to net buy and sell orders off against each other.

opposed to "single manager"). Many leading funds of funds now insist that all their investee managers use a common hedge fund platform, and will monitor exactly what they are doing on a daily basis, albeit necessarily 24 hours in arrears.

Apart from its obviousness as an ongoing due diligence issue, the monitoring of trades is also very important for one specific issue which we will look at later in this chapter, namely tilt drift.

Along with the use of leverage and derivative positions, it is this lack of transparency which sets the world of hedge funds apart from just about any other type of investment fund. Note however that it is a charge which might also be levelled at active currency, which we will be treating separately from hedge funds, though it is less serious a concern in that case.[4]

HOW HEDGE FUNDS INVEST – AN OVERVIEW

It has been said that all hedge fund investment strategies ("tilts") can be grouped into one of three categories. This is almost certainly being too simplistic. For example, event driven strategies, which we will examine shortly, do not seem to fit naturally into any of them, and could indeed fall across more than one. So, it is probably more correct to say that the great majority of them can, but it will do no harm to be clear about what they are.

Long and Long/Short

These are strategies which deal principally in equity exposure; that is, buying and selling derivatives which relate to company shares (stocks). As the name suggests, the latter phrase refers to situations where a manager will be taking both long and short positions simultaneously (effectively calls and puts). Traditionally, "long only" strategies were used only in markets which did not allow short selling, and where such a position could not be replicated by the use of derivative exposure.

However, many believe that as the noughties unfolded most managers in this category moved increasingly towards a long only approach. The reason was simple: in a long bull market for equities, who wants to be short the market? Assuming that you are correct in your prognosis that prices will continue to rise in the short term, then, if you have borrowed shares and sold them (the real meaning of "short selling"),

---

[4]Again, it is dangerous to make generalisations, but active currency managers probably take relatively fewer positions, certainly if measured against hedge fund managers who use anything like a program trading approach.

you will have to buy them back later at a higher price, while even if you have simply bought a put option it will be "out of the money" and therefore worthless, so you will have lost whatever amount you paid for it in the first place.

Thus, the detractors argue, if hedge fund managers were now adopting a purely long only strategy then they were not really offering any more than any mainstream active equity manager, whose normal investment strategy was simply to buy shares and hold them. Yet, though they were merely duplicating something which you could buy from an active equity manager, perhaps even a mutual fund, they were charging very much higher fees, and thus your net return was actually likely to be less than you might earn with the ordinary active manager.

There is a great deal of force to this view. However, it is inaccurate to say that the hedge fund would simply be duplicating the sort of portfolio that an active manager might hold. The active manager would actually be sitting on a share portfolio, whereas the hedge fund would be more likely to contain derivative instruments such as options, and to be highly leveraged by debt. This clearly adds greatly to the portfolio's risk, however one wishes to define that most complex of terms.

As long as the market goes up, your returns will be higher than they would otherwise have been by sitting on a basket of shares, but should the market suddenly go down unexpectedly (and it always does seem to be unexpected) then disaster threatens. The active manager will still have the market value of his shares, though this will now be less than it was before. If a hedge fund manager has only a drawer full of call options these will now be worthless, and if their purchase was financed by debt then the hedge fund has now gone bust, since it does not have the asset value with which to repay the loan.

It was also, so the argument goes, not only market dynamics which pushed some hedge fund managers into such an aggressively leveraged one-way bet, but the high levels of fees and carry being charged, modelled deliberately on private equity practice. In order for the fund to be able to afford these fees and still out-perform, extra leverage, extra capital risk, was the only possible solution.

Again, there is force to this view, but it begs a couple of important questions. First, if it was really so obvious to investors that all many hedge fund managers were offering was long only exposure, then why did they invest with them rather than with the cheaper and less risky active equity managers? Second, why were investors prepared to pay hedge fund managers private equity type fees when it should have been obvious that hedge funds could not consistently produce anything like a private equity type return? Nor did they claim to. Indeed, many hedge funds were sold on the basis of their ability to "reduce risk" in a portfolio, rather than to boost returns. We will look at this last point in more detail later in the chapter.

Credit Based

As the name says, this strategy group would embrace all those hedge funds who deal not in equity exposure, but in what has become known collectively as "credit". The term is here being used in its broad sense of any entering into an arrangement for the deferred repayment of a principal sum. Thus, it would clearly include something like a government bond. It can, however, also be used in a narrower sense to mean the lending of money to a company by a bank or finance house.[5] During the early part of 2009, for example, there was much talk of investors buying from banks at a discount some or all of their corporate loan books. In this sense, "credit" is clearly different from fixed income securities.

In its broader sense, though, it embraces everything from a blue chip government bond downwards ("downwards" in terms of perceived creditworthiness, or "upwards" in terms of default risk). It is rare, however, to find a hedge fund investing in anything as boring as a government bond (though many, including Carlyle Capital Corporation, did invest in something they considered almost as safe, because of the unstated but implicit backing of the US government – securities issued by the mortgage corporations Fannie Mae and Freddie Mac, each of which was a GSE[6]).

It is much more likely that they will be dealing in derivative positions over the fixed income securities issued by corporations (or perhaps even by South American governments). Equally likely is that they will also be investing in things like credit default swaps and interest rate swaps, often matching these against each other or against some supposedly related instrument in the way we considered a little earlier.

An area of particular interest in recent years has been the Collateralised Debt Obligation (CDO) market. CDOs are effectively pieces of paper each of which represents many different loans which have been bundled together and sold by the lender into the market. In theory, the default risk of any single loan can in this way be diversified away. As the events of late 2007 and 2008 were to demonstrate, however, theory and practice do not always happily converge.

---

[5] It can also of course be used to mean the grant of goods or services to a company or individual on terms that they may be paid for at a later date, but we will not be concerned with this category of credit.
[6] Government Sponsored Enterprise.

2007 was a year beset by hedge fund bankruptcies and rumours of hedge fund bankruptcies. Yet during the first half of the year, while plentiful leverage could still be obtained in the prime brokerage market, some hedge funds made a great deal of money for their investors by persistently shorting the CDO market.

Global Macro

These funds position themselves to take advantage of something which they believe is likely to occur in the wider environment. This could be something as mundane as a change in interest rates, or as exotic as a change of government, or even a war. Many people have classified George Soros's understanding that sterling could not remain within the European Exchange Rate Mechanism in the face of a sustained assault as a global macro approach.

Much of the time global macro approaches are relatively straightforward, however, and involve taking positions at the level of national or even regional markets. For example, a manager might go short German equities and long emerging market equities, or play off against each other the yield of the same bond over different periods.

Obviously these approaches tend to be both subjective and instinctive. You may be able to calculate that German equities seem overpriced in the short term relative to emerging market equities, but you cannot calculate why this is and to what extent the prevailing assumptions are justified. We are here in the area of personal judgement.

Attempts have indeed been made to create "systematic" macro investing (to distinguish it from the "discretionary" macro of personal judgement) using the same sort of hardcore quantitative models which are to be found supporting other tilts, but, while hard figures are not available, it is believed that such attempts have generally not proved successful, largely because of the amount of subjective input, or filtering of input, that turns out to be required. The only possible exceptions in this area have been in the fields of currency and commodities, both of which we will be considering separately.

SPECIFIC STRATEGIES

Again, let us be clear about the level of imprecision and ambiguity here. There is no general understanding as to exactly how many separate strategies exist, what they are or how to describe them.[7] Indeed, even

---

[7]For example, the author has heard examples of all the arbitrage tilts listed above referred to as "relative value arbitrage".

the various hedge fund industry data providers do not use the same classifications. The following are offered as examples of some of the most popular, and though their descriptions are brief, they are broadly correct. Again, please bear in mind that we will be looking separately at commodities and currency based funds later in the book. The first three are equity based, whereas the remainder operate across a range of asset classes, including credit derivatives.

Long Only

An equity based strategy operating in much the same way (or at least giving much the same exposure) as a traditional active equity manager. In some markets, this is the only such exposure possible as either short selling, options, or both may be unavailable. Such funds are often classified separately as "emerging markets".

Long/Short

This is a more sophisticated technique which adds going short (whether by short selling or the use of put options) into the mix. Some classify such funds as "equity hedge", although this phrase can also be used as a description of funds which are highly geared and/or maintain over 100% exposure and this can do either very well or very badly during periods of unexpected market volatility.

(Equity) Market Neutral

These are effectively absolute return funds, in the sense that they look to make a low positive return regardless of whether the return of the relevant stock market as a whole is positive or negative. They work by identifying within each sector a pair of shares, one of which they think is likely to go up by more than the other, and one of which is likely to go down by more than the other. They then simply go long the first and short the second.

This technique worked well during the period of negative public equity market returns from the middle of 2000 to early 2003.

Convertible Arbitrage

Any description of a fund or strategy which contains the word "arbitrage" refers to an approach whereby differences in the pricing of two closely related things can be exploited. In this case, the hedge fund will typically be short in a particular share and long in the convertible bond of the same company.

This was a successful strategy for many years, since (1) companies typically sold what was effectively a right to buy their shares too cheaply in order to be sure of getting the bond issue away, (2) the coupon payments on the bond covered some or much of the cost of selling the shares short and (3) in rising markets the value of the bond could rise steeply once the strike price was reached, or even approached. As usually happens, however, capital chased returns and large amounts of money came into the strategy, squeezing returns and tempting managers to make increasingly bigger bets at increasingly higher odds.

In 2005 many such funds lost money and were closed, with fair weather investors pulling out and looking to redeploy their capital elsewhere. The strategy picked up again in 2006, and many funds transitioned into what has become known as "capital structure arbitrage" under which the company's senior debt is added to the mix. Such an approach was widely tipped to yield high rewards during the credit crisis which began in mid-2007 but it is unclear from the available data exactly to what extent this has proved to be the case.

Statistical Arbitrage ("Stat Arb")

Many do not consider this to be a separate approach but lump it under long/short, convertible arbitrage, or some other strategy, but it is sufficiently distinct as a tilt to warrant its own description. Stat arb works on the principle that there are certain pairs of securities which typically move together, such as different classes of share or different types of instrument, that the pricing of these occasionally gets out of kilter, and that advantage can be taken of this to make money.

What sets stat arb apart is (1) that it is a solely quantitative approach, using a sophisticated proprietary computer model (the fund's much-vaunted and closely guarded "black box") to analyse trends and prices and (2) that it is an extremely short term approach, since such opportunities might exist only for a second or two, largely because there are a great number of similar managers out there looking to take advantage of exactly the same opportunity. For this reason, such funds will use program trading, whereby stock market trades are generated directly by their computer without the need for human intervention. In volatile market conditions, thousands of such trades may be generated each day.

While it is difficult to distinguish specific stat arb returns from the mass of available data (because such funds are often classified under different headings), there is general agreement that for a long time such "black box" quant approaches worked well. However, they rely of course on market liquidity to be able to trade in and out of position instantly, and many unravelled helplessly and expensively when such liquidity began to disappear in mid-2007. Indeed, many argue that they in fact contributed to the ensuing market turmoil, a charge which had first been levied in respect of Black Monday (19 October 1987), which shows how long this approach has been around. There is undoubtedly some justification to these charges; some believe that program trading is capable of manipulating markets, particularly on days when options expire, and there have been calls for it to be banned.

Merger Arbitrage

Here the fund will try to identify potential take-overs, and will go short the likely acquirer and long the likely target. This approach works on the simple principle that when any such take-over is launched, whether hostile or agreed, the bidder will always have to pay a premium over the existing market price for the shares in the target company, whereas the price of the bidder's shares will typically go down, partly because they may be proposing to issue new shares as part of the deal and partly because they may be seen (often with justification) to be over-paying for the target when the price is measured against any likely merger benefits.

Fixed Income Arbitrage

Here the arbitrage centres around irrational difference which may open up in the pricing of fixed income securities such as government bonds. The example most often given was that long term investors in the US typically wanted to hold 30 year bonds, to the extent that bonds with 29 years left to run had a lower price than simple arithmetic would justify. The problem is that such differences are usually very slight, and so very large positions have to be taken in order to generate any significant profit, which in turn means that the fund has to borrow heavily. Thus, while investing in assets which are traditionally seen as "low risk", the fund itself could properly be classified as "high risk", since its highly geared position makes it impossible to withstand any prolonged period of supposedly irrational market behaviour. As Warren Buffett memorably put it: "markets can remain irrational for longer than you can remain solvent".

Over the strategy hovers Banquo's ghost in the shape of LTCM (long term capital management) a hedge fund that was set up by John Meriwether in 1994 and which included the Nobel prize-winner Myron Scholes. Briefly put, LTCM and its distinguished crew demonstrated that traditional finance theory turns out to be deeply flawed if you try actually putting it into practice, not least the statistical assumption that highly unlikely "tail" events will not occur, notwithstanding that if they *do* occur they may have a devastating impact.

LTCM failed to predict the Asian debt crisis which erupted, initially triggered in Thailand, in mid-1997 or the Russian debt default which followed in 1998. They found themselves having bet on pricing returning to normal, but such "normality" stubbornly refusing to occur, and with very large positions which it was almost impossible for them to off-load. So large, in fact, that the Federal Reserve organised a multibank bail-out of LTCM for fear that its total collapse might cause a global meltdown in financial markets. When viewed from a post-2007 perspective, the reader will appreciate Karl Marx's observation that history repeats itself, the first time as tragedy and the second time as farce.

Global Macro

This approach has already been described above, but it may be convenient to differentiate it from "event driven", with which it is often confused.

Event Driven

At the risk of causing yet more confusion, this category can also be labelled "special situations". It is distinguished from global macro in that there the anticipated happening is thought likely to occur in the wider environment (such as the devaluation of a currency, or worse than expected economic figures) whereas in event driven tilts it is thought likely to occur in relation to the company or issuer itself. It can, for example, relate to corporate reconstructions or spin-offs, in which case it can also be described as "corporate life cycle" investing. There is also a very specialist sub-sector within event driven tilts that focuses on restricted trading stocks in the US, commonly referred to as "regulation D". These are shares or bonds which are effectively trading on a grey market while awaiting formal listing approval from the SEC.

Distressed

This approach, too, suffers from overlapping and ambiguous terminology. Originally it was called "distressed securities" and was based around selling short the shares of companies which were being adversely impacted by corporate reorganisation, credit downgrading, etc. However, the "securities" part got dropped as funds increasingly bought the debt or convertible instruments, rather than the equity, of troubled companies. This tilt is now frequently coupled with an "activist" approach, whereby the fund, having bought a large position in a particular slice of a company's capital structure, will try to force a particular business plan upon the company's directors, or a particular refinancing scheme upon its lending bankers.

Fund of Funds

Not really a separate strategy at all, though it is listed as one. It is, rather, a different approach to hedge fund investing, allowing an investor to appoint a manager to make their individual fund selections for them, thus ideally (1) diversifying away the risk of any one individual fund, (2) ensuring professional excellence in the selection and due diligence processes and (3) obtaining access to "invitation only" funds. A further attraction is that the best fund of funds managers offer daily monitoring and risk analysis of the portfolios of underlying funds, something which is essential, yet simply beyond the capabilities of ordinary investors.[8]

Originally, the approach was similar to that found in private equity, with a dedicated blind pool being raised to which an investor would commit funds on a blind basis. However, many fund of fund managers also offered a managed account service, under which a specific portfolio of funds could be put together to match the particular circumstances of an individual investor (a short term investor, for example, would have different requirements and tolerances to a long term investor).

Such a composite approach is frequently referred to as "multi manager", as opposed to investing in individual funds, which is called "single manager". Again, for the sake of eliminating as much confusion as possible, it should be pointed out that these terms refer to the funds involved rather than the approach itself.[9]

The above is far from exhaustive as a list of hedge fund strategies, though it certainly covers most of the leading contenders. As will by now be readily appreciated, the hedge fund industry is riddled with jargon, much of it unnecessarily confusing, and little of it helpful.

Before we leave this section on hedge fund strategies, let us just note for the record three matters which have all been mentioned elsewhere.

---

[8]Which did not, however, prevent many of them investing in single manager hedge funds.
[9]In which case it would logically be the other way around.

Funds which employ active currency strategies are, for the purposes of this book at least, being treated as a separate type of asset and have been accorded a chapter of their own.

GTAA funds have already been discussed in a previous chapter and are not considered further here, although many would argue that they constitute yet another distinct hedge fund strategy.

Managed futures funds will be discussed in the chapter on commodities.

By way of justification for these decisions, should any justification be needed, it should be noted that many investors around the world do in fact treat them as separate areas for asset allocation purposes, yet further evidence of the growing difficulty of arguing that a single discrete asset class called "hedge funds" does in fact exist and, even more problematically, that it is possible to list exactly what sorts of funds and approaches it comprises.

THE HEDGE FUND MODEL – PROS, CONS AND THE FUTURE

At the time of writing (mid-2010) there is considerable uncertainty about the future of the hedge fund industry, facilitated in part by an ongoing debate as to just how representative the industry benchmarks may be of underlying fund performance. Supporters will point to the very successful year which the industry enjoyed in 2009 according to the HFRI composite index (just over 20%), with some tilts (such as fixed income and convertible arbitrage) up over 60% year on year. Detractors, however, will remind us of the spectacular bankruptcies of some individual funds, and the almost total failure of the asset class to provide liquidity when it was required (albeit in the panic-stricken circumstances of a fire sale).

Without getting bogged down in nit-picking over the available data, it is possible to make some general comments about hedge funds, and in particular about the whole basis of what might be called the hedge fund model. It might be helpful to define our terms here. The "hedge fund model" might be described as the provision to an investor, for a fee, of specialist investment techniques which would not otherwise be available to them. Further description might provide that these techniques would normally be confined within a particular strategy or "tilt", and offered by way of a dedicated open-end fund vehicle subject to restrictions on capital redemption ("lock-ups") under certain circumstances, and usually highly leveraged with debt at the fund level.

The "pros" of such an approach have already been briefly stated. Tilts such as stat arb will not be available to the average investor;

therefore, if they wish to avail themselves of them it must surely be beneficial that there are third party managers ready to provide them.

Another pro which is rarely mentioned is that, far from being the "high risk" investments that people so readily envisage, many hedge funds are sold on the basis that they will *reduce* the overall risk within an investor's portfolio, and do in fact do so – at least if you accept that volatility and risk are one and the same. It is worth noting, however, that though your Sharpe Ratio[10] may indeed be lower, so will your overall return. How many investors really understand that in many cases they will be paying an *additional* management fee for a *lower* return, all in the cause of "risk reduction"?

Yet another pro, which is in a sense related to the last, is specific to market neutral funds. However much one might quibble about the validity of the available return figures, there is no doubt at all that they did exactly what they were supposed to do during the last bear market between 2000 and 2002, and it also seems highly probable that they performed in similar fashion during 2007 and 2008, despite their investors' determined efforts to derail them by asking for their money back at exactly the wrong time.[11]

Most investors, if asked to list their "cons" would point to high fees, problems with liquidity and/or redemption, and (perhaps surprisingly) headline risk.

The first is undeniably a problem and one which, unlike their counterparts in the private equity space, hedge fund managers really are going to have to confront and solve. Hedge funds have traditionally charged a private equity like fee structure of 2% annual fee and 20% "carry" or profit share. In some individual cases, much higher amounts have been demanded: at one stage Renaissance was charging a 5% fee and 44% carry, while SAC's carry reached the giddy heights of 50%.

The problem with all of this is that it seems unlikely that hedge funds could ever achieve the sort of returns which their private equity counterparts have achieved, at least not consistently and over many years. First, many hedge funds aim not to earn high returns, but to decrease volatility. Second, private equity returns are measured as compound returns over many years, not just one-off annual returns of one individual year. Third, during the equity bull market leading up to mid-2007, many long/short hedge funds effectively became long only, and thus did not

---

[10]Which measures the excess return of a portfolio relative to the standard deviation of the excess return.

[11]Anyone who believes that all investors are rational should ask themself why, when market neutral hedge funds only show superior returns during periods of falling stock market prices, should investors be anxious to invest in them while stock markets are rising, yet anxious to disinvest from them when stock markets are falling.

really offer anything different (apart from leverage and therefore extra risk) to a conventional long only active equity manager.

Of course, one hears stories of funds who really do out-perform year after year (though many of these came to grief in late 2007 – a Renaissance fund lost nearly 10% of its value in a few days, for example), so perhaps there is a Golden Circle just as there has been for US venture capital, but across the industry as a whole this picture of a mis-match between manager fee expectations and excess return delivered to investors is a valid one. In order to address this issue, many of the world's largest investors are now exploring the creation of what might be called internal hedge funds, whereby they lure successful managers and analysts away from hedge fund groups to run internal allocations using hedge fund techniques. Yes, they command large salaries and bonuses, but these amounts are small relative to what the investor would have to pay to a single manager hedge fund.

Another threat to the traditional model comes from what may seem unlikely sources, namely ETFs and spread betting. Whereas in the past it would have been extremely difficult for most investors to implement hedge fund type approaches even if they had wanted to, today even the humblest retail investor could, for example, buy an ETF representing physical gold, and at the same time take the spread betting equivalent of a long or short position on the US dollar.[12]

It remains to be seen how this particular issue will play out. Certainly there has already been a visible shift in practice at the fund of funds (multi-manager) level, with fees having been slashed and more flexible, managed account type approaches being offered. Ironically, it is with the best fund of funds managers that real value for money may now be seen, given the great advantage which they offer of expert selection, due diligence, daily monitoring and risk analysis, and yet many investors have seemingly been happier to invest directly with single manager funds, apparently believing a fund of funds approach simply to add a further level of fees for no discernible extra benefit.

Redemption/Co-Investor Risk

This issue is explained fully in the chapter on real estate when considering property unit trust type vehicles, and suffice it to say that it emerged during the crisis as the major threat to the traditional hedge fund model. It is one thing to suffer outflows from investor redemptions as a consequence of poor performance. It is quite another to face a barrage of

---

[12] With the added attraction that betting gains are tax-free in the UK, whereas investment gains are not.

redemption calls which, if all of them were honoured, would result in having to unravel positions at a disadvantageous time and price, thus artificially creating poor performance which, had the hedge fund been left to its own devices, might well never have occurred.

This is a massive, yet still largely unappreciated, problem overhanging the industry. Investors blame managers for having sought protection by invoking lock-ups. Managers blame investors for having been driven by panic rather than investment fundamentals. Certainly logic seems to have flown out of the window. After all, many investors had invested in hedge funds to "de-risk" their portfolio, so how did it make sense to sell these assets in what the investors perceived to be a high risk environment? Certainly in the case of market neutral funds, for example, it would have seemed more sensible to buy, not sell.

Three comments are probably worth making. First, traditional finance is clearly wrong in assuming that investors will always be driven by reason rather than emotion. Second, traditional finance is also clearly wrong in believing that all the material risk of any investment to any investor can be measured by the volatility of its historic returns. Third, the avoidance of co-investor risk is yet another powerful argument for the world's largest investors to seek to run their own hedge fund type programmes in-house in future.

SOME FINAL THOUGHTS ON HEDGE FUNDS

Running through this chapter, and certainly through this last section, has been a disturbing theme. Investors, as Warren Buffett memorably put it, should not invest in anything which they do not understand. Yet the recent history of the hedge fund industry has demonstrated all too clearly that this is exactly what many investors have in fact done. Hearsay evidence abounds, for example, of pension trustees agreeing to invest in, say, a convertible arbitrage hedge fund not only not understanding what convertible arbitrage is, but not understanding either what a convertible instrument is or what a hedge fund is.

Let it be clearly stated at once that while investing in such circumstances is very much the fault of the trustees, their lack of knowledge is only partly so. It is the duty of investment managers and pension consultants to explain complex financial matters in clear, simple, jargon-free terms. To do so is a considerable challenge, which is why those tasked with doing it are paid high salaries. That they should consistently fail in their task is only slightly less understandable than that trustees should allow them to get away with it.

Finally, it would be wrong to leave the subject of hedge funds without mentioning regulation. Surprisingly, given their potential for fraud, money laundering and market manipulation, many of the world's hedge funds and their managers operate entirely without regulation or supervision. At the time of writing there are already proposals afoot for the European Union to impose thud and blunder type regulations indiscriminately across the whole gamut of alternative asset managers, and these have already been countered by hedge fund managers announcing their intention of quitting the European Union in order to avoid them; Hong Kong, for example, has seen a significant increase in the amount of hedge fund capital under management. While there seems to be a certain fitting irony in the prospect of such ill-conceived rules completely missing their most valid target, it does seem troubling not only that so many hedge fund managers should be so keen to operate completely without regulation or oversight of any kind, but also that so many investors should be prepared to entrust them with their money.

Those who are professional and responsible within the hedge fund industry (and there are many) will hopefully appreciate all too well that these issues of fees and regulation must be resolved, and quickly. The hedge fund industry continues to have much to offer the world's investors, but if it is to have a viable and successful future then the traditional hedge fund model needs to be reconsidered, and the rival interests of investors and managers more closely aligned.

SUMMARY

Hedge funds are investment vehicles which invest almost entirely in derivative instruments, or by creating derivative-type exposure by short selling. Where they do not, it is because such a methodology is not legally possible in a particular market.

Unlike conventional investors, who use derivatives to hedge an underlying position or liability, hedge funds use derivatives without an underlying position or liability for purely speculative purposes.

In addition to the gearing naturally provided by the derivatives themselves, many hedge funds have in the past been very highly leveraged with debt.

Hedge fund trades are typically carried out in matched groups, such as pairs, and may seek to exploit perceived aberrations in pricing, or expected economic or corporate events.

Strategies are called "tilts" and may be thought of as grouped loosely into three broad categories: equity based, credit based and global macro. A full list of hedge fund strategies is listed above. For the purposes of this book, we will be treating active currency separately as an asset class in its own right.

Fee structures have emerged as a major issue within the hedge fund industry, with some detractors arguing that managers have charged private equity type fees for quoted equity type returns. Despite these reservations, at the time of writing, fundraising appears to be picking up once more, and inflows to existing funds currently outnumber outflows.

So too has the issue of co-investor risk, which is dealt with more fully elsewhere. In response to both these factors, it seems likely that large investors such as Sovereign Wealth Funds may increasingly seek to create their own hedge fund type programmes internally.

Hedge funds will remain a major candidate for inclusion in institutional portfolios, and have some major perceived advantages, such as their ability to lower both volatility and correlation. However, it is to be hoped that any such allocations will in the future be made on a more sophisticated and better-informed basis than has been the case in the past.

7

Infrastructure

"Infrastructure" seems to have become a new buzz-word among investors, and is being hailed as one of the next hot areas of asset allocation, even by long-time champions of other asset types such as Leon Black (debt) and Henry Kravis (mega-buyout).[1] While this is gratifying, since infrastructure is indeed an interesting and attractive area which is worthy of any investor's serious consideration, it is also somewhat baffling since these same investors have had the opportunity for at least the last decade to take advantage of this opportunity while it was still genuinely an "opportunity", yet have consistently failed to do so.

For until the last year or so, infrastructure exhibited exactly the sort of project rich/capital poor conditions which made possible (or at least greatly facilitated) the glory days of US venture and European buyout returns in the early to mid-1990s. Infrastructure funds were relatively small, and often struggled to raise much money outside their own country, while many of the world's institutional investors simply ignored the asset class, in many cases (believe it or not) because they did not know how to classify it rather than because they had considered it and found it unattractive.

As we have seen elsewhere, this obsession with being able to attach a label to something, so beloved of regulators, auditors and risk managers, is one of the major bugbears of traditional investment practice, and one of the most important barriers to be overcome in order to be able to operate in a more modern and (hopefully) rational fashion. For what should matter more: what something is called, or how it might behave within your portfolio?

It is with infrastructure that we find this paradox at perhaps its most extreme. Remember that in an earlier chapter we categorised infrastructure as one of the three "private" asset types, alongside private equity and private real estate. Like them, it is highly illiquid, both in terms of the type of investment vehicle which is used and in terms of the underlying assets which these vehicles buy and hold. Like them, it is a long term asset type, indeed in many cases the longest of all, since infrastructure projects can generate cash flows stretching far into the future.

---

[1] Interviewed at Super Return, February 2010.

So much for the similarities. There is, though, one very important difference, and it's here that the labelling paradox comes into play. With both private equity and private real estate the cash flows of an investment are unpredictable both as to their timing and their extent; wholly in the case of private equity, and mainly in the case of private real estate, since while rental payments may be predicted, the time at which properties may be bought or sold, and the amount agreed by way of price in each case cannot. In the case of infrastructure investments, however, particularly with those which we will shortly describe as "secondary", both the timing (certainly) and the amount (often) of cash inflows may be modelled with comparative certainty.

The former will be either because the dates on which payments are to be received will be fixed contractually in advance, or because the infrastructure vehicle, or the project level company in which it has invested, has the contractual right to receive revenues directly from the project users. The latter will be because there will often be a period when revenues are guaranteed at either a fixed or minimum amount, and in any event usage rate assumptions will have been used when modelling the project in advance, and can be adjusted as it progresses should they prove to have been inaccurate.

Hence the paradox. Here we have something which by any investor's standards they would label as an "alternative" and yet which exhibits many of the characteristics of a bond. In fact, if guarantees have been entered into by a governmental body, then it may even exhibit many of the guarantees of a government bond. Yet, such is the tyranny of the labelling fetish that an investor who is seeking a 30 year bond may well be prepared to pay more, perhaps significantly more in the shape of lower returns, for the bond than for a comparable interest in an infrastructure project, or even a basket of infrastructure projects. In addition, an investor may well be looking for an index-linked bond but have to settle for a fixed rate one because of limited availability of index-linked long bonds, when the cash flows of the infrastructure project may well include a contractually agreed annual increase in line with inflation – exactly what the investor was in fact looking for. So, what's in a name? As Shakespeare pointed out, in *Romeo and Juliet*, even if you were to call a rose something else, it would still smell like a rose when you raised it to your nose.

Of course if you want to hold an asset as a source of short term liquidity then you would choose a bond, but, as is being increasingly pointed out,[2] if you want a source of long term cash flow yield then

---

[2] See for example Inderst, G. *Pension Fund Investment in Infrastructure*, OECD Working Papers, 2009.

infrastructure investments may make ideal liability matching assets for pension funds around the world and offer a lower price and/or higher yield than a bond. Incidentally, the same study also reinforces the point about how difficult pension funds around the world seem to find it to define "infrastructure", with it being found variously under "private equity", "quoted equities", "real estate", "alternatives", "real assets" or just "other assets"!

Before we get drawn too far into the metaphysics of asset definition, however, let us draw back and take a long look at infrastructure. For a start, we need to be clear about exactly what it is, and consider how we might usefully divide it up into categories.

WHAT IS INFRASTRUCTURE?

A dictionary definition of "infrastructure" is "the systems and services, such as transport and power supplies, that a country or organisation uses in order to work effectively". This is from the Cambridge dictionary, but others offer similar entries. This is not a bad starting point. Investing in infrastructure means providing the capital which enables facilities which provide these systems and services to be planned, built and subsequently operated.

A common way of categorising such investment is by the nature of the service which it is intended to provide. Many infrastructure managers break these into two broad categories: economic and social,[3] with each of these then being broken down into three sub-sectors (Table 7.1).

Since these classifications have been widely adopted then it will do no harm to use them. However, we should note that many infrastructure investors and funds treat airports and sea ports as a separate category

Table 7.1 Economic and social infrastructure

Economic	
Communications	TV transmitters, cable and satellite systems, mobile telephone transmitters.
Transport	Roads, bridges, rail lines and stations, ports and airports.
Utilities	Power stations, gas plants, pipelines, desalination plants. Hydro schemes, water and sewage treatment, irrigation.
Social	
Education	Schools, colleges, libraries.
Health	Hospitals, clinics, nursing homes.
Security	Prisons, police stations, barracks, surveillance systems.

---

[3]This arrangement is adopted by the 2009 Inderst paper.

by themselves, perhaps because they require very specialist skills to operate them once they have been built, or perhaps because, almost uniquely within infrastructure, many of these assets already exist either in publicly quoted form or in state ownership. Indeed, many infrastructure fund managers will be happy to draw to your attention that, given the prices suggested for airport privatisation offerings, it can be cheaper to build a brand new airport than to buy an old one.

Secondary and Primary Infrastructure

There is a further sub-division of all these types of infrastructure, and that is into primary and secondary infrastructure investments. At this point, however, a warning note should be struck since these words are not used in their more usual sense. When we talk about secondary private equity or private real estate investing, for example, we are talking about interests in private vehicles such as limited partnerships, which are sold by one investor or another. This is of course also the sense in which the words are used in the bond and quoted equity markets, hence the primary and secondary desks of investment banks. The primary desk markets the instrument when it is first issued by a company or government, and the secondary desks deal the instrument thereafter as it is traded from one investor to another.

In the world of infrastructure things are different, as we are not talking about an interest in a fund but about the underlying project or projects. Basically, primary infrastructure relates to the planning and building phases of a project, while secondary relates to the operating phase. This is a sensible distinction to draw in terms of investment theory, since the characteristics of these two stages of a project's life are very different from an investment point of view. Primary infrastructure offers at least the possibility of a fairly quick payout, and the main risk is constructions risk, the risk that the project will run over time or over budget. By the time the secondary phase is reached, the payout profile has become that of a series of cash flows stretching away into the future, and the main risks are operational hitches (as in Eurostar "train stuck in the tunnel" syndrome) and usage deficiency (the number of users falling short of the originally projected totals).

The distinction is a sensible one to draw in practice too, since different types of investor have developed who favour one or the other type. Long term investors, such as pension funds and life insurance companies tend to favour secondary infrastructure because they find the idea of long streams of cash flows attractive. There are others, however, who prefer the idea of a relatively quick "bang for their buck" rather than waiting 25 years or more to harvest the fruits of their labours.

As a result, infrastructure managers are springing up who specialise in one type or the other, or perhaps offer both in segmented funds or pools. This is further evidence of the growing sophistication of an asset type which was only a few years ago regarded as frankly marginal by many investors around the world.

Even so, there are many who have failed to grasp this very real distinction, or who perhaps lack the imagination to see the possibilities which it opens up. Why should primary infrastructure not be, for instance, a possible solution to the problem of what to do with capital which has been allocated to private equity but which is as yet uninvested?

Regulated and Demand-Driven

Before moving on, it is worth noting that some commentators also divide infrastructure into that which is regulated (water, gas and electricity) and that which is demand driven (such as roads and bridges). There are two important points to grasp here. First, what is being talked about is primarily regulation of *pricing*; after all, hospitals, prisons, toll roads and bridges, airports and sea ports all operate within operational environments which are regulated to some degree or other. Indeed, it could be argued that this is something of an artificial distinction; roads and bridges should also fall within the "regulated" category since their pricing is usually periodically fixed, while the amount of money received by utilities (as opposed to the pricing of their product) is clearly determined by levels of consumption. Second, even when talking of "regulated" infrastructure, one is only referring to the utilities themselves; it would not, for example, refer to a company which built and fitted out desalination plants, nor to a business which had developed a new type of sewage treatment technology.

DRIVERS

One of the main reasons why infrastructure has grown so rapidly as an asset type is that it represents a marriage made in heaven. On the one hand is the desire by governments to make the most of tax revenues by economising on expenditure, while recognising the need to build infrastructure. On the other hand is the hunger on the part of investors around the world for stable and reliable long term cash flows. Add to this the ability for large construction companies and civil engineering firms to create business for themselves, and it becomes not so much a marriage as a highly congenial *ménage à trois*.

GOVERNMENT

The need for government to involve the private sector in building and operating public infrastructure projects was perhaps grasped earliest and most decisively in Australia, which market pioneered the development of unquoted infrastructure (a definition which we will explore shortly). As these Australian managers became more experienced and more ambitious, they then began to spread their activities into South East Asia and beyond. To this day, there remains a preponderance of Australian accents in the offices of infrastructure funds worldwide.

This governmental driver embraces not just countries where infrastructure is being laid down for the first time (in the case of somewhere like India, even to the extent of whole new towns being built) but also countries where tired old infrastructure needs to be either developed or replaced altogether, often after decades of neglect and under-investment. Perhaps surprisingly, countries such as the US and Great Britain are leading contenders here. In both countries, for example, there is talk of major new railway projects, while in Britain prisons are full and in America bridges can and do fall down. Britain is slightly ahead of the game here, as we will shortly see.

Investors

It is premature to speak, as some people do increasingly at investment conferences, of fixed income and real estate assets being replaced in investors' portfolios by infrastructure investments. Indeed, it seems highly unlikely that fixed income (bonds) or real estate should *ever* disappear from portfolios; they both have a very valid role to play. It is true, however, that an increasing number of investors are either already investing in infrastructure, or strongly considering such a move. It really makes little difference whether they are considering this a subset of their private equity allocation, an asset type in its own right or a marginal oddity. The fact remains that the way in which infrastructure behaves in delivering returns is beginning to attract a growing number of fans. With large investment managers such as KKR entering the market for the first time, this is a driver which can only increase in power.

Industry

Infrastructure projects have been a boon for the companies in the construction, development and civil engineering sector, generating a large amount of work which might not otherwise have been available. Of course, other business areas have profited as well, most notably building materials, such as aggregate for road-building, and facilities management. However, it is the aforementioned companies which have developed specialist infrastructure expertise, playing a key part in the highly complex syndicates of planners, consultants, developers and finance providers which are required to build and operate these projects.

It is no over-statement to say that infrastructure has prompted a radical overhaul of the construction sector generally, with many companies re-positioning themselves in consequence. To give but one example, the British public company John Laing, traditionally known for its house-building activities, underwent a complete restructuring in 2001 to become "a specialist owner, operator and manager of public sector infrastructure assets in the UK and internationally".[4] So successful did this transformation prove that Laing were acquired by Henderson Infrastructure in 2006 and now have current infrastructure projects all over the world, including Australia – surely the ultimate accolade.

The depth of these new required skills should not be under-estimated. Putting these consortia together is a hugely complex task, calling for both specialist professional knowledge and sound practical experience. The ability to act as the focal point of such a consortium has become an essential skill for any large construction or civil engineering business.

THREATS

Regulatory/Governmental

It is a truism that if an investor has an opportunity to invest in a regulated or an unregulated industry then they should choose the latter (unless, of course the industry in question is financial services and the "investment" in question takes the form of entrusting money to an investment fund or manager). The rationale is obvious. Regulation always imposes an extra cost burden upon a business because of the need to satisfy compliance requirements by monitoring, training and reporting. Also, certain types of regulation may impose artificial constraints upon pricing, sourcing or market share.

Sadly in many of the areas with which infrastructure is concerned the dead hand of the regulator is firmly on the tiller. Flippancy aside, it is obviously right that this should be the case, particularly where public safety is at issue, hospitals and airports being but two obvious examples. The whole business of complying with such regulation is a vital

---

[4] www.laing.com.

part of the consortium's planning and operating processes, calling for the drafting and implementing of codes, guidelines and regulations.

A distinction should be drawn, however, between the construction and operation of a facility on the one hand, and the regulation of how the project is tendered, structured and financed on the other. It is here that difficulties arise. If investors' freedom of action to structure the funding of a project is restricted, for example, then sub-optimal outcomes from an investment return point of view can, and do, occur.

A well known example took place in Britain under the Public Finance Initiative (PFI), a programme which we will consider in more detail below. A hospital project in Norwich underwent a financial recapitalisation as a result of which the private sector investors made a higher financial return than they would otherwise have done. This aroused the anger of many politicians who, it seemed, were happy to make use of private equity type funding to fill a potential black hole in public finances, but not to allow the investors to make a private equity type return. In vain did the local Member of Parliament point out that the contracts had been freely entered into by all parties with the advice of specialist lawyers, and that the British Department of Health had expressly decided not to include a refinancing clause which would have allowed the hospital to receive some benefit itself from any recapitalisation.

Unsurprisingly, this spooked the UK PFI market for some time. The planned redevelopment of St Bartholomew's Hospital ("Bart's"), for example, was repeatedly postponed. When activity resumed, it was on the basis of a standard provision that in future the benefit of any recapitalisation must be shared. This does, however, point up the essential intellectual contradictions inherent in any such scheme when viewed from a left wing political viewpoint. Public projects, such thinking would run, must be built whenever and wherever they are needed, and built with public money for the public good. Since the collapse of the socialist utopia that was the Soviet Union, however, has come a new reality even in the most idealistic of governments around the world, a recognition that public money simply is not available in sufficient quantities to allow this to happen, nor is it ever likely to be. So, the involvement of the private sector is unavoidable, and to expect them to tie up their money in a project at only a few percentage points above the risk free rate seems unrealistic. Thus, any such scheme, in whatever country, is always going to represent a compromise between government paternalism and hard-nosed commercial reality.

As a report commissioned by a British trade union stated in 2009, PFI/PPP projects (see below) "are subject to quite intense political risk, because there is almost universal distrust and resentment of them, and constant pressure to renegotiate or terminate".[5]

Funding

We referred above to the desire of new capital to enter the sector as constituting a major driver, and so it does. Paradoxically, however, it could also represent a very real threat. When traditional finance theory is exposed to the harsh light of investment reality, it often does not stand up to it very well. In some respects, though, traditional finance is impeccable, and nowhere more so than in the idea that all investment opportunities will ultimately get arbitraged away. Put simply, where investors see high returns being made by a particular asset type then sooner or later they will make large allocations to that asset type, and the weight of this new capital will flood the market, driving up valuations and depressing returns until the "opportunity" is no more and the asset type no longer looks attractive. Then (possibly) a new cycle may begin.

Fortunately most investors take a long time to get around to this. The real opportunity for both US venture capital and European buyout funds, for example, started in about 1990 and probably ended (at least in the sense of the very high returns which were earned by some managers during that period) in about 1999 and 2001 respectively. Yet, at the time of writing (2010), 20 years after the opportunity began, many investors around the world still have no allocation to private equity at all. Lessons have been learned, however, and it seems likely that investors will not wait so long in future. Sooner or later the same tidal wave of capital that hit US venture capital in 1999 and 2000, and European buyout from 2005 to 2007 will happen to infrastructure. Intelligent investors will try to monitor to what extent, and how quickly, this is happening.

War and Terrorism

Infrastructure projects require a peaceful, stable environment within which to be built and operated. Materials have to be transported to the site. Local labour must be available, and they must be able to work, sometimes in very remote areas, free from threat or attack. Both during and after construction infrastructure assets are vulnerable to physical

---

[5]Hall, David, *Infrastructure, the crisis and pension funds*, Public Services Information Research Unit, London, 2009 (sponsored by Unison).

attack, most notably in the case of pipelines, which may run for hundreds of miles and where it may be possible permanently to guard little more than the intermediate pumping stations. Even offshore oil rigs are regularly occupied by terrorists – for example off the coast of Nigeria.

Civil war of insurrection brings fresh problems. A new or rival government may, for example, refuse to be bound by contracts entered into by the regime with which one originally dealt, or may even begin nationalising assets, or manipulating legal or economic ownership in less blatant, but equally effective ways.

It is vital, therefore, to conduct a detailed political, military and security based strategic review of an area before commencing operations. If satisfactory findings emerge then it may be possible in certain cases to obtain some comfort through specialist insurance. The real danger is where some sudden and unexpected change takes place in a hitherto stable country or region. Fortunately these occur but rarely, though they can have huge impact when they do. The Islamic revolution which swept away first the Shah of Iran and then the moderate government of BaniSadr might be one such example.

QUOTED AND UNQUOTED INFRASTRUCTURE

Turning now to the ways in which people seek to invest in infrastructure, rather than the types of infrastructure in which they seek to invest, we can divide the asset class into quoted and unquoted varieties. The use of the plural (of "variety") is very deliberate since, as we will see, it is necessary then to sub-divide both "quoted" and "unquoted" infrastructure in order properly to reflect the different ways in which investors have sought to access it.

This ambiguity is unfortunate, but inevitable given that "quoted" and "unquoted" are already being used to refer to various different types of infrastructure investing, so it is necessary to be very clear about what these meanings are, since otherwise much confusion can (and does) arise. Again, we meet these ideas elsewhere in this book, but it does no harm to apply them specifically to each asset type.

Quoted Infrastructure (1): Industrial Companies

A sense in which this phrase is still very commonly used is the attempt to gain coverage of "infrastructure" by means of investing in the stocks (shares) of public corporations (companies) whose business activities give them exposure to it. Some bundles of such securities have been given official sanction by being adopted as indices, which can in turn be used as a basis for investment by tracker vehicles such as ETFs.

Prominent examples include Macquarie's Global Infrastructure series of indices which are administered by FTSE, MSCI offerings and S&P.

Yet any such approach raises some obvious questions and, given that they are so obvious, not ones with which the investment industry has dealt very well. What exactly do you mean by "infrastructure"? How are you proposing to weight your index by market capitalisation, geography and type of activity? Are there some business activities which might be excluded altogether and, if so, on what grounds? How do we differentiate between primary and secondary infrastructure? And so on.

These are all awkward questions, since the answers which they prompt reveal little common practice, and, if truth be told, little strategic thought. In fact, it could be argued that these indices are a classic example of the sales-led mentality of most investment banks. It is far easier, they believe, to persuade investors to buy whatever may be on offer, than to create that which they really need. Blame here must attach to investors too; how many even stop to think about these issues, let alone would be prepared to pay a premium price for a premium product?

Macquarie/FTSE, for instance, give roads, ports and airports as examples of infrastructure, yet its global index includes just three European companies in these categories, none of which owns or operates even a single port, or a single major international airport.[6] Many of the companies which they have chosen from around the world are utilities, whether gas, electricity or water, and some would argue that these do not really come within "infrastructure" at all, but rather constitute their own separate stock exchange category. Yet specialist construction, civil engineering, plant hire and building materials businesses are conspicuous by their absence. So, in the sense of actually providing any exposure to underlying current infrastructure projects, this is really only "infrastructure" because somebody has called it that.

MSCI go to the trouble of breaking out five types of infrastructure (telecommunications, utilities, transportation, energy and social) but their methodology is to weight by market capitalisation, which means that about 94% of the index is represented by telecommunications and utilities![7] Again, all the sorts of businesses which would actually give some sort of exposure to the development of actual infrastructure projects are studiously ignored.

The S&P index is built around three infrastructure "clusters": 20% to energy and 40% each to transportation and utilities. However, 40% is still a lot to have in utilities, which arguably have little to do with

---

[6] Abertis Infraestructuras operates a few very small airports such as Luton and Cardiff in the UK and the Bob Hope Airport at Burbank, California.

[7] Correct at the time of writing (2010) check http://www.mscibarra.com for the current position.

infrastructure at all, and the transportation cluster is heavily weighted in favour of roads.

All these indices are "investable", so all can be used to gain access in a quick, convenient and relatively cheap manner if that is what one wishes to do – but access to what? Certainly not to any significant economic participation in current infrastructure projects. For that, one would expect to see construction businesses which specialise in the field, together with architecture and civil engineering practices, transport and environmental consultants, facilities managers, plant hire businesses, specialist manufacturers and engineers, building product manufacturers, etc. Of course, such an index could conceivably be put together, but it would have to be prepared to accept more and smaller companies. Even this might not offer a perfect solution, however, since many of the businesses we have just described are in private ownership.

Worst of all, however, is the attendant exposure which these indices give us to stock market beta. This can be demonstrated very easily. If we take the yearly returns of the MSCI European infrastructure index since 1999 and compare them with those of the MSCI European equities index for the same period, we find that they are very highly correlated indeed: nearly 90%, in fact.[8] In other words, these "infrastructure" indices will go up and down with public stock markets, not with the fortunes of any underlying infrastructure projects.

As we noted at the outset, a desire for uncorrelated returns (uncorrelated that is with stock market beta) is one of the main motivations for investing in alternative assets in the first place, so why choose voluntarily to import huge amounts of stock market beta into your portfolio (the exact opposite of what you should be trying to do) when you do not have to?

Quoted Infrastructure (2): Listed Investment Vehicles

The second way in which the phrase "quoted infrastructure" is used is a much more natural one, meaning listed investment vehicles which invest in infrastructure projects and assets. It will be at once apparent that, unlike the definition we have just been considering, this one does at least do what it says on the tin, namely to provide exposure to underlying infrastructure activity.

Many of these vehicles are geographically specific, either by country or region. They can take a variety of different forms. Infrastructure India plc, for example, is a closed end investment company quoted

---

[8] Own workings from MSCI data.

on the London Stock Exchange. Some others have more of a hedge fund type structure, allowing for capital redemptions. In fact, the legal form which an infrastructure fund should take has become a very live issue, which arises largely from the investment characteristics of many infrastructure projects. Though more strictly relevant to unlisted funds, it might conveniently be considered here, since it affects all closed end vehicles.

As we noted above, many infrastructure projects are very long term. Some are entirely capable of producing an income stream stretching 30 years into the future. Should you wish to invest in these through a closed end fund, there is then a dramatic mis-match between the nature of the fund vehicle and the nature of its underlying assets. If the fund is set to run for ten years, what do you do at the agreed termination date about the cash flows which are yet to be generated by the fund's assets? Even if the fund is set to run for 25 years this problem is still likely to occur, unless one were able to invest all the fund's capital on day one into projects which all had precisely 25 years to run.

Why is this important? Because most fund managers will be re-munerated partly by way of a performance fee, and the fund documen-tation will need to set out when and how this is to be calculated. At first sight, there would appear to be an obvious route to take, since a listed vehicle will always have a year-end audited NAV figure. Why not simply base the performance fee on improvement in NAV, as most hedge fund type structures do?

Well, it's not quite as straightforward as that. Hedge funds invest in publicly traded instruments which can be valued, or certainly priced, from one moment to another; their "value" is a function of what one investor is prepared to pay another in order to own them. So, year-end NAV really does give a fair picture of how well or badly the manager has performed during the year. Of course, it does not solve the prob-lem of what happens if one very good year is followed by two or three very bad ones, or vice versa, but the basic performance measurement methodology is sound.

With infrastructure funds, though, one is concerned with valuing projects which represent a stream of cash flows stretching into the future, and there is only one way of valuing these, which is by discount-ing them to arrive at a net present value (NPV). There are two problems here. The first is that whenever you are modelling the future you are prey to uncertainty, and no matter how hard you may have worked to draw up assumptions which you think are entirely reasonable, it is very probable indeed that your forecasts will not be entirely correct. The second, is the question of what discount rate you should take. A difference of 1 or 2% in the discount rate can make a difference of millions of dollars in the NPV. Even if you attempt to get around this problem by agreeing the discount rate in advance, you can more or less guarantee that it will not still be appropriate when the time comes to use it, since it would normally be assessed in the light of prevailing interest and inflation rates and you have no way of knowing what these are likely to be even a few years into the future, let alone ten or more.

This means, incidentally, that in strict theory the NAVs of quoted infrastructure funds should, like the price of fixed rate bonds, exhibit very strong negative correlation with interest rates. As interest rates go down then logically so should the discount rate used to value each project, resulting in a higher NPV, and thus NAV. However, it is unclear from the available data whether this does in fact happen in practice or not.

As will now be appreciated, this mis-match between the nature of the fund and the nature of its underlying assets presents a very knotty problem, and one which has for the last few years been taking up the very expensive time of many of the world's leading fund lawyers. As yet, no one universal solution has been adopted. There is of course one practical way of addressing the problem, which is simply to sell the assets at the appointed time, and accept the best price which it is possible to obtain in the marketplace as representing fair value. A second possibility would be to transfer the existing projects into a new fund, perhaps one restricted to investing only in secondary infrastructure, with exiting investors being given the option of effectively transferring to the new fund, though this too would raise very obvious issues of valuation and pricing.

Before leaving this treatment of quoted infrastructure funds, it should be noted that serious concerns have been raised about their payout policy. Whereas with private infrastructure funds, which we will consider below, distributions to investors tend to be driven directly by cash flows from the income and sale proceeds of underlying projects, it has been the practice of many quoted funds to pay out more than they are currently receiving. Logically these extra amounts can only come either from the capital of the fund or from borrowing.

Little (2009)[9] said:

> the long term sustainability of the Macquarie Model has been called into question because shareholder dividends often exceed current revenues and the difference is paid out of capital. In light of increased financial scrutiny and the tightness and cost of commercial credit experienced during the autumn 2008 financial crisis, many have questioned the long-term viability of the model.

[9]Little, Richard G., *Not the Macquarie Model: Using U.S. Sovereign Wealth to Renew America's Civil Infrastructure*, January, 2009. AICP, The Keston Institute for Public Finance and Infrastructure Policy, University of Southern California.

Also noted by Hall (2009),[10] *The Economist* in the summer of 2008 drew attention to the fact that this model might have worked when it was cheap to borrow money from about 2005 to mid-2007, but no longer did so if and when interest rates rose.

The possibility must, therefore, at least be considered that the returns of some quoted infrastructure funds as measured by their investor cash flows may well have been over-stated. We should also note that some of these funds may find themselves having to make adjustments to the capital and debt portions of their balance sheets and/or having to revise their distribution policy.

Unquoted Infrastructure (1): Projects (Typically PFI or PPP Type)

Many investors have invested directly in infrastructure projects, most commonly by way of something which is known by different names and acronyms in different countries but takes a very similar form in each case. Public Finance Initiative (UK) and Public/Private Partnerships (Australia and elsewhere) transactions generally arise where government (either central or regional) publishes a list of desired new or improved facilities and investors then come together in consortia with engineers, consultants, banks, operators and constructors to bid for individual projects. This has the advantage of giving exposure to real life infrastructure projects, but is subject to a few practical disadvantages.

First, putting these consortia together is a hugely complex task, not just procedurally but also in terms of all the legal, technical and financial issues involved. To participate meaningfully, making a practical contribution to discussion and analysis, is simply beyond the expertise and resources of most investors, unless they are prepared to take the time and trouble to put together a specialist team. Perhaps because of this, many investors only in fact invest in bond-type instruments even when they do participate in PPP type projects.

Second, this approach can leave one with a large amount of project specific risk. While it is true that, at least to date, the chance of any one project going spectacularly wrong has proved to be very low in practice, this ignores the fact that a lot of projects are very tightly specified so that, for example, even a short delay in the delivery date can have quite significant financial consequences. Ideally, as with any sort of investment risk, one would be looking to diversify this away.

Third, and this may be less obvious, such an approach is usually restricted to an investor's own country. This may be for a whole host

---

[10] Already cited.

of reasons, ranging from the political impulse to be seen to be contributing to socially worthwhile initiatives right through to unease at operating in foreign legal and regulatory environments. Whatever the case, this tends to be so. The problem here is that within one's domestic market supply of and demand for projects will fluctuate, and the time that an investor chooses to enter the market will typically be when other investors have also announced their intention of doing so.[11] Thus, usually by the time an investor makes up its mind to participate in infrastructure projects, it is no longer the right time, and a focus on the home market will take away the opportunity of looking at perhaps more competitively priced product in other parts of the world.

All three of these disadvantages can be addressed by looking instead at unquoted infrastructure funds, though as with everything in finance this comes at a price, namely the attendant management fees and performance payments.

Unquoted Infrastructure (2): Funds

One must draw a distinction here between the investment vehicle and its underlying assets. It is the former, rather than the latter, to which the description "unquoted" applies. There are, for example, various quoted infrastructure funds which target shares (stocks) or other instruments issued by private companies which are active in building and operating infrastructure assets. We are talking here about funds which are themselves unquoted, what we might refer to as "private infrastructure" in the same way that we talk about "private real estate".

Sadly, many institutional investors and their advisers seem not even to know that such vehicles exist; certainly they seem to ignore them whenever debate arises as to whether an allocation to infrastructure makes sense.[12] Yet, just as private real estate funds can be argued to be the best approximation to actually investing in property assets should direct investment not be possible, so private infrastructure has a strong claim to being the most sensible way of accessing infrastructure projects.

If using a private equity type structure, then capital only needs to be drawn down as it is actually needed. Though this can be argued both ways depending on your point of view, it is undeniably more capital efficient from the fund/project perspective. If money is paid "up front" then there must surely be increasing psychological pressure to invest it as quickly as possible, even should choice and pricing currently be

---

[11]An example of the so-called Bandwagon Effect, also known as herd mentality.
[12]Though there are some honourable exceptions such as the Dutch pension giant ABP.

sub-optimal. If fees are being charged on invested, rather than committed capital, or if (as is frequently the case with PFI/PPP "pools" put together by banks) the capital is only guaranteed available for investment for a limited time, then these pressures may be greatly increased.

As with private equity and private real estate funds, private infrastructure funds provide a ready source of diversification, not just across multiple projects, but also perhaps across different sectors and geographies.

On the other hand, such a fund can also if desired offer focus, perhaps within a single country or on primary or secondary investing. Such offerings could be used to provide diversification away from a purely domestic PPP programme.

Finally, as with private equity and private real estate funds, the management companies will tend to be staffed by specialist professionals with considerable experience of such projects, gained in different fields. Logically, therefore, they are likely to be able to source, analyse, structure and execute such projects much more effectively than generalist investors for whom this is perhaps just a 2% allocation within their overall portfolio.

RETURNS

It is only right to record that one must approach the whole question of infrastructure returns with great caution.

First, as we have seen above, in some cases it is highly questionable whether we are actually looking at "infrastructure" at all, as opposed to some basket of quoted utilities type stocks.

Second, also as noted above, the performance figures of quoted infrastructure funds may have been artificially enhanced by distributions which cannot be linked directly or entirely to the income of the fund.

Third, when it comes to unquoted infrastructure funds there are very few studies available, they each have different (and very small) data sets, and their figures are drawn entirely from Australia. There is also the problem that they deal only with annual returns (presumably so that they can calculate volatility), whereas these are not a good measure of the returns of private asset types (one should look instead at long term, compound, cash flow-driven measures such as IRR) and can often be downright misleading.

For what it is worth, and, after stating all these reservations, perhaps that's not very much, the available sources suggest that at least some selection of private infrastructure funds in Australia made ten year returns to both 2005 and 2006 of about 13.5% with very low volatility and thus very high Sharpe Ratios. However, an IRR analysis would have been very valuable, as it would have enabled some direct comparison with, for example, private equity.

Preqin, a provider of data on a range of private alternative asset funds, does have some IRR figures, and for what it's worth these show an average net IRR of just under 10% for funds which are at least five years old. Again, it is a small data set (less than 20 funds for which performance figures are available), but these figures would seem to indicate a reasonable long term return expectation, given that infrastructure projects could be argued to be less "risky" (depending on which particular definition of "risk" you are using) than investing in quoted equities.

SUMMARY

Infrastructure, properly so called, relates to the planning, funding, construction and operation of public sector assets, some examples of which might be roads, bridges and hospitals.

Infrastructure projects may be divided into social and economic. Social may be sub-divided into education, health and security, while economic may be sub-divided into transport, communications and utilities.

Infrastructure investments are often now split into primary and secondary infrastructure. Primary encompasses the planning and constructions phases, while secondary relates to the operational period of the asset.

Infrastructure projects, at least in their secondary phase, can offer very similar investment characteristics to a bond, with an initial payment buying the right to receive a stream of income over time.

Quoted infrastructure traditionally took the form of buying shares in companies which are exposed to infrastructure projects, and "infrastructure" ETFs continue this approach. It is important to understand, however, that this in no way approximates to investment exposure to actual infrastructure projects.

Despite having represented a major opportunity for some years, infrastructure is still a relatively young asset type, and great caution must be exercised when considering returns data, since some studies cover only very small populations and time periods. They do suggest, however, that private infrastructure vehicles are capable of producing returns which are both significantly higher than, and lowly correlated with, those of quoted equities.

8

Commodities

In *Multi Asset Class Investment Strategy*,[1] the number of "asset classes" (itself now a questionable phrase) considered was in fact relatively small; just three, in fact, apart from quoted equities. There were two main reasons for this.

First, the book was inspired by the Yale Model and the thoughts of its creator, David Swenson. Part of its remit was to examine, critically where appropriate, Yale's actual investment approach, and private equity, hedge funds and real estate were what featured in their portfolio, although to be strictly accurate the latter two were described as "absolute return" and "real assets".

Second, the book was concerned to compare and contrast the Yale Endowment against pension fund performance, and particularly that in Europe. Alas, even this restricted choice proved too rich for these shrinking violets. Many had no allocation at all to either of the first two offerings, and even where they did it was so small as to be little more than a token gesture. Let the grave funding crisis which now seems certain to blight the retirement of millions of people[2] stand as the only judgement and epitaph necessary for such a tragically incompetent approach.

When it comes to commodities, for example, European pension funds did not invest in them, while US ones were actually legally prohibited from doing so. It seemed pointless, therefore, in view of such overwhelming indifference, to include a chapter about them. This, by the way, despite the fact that even at the time many investment observers were arguing for the existence of "commodity super-cycles", and that a basket of commodities had an essential part to play in any portfolio. In fact, since the publication of that book, US pension funds began lobbying Congress to change the law to allow them to make investments in commodities should they wish. However, those who are familiar with the pensions industry in Europe will not be surprised to hear that no similar upsurge of interest has occurred on the other side of the Atlantic.

---

[1] Already cited.

[2] And, in the case of the UK, the formation of two new Government bodies (The Pensions Regulator and The Pension Protection fund), which would otherwise have been arguably unnecessary.

In the context of a book about alternative assets generally, though, it is clearly relevant to include a discussion of this fascinating category of assets, and certainly a consideration of commodities routinely forms part of the consultancy work on investment strategy and asset allocation which the writer performs for institutions around the world. For people have woken up the possibilities offered by commodities, not least the fact that they may offer a source of uncorrelated return. However, as this chapter will show, they are perhaps the most complex asset type of all, and the case for their inclusion is by no means clear-cut.

WHAT ARE "COMMODITIES"?

There are various ways in which one might define "commodities". Let us adopt for the purposes of this book some natural product, which is either grown or extracted, and for which a recognised financial market exists. These are both qualities which are shared by all the investment assets which we will be considering in this chapter. There is however another, which is shared by all commodities including even the ones (gold, oil and gas) which we will be considering separately, and that is that they are "fungible". All this means is that one ton of any one commodity will be the same as any other ton of the same commodity; in other words, the two could quite easily be substituted for each other with no difference in quality or (obviously) in quantity. Thus, unlike when buying a specific cargo at sea, a commodity futures contract relates to a particular quantity of some product, leaving it to the counterparty to decide exactly which batch (or even mix of batches) of the commodity to provide at delivery.

Actually, like most financial principles, this is not universally true. Coffee beans, for example, can vary enormously, even within beans of the same type, consequent on such things as the weather, the soil in which they are grown, and the time at which they are picked, and thus each batch tends to be individually graded. However, it is broadly true of most commodities and at least now we will know what "fungible" means when we hear it mentioned.

Another quality has been suggested for commodities, which is that they are all goods for which there is an underlying business need; construction and manufacturing in China have, for example, been a major driver in the global market for steel in recent years. Yet even here we have to be cautious. Silver, for example, can be held purely for investment purposes, in the same way as gold.[3]

---

[3]Witness the attempt by the Hunt brothers to corner the global silver market in 1979. It is said that they only targeted silver because at that time US citizens were not allowed to hold gold.

For the purposes of this book we are carving oil, gas and gold out from under the general "commodities" label for no better reason than they are regarded differently in practice by the world's investors. Gold, in particular, is subject to all sorts of issues, both financial and emotional, which are unique to it, though even so we might arguably have considered silver alongside it, as we have just seen. Incidentally, this is just one reason why the phrase "asset class" is almost never used within these covers.

In any event, as was said earlier, not only is it becoming increasingly difficult to delineate discrete asset classes, but in a very real sense this is no longer important. There is a growing recognition within investment circles that what something is called does not really matter; all that is important is how that asset is likely to behave within your portfolio. Which brings us neatly back to assets such as gold and oil, which are increasingly being considered as possible sources of uncorrelated return in their own right, whereas the other commodities which we will be considering are usually bundled together in some way.

HOW CAN WE CLASSIFY COMMODITIES?

As we noted above, all commodities are either grown or extracted. By convention, those which are grown are known as "soft" commodities, or just "softs", while those which are extracted are (no surprises here) known as "hard" commodities or "hards".

Soft Commodities

Soft commodities are in turn divided into "agricultural" and "livestock" commodities. These are as follows in Table 8.1:

Table 8.1   Main traded soft commodities

Agricultural	Livestock
Oats	Pork bellies
Wheat	Hogs (pigs)
Corn	Cattle (various)
Coffee (various)	
Cocoa	
Rapeseed	
Soybean	
Soybean meal	
Soybean oil	
Cotton	
Sugar (various)	

In addition, rubber, palm oil and wool can be traded (in Singapore, Malaysia and Australia respectively) but do not usually form part of any major commodities index.

Readers may question the apparently arbitrary make-up of the livestock section. Why, for example, are pork and beef featured, but not lamb, and what is the particular relevance of belly pork? The answer to this question is a classic example of how it is impossible to understand finance and investment without also knowing something of history.

In the nineteenth century most of America's livestock was driven towards Chicago. Railways were created to facilitate this, greatly improving both survival rates and meat quality. Meat packing and processing plants were built to produce and preserve standard cuts. A great port grew up to export these meat products around the world. Innovations in refrigeration offered a quantum leap forward as meat could now be frozen. It was in Chicago, too, that a futures market in such products grew up quite spontaneously as meat processors and exporters sought to hedge their costs, and livestock producers sought to reduce the uncertainty of their income.

Pork bellies were a case in point. Before the days of refrigeration, drying, salting, smoking and curing were the only known ways of preserving meat. Bacon made from pork bellies became the staple fare of the American West for settlers, miners, soldiers and railway workers alike. Hedging the price which they had to pay for their raw materials, therefore, made good commercial sense for the bacon producers in Chicago. Thus, unlike the history of gold, which is, at least in modern times, largely Euro-centric, developments in soft commodities trading have been largely driven from the US; because the great Western adventure of the mid nineteenth century required bacon for its wagons, there is today a global futures market for frozen pork bellies.

Hard Commodities

Hard commodities are divided into precious metals and industrial metals. gold is included below for the sake of completeness, but is of course dealt with separately within this book.

As with soft commodities, there are some historic anomalies. As pointed out in the note to Table 8.2, it seems strange indeed that steel, that most necessary of industrial metals, should never have been officially recognised or traded as a commodity. Probably it had a lot to do with standardisation; there can be great variation in the quality of steel produced by different plants and processes, and particular alloys and compounds are often specified for particular purposes. Innovation with

Table 8.2   Main traded hard commodities

Industrial	Precious
Copper	Gold
Lead	Platinum
Zinc	Silver
Tin	Palladium
Aluminium	
Aluminium alloy	
Nickel	
Steel (various)*	

*Steel is traditionally not classified as a commodity at all, and only recently started trading on the London Metal Exchange, though there had been for many years an effective private market in standard industrial steel rods (which can be stacked in ports, warehouses and factories around the world, but particularly in China and South East Asia). There is also a market for recycled steel in Amsterdam.

the incorporation of tungsten, for example, greatly improved the efficiency of armour plate for tanks and warships.

Thus, it was perhaps difficult to arrive at a standard guaranteed quality, though this difficulty seems now to have been overcome, and so was probably never insuperable, certainly not once the international testing industry really developed in the 1960s. Whatever the case, it does raise questions about the suitability of various commodity indices which claim to represent "global commodities" and yet do not include steel. Not only is it the most essential of industrial metals (and probably has the highest sales volumes of all – perhaps even more than all the others put together[4]), but many consider the steel market to be a bell-weather of global industrial output and demand.

Similarly, both iron ore and manganese ore enjoy active markets, though technically these do not satisfy our description of goods which have been "extracted", being rather raw materials from which commodities are created.

WHAT ARE THE RETURN DRIVERS?

Clearly all commodity prices will be driven by fundamental factors of supply and demand, whether actual or perceived. The price drivers of soft commodities, particularly agricultural ones, will tend to be natural events, especially the weather; weather risk in different parts of the world at different times of year is the major source of uncertainty in

---

[4] 1.2 billion tonnes in 2009, according to Anglo-American's annual report.

the price of coffee, for example. This has a direct ripple effect up and down the chain of supply and consumption; it was a poor harvest in Colombia one year which killed off the traditional one dollar cup of coffee which was for so long regarded as the inalienable right of any New Yorker on the streets of Manhattan. Sometimes this can be less direct, or at least less obvious. When Hurricane Katrina devastated New Orleans it also destroyed, according to some estimates, as much as one third of the total number of unroasted coffee beans in the world.

Hard commodities will tend to react to basic industrial drivers, though it can be hard to observe or measure direct cause and effect as producers react to increased demand by bringing increased supply on stream and some major customers will build stockpiles when prices are low. Investment conferences in Australia repeatedly speculate about likely industrial activity in China, for instance, since Australia's economy is heavily commodity driven and China is its main industrial market for most of those commodities.

COMMODITIES BETA

Prices and Indices

As we have seen, part of our definition of a "commodity" is that it must enjoy a discrete and recognised financial market. Thus, the price of each commodity is constantly quoted, and this will form its beta return. This assumes that an investor can access it, directly or indirectly, through an underlying futures contract and/or options written upon it.

As mentioned above, there are also various indices which represent baskets of commodities. The two main ones are, as might be expected, from S&P and Dow Jones (DJ). Each covers a broad basket of commodities, including gold and various oil products. However, they are not identical. The S&P contains more components than the DJ[5] and thus has some that the latter does not (lead, for instance). The index weighting methodology is also different; for example, the DJ index does not allow any component to be less than 2% of the whole, whereas the S&P index does.

In addition, each index provider offers products which track commodities sectors and sub-sectors. Examples would be livestock, light energy and agricultural. Sometimes the specialisation is by exclusion, such as with "non-energy".

---

[5]The Dow Jones commodity index is issued jointly with UBS (but was previously issued jointly with AIG, so that many archived articles refer to the DJ-AIG index). The S&P commodity index is issued jointly with Goldman Sachs.

As with any asset type where one encounters multiple indices, this is far from being an ideal situation, particularly when the indices not only have different components but different methodologies as well. While it is clear what the beta of any individual commodity might be, it is arguable that there is no real beta for commodities as a whole if one cannot even agree what should be included and what should not.

In practice, no matter how suspect an approach this might be as a question of pure financial theory, probably little harm is done in accepting a basket of different commodities as representing some approximation of how the group as a whole might behave. We are trying to find a group of assets in which we can invest, and an index which we can use (1) to define the group, (2) to provide an access point to it and (3) to benchmark our performance. We are not trying to research exactly how commodities as a whole have performed as an asset class. Even if we *were* attempting the latter exercise, we would still have to decide exactly how we were going to define "commodities", and how we would weight our selections. Equally? By production volumes? By trading volumes? We would also need to decide whether we were going to use spot or forward prices as the basis of our calculations (see below).

Is It Investable?

Any time you have a futures contract underlying a spot pricing mechanism then you have an investable product. There remains of course the issue of how representative the futures contract may be of the spot price, and of whether this is even a valid question to be asking, but one thing is certain, this is something (an exchange traded contract in this case) which is investable.

This statement requires qualifying, however. As we see when looking at other assets within this book, such as gold and oil, it is all very well to assume that an investor can just go out and buy a futures contract. In practice, this has all sorts of implications as regards size (the minimum contract volume for cocoa, for example, is 10 tons[6]), trading and settlement, the appointment and monitoring of a dealer, and the ability and expertise to "roll" a position so as to ensure continuing access (and not having to take physical delivery). Fine perhaps for a large, sophisticated investor such as an endowment or a sovereign wealth fund (SWF), but certainly not for retail investors or even for relatively small and/or unsophisticated institutional investors, such as most of the world's pension funds. Even for the SWFs, this all

---

[6]On the NYBOT (New York Board of Trade) exchange.

entails a lot of time and trouble, particularly since the investor would presumably want exposure to a number of commodities rather than just one.

It is here that commodities ETFs come into play. These are quoted vehicles which buy a basket of underlying assets which represents exactly the capital contributed by its investors.

In the case of an equities ETF they will reproduce an index or sector index, and where no sector index exists then they will create a representative basket of stocks. We have already seen that there are certain cases (where one wishes to invest in a particular index, such as MSCI World) where this works excellently, and certain cases (where one wishes to gain exposure to, say, underlying infrastructure assets) where it works very badly, although to be fair the ETF provider would argue that in fact the product is doing exactly what it promises to do. The problem, they would claim, with every justification, is not that the product is not achieving its objective, but rather that there is no product available whose objectives are the same as your own.

In the case of commodities ETFs they will replicate an index by putting together the appropriate basket of commodities. Since they do not wish to take physical delivery any more than their investors do, this exposure will be by way of the underlying futures contract, or instruments written around it such as options and swaps, particularly total return swaps.

These are tracker funds, in other words. They provide beta exposure, and they do it very well, producing very low tracking errors at very low cost to the investor. In particular, they seem to be immune to stock market beta (unlike REITS, for instance), largely because the market realises that these are not in any way operating businesses, but simply parcels of assets; in other words, they are not equities.

In a sense this does no more than state simple market reality, certainly in these days of instantaneous pricing and trading. If an ETF were to trade at a premium to the value of its underlying assets, then any holder of the ETF would simply sell the ETF and buy the assets instead. Were it to trade at a deficit, then the opposite would happen, as indeed used to be seen on the London Stock Exchange; when an investment trust traded at a sufficient discount to NAV then "trust-busters" would take over the trust, sell its assets, and distribute the proceeds to shareholders.

There are however two issues with ETFs which should be stated explicitly, since both of them are widely ignored by investors. Both are technical points and both probably of more impact in the short term than the long, but both bear considering. In addition, we should at least be aware of the "renewal effect".

US Dollar Currency Risk

The first is that the overwhelming majority of the world's ETFs are dollar denominated. We can deal with this point fairly succinctly here, since we are concerned with commodities, and the prices of individual commodities are themselves quoted in dollars, so no harm is done; the investor is placed in exactly the same position as if they held the underlying assets. However, it remains the case that a non-US dollar denominated investor can only make an allocation to commodities if they are prepared to import a considerable amount of US dollar currency risk into their portfolio. As we have just seen, this will be so regardless of whether the allocation is invested directly in individual commodities contracts, or indirectly through ETFs.

What does this mean? That you must be prepared for the value of your commodities holdings to go up or down with the price of the dollar relative to your own currency. This is clearly "risk" both in its traditional sense of "likely volatility of future returns assessed on actual historic performance", and in two more sensible meanings: "uncertainty of outcome" and "the chance that something unpleasant may happen". It would be galling, for example, to find that your brilliant asset allocation decision to move into commodities immediately preceded a rise of 20% in your chosen index and/or ETF, but that the US dollar had fallen 25% against your own currency in the meantime, thus leading to a small loss instead of a thumping profit. Yet, if you are not a dollar investor then this is precisely what you must be prepared to see happen.

One possible answer would be to run a permanent short position on the dollar, or perhaps a slightly more sophisticated approach might be only to switch on your short position when the dollar exchange rate reached a certain level and, yes, there are currency ETFs as well which will allow you to do exactly this. What you must do is at least to address the problem and decide whether you want to do anything about it and, if so, what. Simply to ignore the issue or, worse still, never even become aware of its existence, is inexcusable; this is a key factor which may have a significant impact on the value of your portfolio.

To take but one obvious ramification, what about rebalancing? All investors will rebalance their portfolios at least once a year and in many cases once a quarter. In principle, this is a sensible thing to do as it forces investors to buy low and sell high, whereas their instinctive tendency is often to do the opposite. For this reason, rebalancing has been described as a free lunch. Practice, however, is more complicated. It can take several years, for example, to have much impact on the size of, say, a private equity programme, and the other private asset types suffer from similar disadvantages. This is why possible fluctuations in value due to exchange rates must be discussed in advance and a policy agreed. There are many valid views on this, ranging from the argument that a genuinely long term investor should simply ignore short term currency effects, to a desire to have an overall currency hedge permanently in place. So, your policy towards this might take any one or more of a number of forms; the only unacceptable policy is not to have one.

The second issue has already been touched upon. To what extent do commodities ETFs really track the "value" and/or "return" of the underlying assets?

Are They Representative?

This is a slightly contentious issue. We have already seen that the index providers have been somewhat arbitrary in their choice of constituents and, in particular, steel seems to be a surprising omission, for all that it was not traditionally viewed as a "commodity" at all.[7] The inclusion of both gold and oil can also cause difficulties. For example, some investors may already have a separate allocation to gold and not wish to "double up", while others, such as some SWFs, may wish to avoid oil exposure in order to have as little correlation as possible between their investment performance and the price of oil, on which their national revenues may be based. However, let us leave this point to one side.

More serious is the argument that has been raised by many observers that while commodities ETFs do a very good job of tracking the underlying futures contract around which they invest, they do *not* track the relevant spot price. This is actually a long-standing objection to commodity ETFs on the basis of something which has been referred to variously as "the contango effect" or "negative roll yield". Let us rehearse the argument first, and then consider it.

The natural state of a futures market is contango, that is when the price for future delivery is higher than the spot price; were it otherwise, according to strict financial theory, then investors could simply sell the commodity and buy the futures contract. The opposite condition, backwardation, is regarded as an aberrant situation which only arises infrequently and for short periods,[8] usually forced by extreme unexpected

---

[7]There is a separate Steel ETF, which is based around the DAX Global Steel index, but be warned that this is an equities ETF, not a commodities ETF.

[8]Though for the sake of completeness it should be pointed out that there is an ongoing debate about this, which lies beyond the scope of this book and belongs in a specialist work on derivatives markets. For the record, John Maynard Keynes argued in his *Treatise on Money* (London: Palgrave Macmillan, 1971, originally published in 1930) that backwardation should be a normal expectation in commodity markets, arising from the eagerness of commodity producers to hedge their anticipated sales revenue.

events, such as the effect which the Iraqi invasion of Kuwait had upon the oil market.

Any holder of a futures contract who does not wish to take delivery under it will need to renew it on a regular basis, and where a market is in contango the contract will typically be "out of the money", have no surrender or resale value, and require an extra cost to renew (this extra cost was traditionally but confusingly known as a "contango"). It is these regular extra costs incurred in renewing or "rolling" the position which are known as negative roll yield, or the contango effect and which, it is claimed, eat into the investor's returns, thus leading to a discrepancy between the performance of the ETF and the spot price of the underlying commodity.[9] The investor, who is expecting the ETF to track the spot price of the commodity, will thus be confused and disappointed by actual performance.

In fact, it is widely accepted that negative roll yield does indeed impact on ETF performance. Let us take oil as an example. Crude oil futures contracts are available for each month of the year and ETF managers typically buy what is called "the near month" contract, that is the one for the next available month, selling it before expiry to avoid having to take physical delivery, and then buying the next near month contract. Clearly, there is a cost involved, as noted above. However, there are a number of other issues which should to be considered.

First, as a matter of financial theory, the futures price and the spot price of a commodity will converge steadily as the futures contract nears its expiry date. This is because the futures price has considerable notional carrying costs (chiefly storage, insurance and interest payments) built into it, and these diminish and finally vanish when the delivery date occurs. Of course, this issue can never be entirely eliminated unless an investor in the futures contract is prepared to take physical delivery from time to time, but it does suggest that there is at the very least considerable "wriggle room" in skilled hands.

Second, some ETFs no longer invest in the futures contract itself, chiefly because they acknowledged that the contango argument was valid at least in part, but in instruments based around it, such as total return swaps, which can run for much longer than one month.

Third, an ETF will only need to invest a small part of its capital at any one time in the current contract, since only a deposit or margin payment will be required. The rest of the money is placed on deposit and will earn interest which will be offset against the roll costs.

Fourth, in order to be able to trade at the spot price an investor would have physically to hold the commodity, and there would be very

---

[9]See, for example, an article by Moonraker Fund Management in March 2010 for *ETF Express*.

significant carrying costs involved in maintaining this position too. A physical gold ETF, for instance, will need to pay a bullion dealer to buy, hold, number and register gold bars on its behalf.

The fifth point, and the ultimately fatal one for the argument set out above, is that ETFs do not pretend to track the spot price of a commodity, but only to replicate an unleveraged position in the futures contract, which is precisely how the relevant index is calculated. Thus, the investor gets exactly what they contracted for; an instrument which tracks a specified commodity index. If they are expecting anything different then they clearly have not read the label on the tin.

Let us be clear, though, that this is admittedly not the same thing as physical ownership of commodities. Some critics have suggested that ETFs should be seen as short term trading vehicles, and "that long term investors should avoid them if they want a long term exposure to commodities as an asset class".[10] Yet what is the alternative? Holding the commodity itself, with the possible exception of physical gold is clearly not an option, not least because the agricultural ones are perishable.

What seems to be being suggested is that investors should instead choose funds whose managers have freedom to invest not only in the commodity itself but in the stocks of companies whose businesses are related to the commodity; in other words, exactly the sort of quoted vehicle approach that we have already examined and rejected. As 2008 clearly demonstrated across all asset classes, far from resulting in uncorrelated return, such an approach is likely simply to import large amounts of stock market beta back into the investor's portfolio.

Counterparty Risk

There are some ETF experts who argue that commodity ETFs are not really ETFs at all. This is not strictly true, but behind the statement lurks a very important fact, which is not generally appreciated.

Not strictly true because the fund itself is indeed exchange traded. The underlying derivative instruments, however, are not. Thus, we encounter the issue of counterparty risk, which until the collapse of Lehman Brothers nobody thought significant, but which now ranks high on any list of factors for risk assessment purposes.

It is, therefore, theoretically possible that the fund could be sitting on a derivative position which was heavily in the money and yet find that on the strike date the party that had written that option or swap was unable to honour it. In those circumstances the fund would be in

---

[10]The Moonraker article already cited.

danger of losing not just the potential profit, but also the cost, if any, of establishing the exposure in the first place. There would also be practical ramifications which would be equally vexing, not least the amount of time and effort needed to agree new documentation with replacement managers and counterparties to be able to re-commence the fund's operations.

In passing, it is worth noting that this problem may disappear, since the Obama administration is currently outlining proposals heavily to reform derivatives trading, and one of the more radical ideas is to ban OTC instruments altogether. Clearly if all derivatives had to be either exchange traded or issued under the auspices of a clearing house, then counterparty risk would all but disappear since settlement would be guaranteed by the exchange or clearing house as appropriate, secured in each case by members' deposits.[11] Because of this extra burden of having to provide margin cash, this move is currently being opposed by those who write derivatives, and thus at the time of writing it is impossible to predict in which way the situation may develop. That said, let us revert to considering the situation as it actually is rather than as it might be one day soon.

The point is unanswerable. Clearly if the settlement of an instrument is not guaranteed by either an exchange or a clearing house then there *is* counterparty risk. It is for the individual investor to assess just how trivial or significant this risk may be in any particular situation, and the impact of highly improbable but highly significant events should no longer be ignored. The holder of a total return swap from BP could say with every justification that BP was one of the world's biggest energy companies – but then so was Enron.

In a sense, though, the same sense in which we discussed an earlier point, the argument is academic. It is not for us to place an investor in an ideal position, a commodity ETF would argue, but only to place them in the same position they would be in if they held the ETF's underlying assets directly. All we offer is a securitised access route into those assets; instead of buying them directly, the investor can buy the ETF instead.

If the investors wanted exposure to the commodity but the ETF did not exist then, as we have already seen, the investor would have to hold derivative contracts. The ETF simply replicates this position; it offers convenience, not security.

The question for any investor therefore remains the basic "should we make an allocation to commodities?", with "what do we think about counterparty risk within commodity ETFs?" as one of the follow-up

---

[11]Exactly as is being done with European (currently chiefly UK) property derivatives.

questions to be considered as part of the strategic discussion. The point is nonetheless important. You cannot compare the returns of a commodity ETF directly against those of, say, the FTSE Total Return index, for example, since the former carries default risk, no matter how seemingly slight, while the latter does not. There must therefore be either some element of out-performance or some other strategic advantage offered by the former relative to the latter to justify its inclusion within a portfolio.

Renewal Effect

There is one other aspect of synthetic exposure which should be considered, and that is something which is often called the renewal effect. In fact, it is not relevant here, but it is worth being aware of the argument, since it does impact on other areas of investment.

If one buys a parcel of shares, the argument goes, and their value goes down, you can simply sit on them, hoping that sooner or later they will return to at least the same price as that which you paid for them. If, on the other hand, you have taken a long position (say a call option) and the shares decline in value, then your option expires out of the money and you have to buy a new one. In other words, if you are a long only investor in a bear market then as a stockholder you will be suffering a paper loss on your portfolio, but there is no cost to actually maintaining your position. As an option holder, on the other hand, you will suffer recurring costs to maintain your position; this is exactly the same (so far as the practical outcome is concerned) as the contango effect, or negative roll yield referred to above.

Suppose that you were an option holder, and this was to happen to you for six or seven periods in succession. Might there not be a great temptation for you to decide to "sit this one out", on the basis that this period was likely to be negative as well so why throw good money after bad? That, in a nutshell, is the renewal effect. With each succeeding period of loss it grows progressively more difficult psychologically to "re-up". We saw an example of this in the period leading up to mid-2007 with many hedge funds that were officially "long/short" becoming in reality "long only" as they grew tired of taking out losing bets on falling prices.

With commodities ETFs this is irrelevant as they are legally obliged to maintain the position, but it is worth being aware of the argument because it *is* a valid issue to consider when discussing in more general terms whether to seek physical or synthetic exposure to a particular asset type.

COMMODITY RETURNS

Let it be noted straight away that when it comes to commodity returns, the investor will be confronted by any number of conflicting claims, studies and observations. There were many, for example, who claimed back in 2005 that we were in the grip of a commodity super-cycle of inexorably rising prices, yet five years on commodity indices are showing negative five year returns.

Part of the problem lies in agreeing common parameters such as time periods and underlying data. Part too in the fact that the available research all took place in an environment of steadily positive equity returns, thus raising the question of what "equity-like" returns should really be taken as meaning in a post-crisis world.

Research by Vanguard, for instance, stated that commodity futures have experienced long periods of significant returns. From 31 August 1969 to 30 April 2009, commodity futures produced an average annual return of 9.8%, compared to 9% for US equities over the same period. Vanguard also researched the potential diversification benefits offered by commodity futures and concluded that commodity futures returns and equity returns have historically had very low correlation.[12]

Gorton and Rouwenhoorst (2006)[13] studied a period from 1959 to 2004 and concluded that commodities futures offered near-identical returns and Sharpe Ratios as US equities, but with very low correlation. They also argued that commodity futures returns showed strong correlation with inflation, including unexpected changes in inflation, which would suggest that they should be attractive to any investor seeking to hedge away inflation risk, such as pension fund paying index-linked benefits.

Erb and Harvey (2006),[14] point out that the returns of individual commodity futures during that same period were approximately zero. In fact, this refers to the overall position; of the 36 individual commodities studied by both research teams, exactly half (18) had positive returns, while the other 18 were negative. Significant returns, they argue, can be generated only by bringing different commodities together into a basket; and very significant returns only by successfully choosing which commodities to overweight at which time.

---

[12]Quoted by IFAonline 23 March 2010.
[13]Facts and Fantasies about commodity futures, *Financial Analysts Journal*, Vol.62, No.2, April 2006, but originally written in 2005.
[14]The Strategic and Tactical Value of Commodity Futures, same volume of *Financial Analysts Journal*.

They ponder the apparent anomaly that, as Gourton and Rouwenhoorst's paper seems to show, a diversified portfolio of commodity futures can generate equity-like returns, while both the median and the average excess return of its individual constituents is zero. They suggest that this is partly due to a combination of low correlations and high volatility, and partly to the effects of regular rebalancing.

The author's own research, deliberately based upon a different index (the DJ-AIG/USB rather than the GSCI) and a different time period (1991–2009), suggests average annual returns of about 3.6% (and so probably no excess return) and a Sharpe Ratio of roughly zero.

Faced with such a mass of conflicting evidence, what is one to think? Both Erb and Harvey and the author's own figures seem, for example, to contradict Gorton and Rouwenhoorst's claim that commodities are highly correlated with inflation. Let us try to extrapolate what little can be stated with any certainty from this confusion, and then try to identify any other relevant factors.

What can be Stated?

There seems to be general agreement that in order to generate significant returns over a long period, it is necessary to put together a basket of commodity futures rather than choosing individual ones. However, even here we need to be careful, since we have seen elsewhere in this book that both gold (and probably silver) and energy commodities (notably oil) can usefully be split out and treated by investors as separate asset types.

This is of particular importance, since they feature largely in commodity indices, and thus if we choose to take an index-based approach (such as through broad commodity ETFs) we run the real risk of double coverage.

There also seems to be general agreement that commodity returns are lowly correlated with quoted equities. Indeed, the author's own calculations suggest low correlation with most other asset classes (global macro hedge funds, at about 50%, seems to be the highest). In principle, then commodities appear to be a prime candidate as a provider of uncorrelated return. Against this must be measured the fact that when uncorrelated performance was most needed by investors (2008) commodities nose-dived (though, in fairness, 2001–2003 was a different story).

Since there have been occasional periods of very heavy negative returns, calculating the return of commodities will be strongly influenced by which period, and in particular which starting date, one chooses. For example, the GSCI index, having been steadily positive from 2001 onwards, collapsed in 2008 to below its 1999 level. We will examine this point a little more.

What other Factors are Relevant?

In common with most academic finance papers, the ones referenced in this chapter ignore the time value of money. Specifically, they think of returns in one of two different ways: either as an average periodic (annual, quarterly, monthly, etc.) return or as a geometric mean. The latter sounds complicated but isn't; it simply calculates the average percentage increase or decrease over various time periods.

The explanation for this approach is that finance academics believe that all the material risk of an investment can be measured by the volatility of its historic returns, and that without using periodic returns then it is impossible to carry out this calculation, and find its "risk adjusted" return (of which the Sharpe Ratio is one measure). It is not for this book to discuss whether this view is correct or not, but simply to point out that it *is* the prevalent view, and therefore colours every approach to financial research.

Note please that both views share two common qualities. First, they think in terms of a number of different time periods, and second they assume that the impact on the return of every time period is the same. How valid are these assumptions in practice?

It is strongly arguable that what is important to an investor is not that they hold an investment over a certain number of time periods, but *when* they buy it and *when* they sell it. For example, had you bought commodities at the beginning of 2008 your investment would have lost well over a third of its value in the first year – a loss which it would have struggled to make up perhaps for many years (following an initial loss of 37%, it requires a subsequent gain of nearly 59% to restore the investment to its original value). If, on the other hand, you had bought at the beginning of 2002, you would have made an initial gain of over 24%.

Then, of course, there is the little matter of the time value of money, which the use of periodic returns and geometric means completely ignores.[15] Surely it makes more sense to consider the whole range of ways in which returns can be viewed, rather than just one or two, particularly if the remainder might represent the reality of how an investor buys and holds assets? Measures of compound returns, such as an

---

[15]Apologies – this is one of those moments when the curtain slips and we have to view reality as it is.

IRR,[16] capture this while periodic returns, whether annual, quarterly or monthly, arguably do not.

Erb and Harvey (2006) actually start groping towards this idea themselves, but never quite get there. They recognise that rebalancing can have a significant effect on returns, but fail to take the logical next step of recasting their returns data in such a way that the effects of rebalancing can properly be portrayed. After all, what is the reality of rebalancing? That the investor will experience cash flows, either in or out, as they sell or buy the asset to rebalance it to its original level. Together with the initial outflow when the investment is bought, and the final inflow when it is sold, surely this represents the economic reality over the lifetime of the investment?

Running some IRR calculations of commodities returns gives a broad range of results since, of course, the timing of the investment is now critical, as pointed out above. At the high end, commodities can achieve a long term compound return in excess of 10%, which would clearly be acceptable. At the lower end, the situation becomes much more marginal.

Thus, as is usual with finance, the situation is actually much more complex than is assumed by the parameters of academic studies. An added complication in this case, outlined in an earlier chapter, is exactly what might be expected by way of an "equity-like" return in the future, since this might define the benchmark for what might be acceptable in the case of a different but lowly correlated asset type.

THE CASE FOR COMMODITIES

This chapter began by saying that "(commodities) are perhaps the most complex asset type of all, and the case for their inclusion is by no means clear-cut" and hopefully the intervening pages have served to justify those statements.

Many of the criteria for inclusion seem to be met. There is a beta return available which is investable and broadly representative, subject to two caveats. The first is that commodities ETFs are subject to counterparty risk at the level of the underlying derivative instrument. The second is that if we wish to include, say, gold and oil in our portfolio separately then we will need to build up our own commodity baskets (say agricultural commodities and industrial metals) rather than relying on the broad indices, or we shall suffer double coverage.

---

[16]Internal rate of return, a measure of the compound return which can be earned by a stream of cash flows over time.

So too is the criterion that returns should be lowly correlated, and here it seems the argument for commodities is at its strongest, since diversified commodity returns seem to be lowly correlated not just with quoted equities, but with most other asset classes.

The two areas of uncertainty revolve around inflation and returns.

Gorton and Rouwenhoorst (2006) echo much traditional hearsay when they say that their results suggest strong correlation between commodities and inflation. Erb and Harvey (2006), however, disagree and the author's own calculations seem to favour the latter view. Perhaps, like gold, commodities require a very long period for this correlation to become apparent. Whatever the case, it would seem unwise to assume that investing in commodities will provide a hedge against inflation risk in the absence of a great deal more consistent research on the point than currently exists.

Returns are a real puzzle. The author's figures seem to support the view of Gorton and Rouwenhoorst (2006) that broad commodities should over time exhibit roughly the same volatility of returns as quoted equities. The questions that investors thus need to ask themselves are: (1) what exactly do we currently mean by "equity like" returns?, (2) do commodities exhibit "equity like" returns? and (3) would that level of returns, whatever it might be, provide the individual investor with an acceptable return given their own particular targets and objectives?

The opening chapter of this book suggests that the answer to the first question may be a much lower level of return than was assumed before 2007, perhaps no more than a couple of percent above inflation. The second question is difficult to answer with any certainty, but assuming the answer to the first question just stated, then one could say "probably". The answer to the third question will have to be assessed individually by every investor according to their own requirements. Assuming that they were comfortable with out-performing inflation by some small margin, then commodities would become a valid candidate for inclusion, and at this point their low correlation with other asset types would begin to weigh very heavily in their favour.

SUMMARY

Institutional investors, particularly pension funds, have traditionally ignored commodities as an asset class within their portfolios. In the case of American pension funds this was because they were legally incapable of investing in them.

Commodities can be classified as either "soft" or "hard", with each category being further sub-divided as set out in the tables above. Note that there are some surprising omissions, notably steel, which enjoys its own separate market.

Beta returns are provided by various indices which are investable by means of ETFs. Care must be taken when evaluating these, as different index providers have adopted different constituents and methodologies.

With the exception of physical gold, commodities ETFs do not take physical delivery, and thus cannot make use of spot pricing. Instead, they achieve synthetic exposure by reference to the underlying futures contract. Note that while the fund itself is exchange traded, the derivative instruments in which it invests are not, and thus there will always be some element of counterparty risk, at least for the time being (since reform of OTC derivatives is currently under discussion).

It seems clear that a basket of diversified commodity futures will be lowly correlated not just with quoted equities but with most other asset types as well. In principle, they seem therefore to offer a source of uncorrelated return within an investment portfolio.

They also seem to exhibit roughly the same level of volatility of historic returns as quoted equities. It is necessary therefore to enquire whether they also exhibit equity-like returns.

The answer to this question is complex, not only because the answer will differ according to the time period and measure of return chosen, but also because conceptions of just what an "equity-like" return might be may have changed significantly in recent years.

Unless and until evidence to the contrary becomes available, it would seem sensible to adopt the relatively conservative view that both commodities and quoted equities should, over a long period, out-perform inflation by anything up to about 2%, but exhibiting low correlation with each other. However, the phrase "long period" should be stressed, and the author is thinking in terms of compound returns over time. Periodic returns may fluctuate wildly, and fall considerably short of this target, particularly should a rapid and/or unexpected rise in the rate of inflation occur.

9

Gold

INTRODUCTION

This book seeks to split out gold as a separate asset for consideration because although many might regard it as part of a generic "commodities" pool, it has certain particular characteristics which set it apart.

Gold is one of the earliest known precious substances whose value was recognised on a more or less universal basis across nations and cultures, yet until the exploitation of the New World by the Spanish and Portuguese it was in relatively short supply in Europe, leading to it being particularly highly prized. Until the arrival of gold from the New World, funding large financial transactions was highly problematic. The value of currency was held to be equivalent to the value of the commodity from which it was made; thus the amount of silver in a silver coin would determine the value of that coin, and so forth.

The reason that the English, and subsequently British, unit of currency is called the pound, for example, is that it was originally composed of 240 silver pennies, the collective silver weight of which was precisely one pound, although in practice the "mark" (13 shillings and four pence, two thirds of a pound) was more widely used in medieval times. The mark was to become the standard currency of many countries in the Nordic and Germanic regions, although here confusingly it was often used to mean half a pound of silver, rather than two thirds.

Until the reign of Edward III (1327–1377) the silver penny was the highest value coin in circulation. At the time of his grandfather, Edward I, this meant that during his numerous military campaigns in Wales and Scotland his troops' pay had to be carried around by trains of pack mules, each requiring a considerable escort, and frequently leading to problems in finding enough coins in circulation to bring together for the task.

In countries where even silver was in short supply, the problem was still more acute. In Sweden, the most valuable naturally occurring commodity was copper, and so the Swedes had no choice but to use this as currency. Some lumps of copper "currency" weighed as much as 15 kilograms, and so when merchants travelled to do business they had to take with them not a purse but a donkey, which could carry two of these large copper sheets. A "donkey" of copper thus became an established approximation of value. In the more venal and exotic world of Italy, a donkey load of gold or silver would become established as a unit of value in the sale and purchase of votes in the college of cardinals at the time of a papal election.

The sudden influx of gold from the New World would transform the situation. However, even before this we find Europe's first gold coin to become widely accepted: the gold florin, first minted in Florence in 1252 and which was to remain a universal unit of currency across the continent for 300 years. In England, the gold "noble" was introduced by Edward III, being equivalent to a third of a pound, so that two nobles equalled one mark. From now onwards, gold became the standard fallback position in any monetary discussions. Faith in currencies might wax and wane, particularly once paper money was introduced, but gold was the financial world's comfort blanket.

Most currencies were tied to gold either explicitly or implicitly. Most banknotes were "representative money" meaning that although you held a piece of paper it represented a quantity of gold or silver sitting in the vaults of whichever bank had issued it, and into which you could convert your banknote by presenting it for exchange at the counter of the bank.

Under the Bretton Woods agreement after the Second World War, the US sought to secure the world's monetary systems by anchoring the dollar to gold, and every other currency to the dollar (the fact that this guaranteed that the dollar would become the world's standard reserve currency and be adopted universally by a range of industries such as oil, shipping, hotels and airlines might be seen either as a happy coincidence or as an attempt by the US to dominate the world's economic mechanisms, depending on your point of view). This system was abandoned in 1971, after which time all currencies were allowed to fluctuate, although in practice for many years an official exchange rate for each was fixed and enforced by central banks.

Through all of this, gold has remained constant, traditionally viewed as the asset to which investors flee when everything else seems to be falling apart around them; the defensive investment *par excellence*. Let us explore a few reasons for why this might be the case.

Inflation

We know from the Old Testament that at the time of King Nebuchadnezzar one ounce of gold purchased 250 loaves of bread. Today, that is still broadly correct. Another, more recent, example often cited is that in New York at the time of the American Civil War an ounce of gold would buy a decent suit of men's clothing, still broadly the case today.

So, it does seem to be the case that provided one is dealing with long periods, perhaps even very long periods, then gold provides a perfect hedge against inflation, and can be counted upon to produce a return which exactly matches it.

The rub here is talk of "long periods". While the last paragraph is correct, it ignores the fact that over shorter periods gold is highly volatile, and, as a result, over these shorter periods the above assumption does not hold true. For example, for the period from 1986 (a convenient one if one seeks to measure correlation with, say, UK quoted equities since this matches the lifetime of the current FTSE 100 index) gold shows an average annual return of 5.34% compared to an average UK inflation rate of 3.49%, and actually exhibits *negative* correlation with it (−19%). Given that we can be pretty certain that over the long term that correlation figure should be about *plus* 100%, this is a striking anomaly.

The answer of course is volatility. If one adopts the standard deviation as a proportion of the average return as a measure of volatility, gold scores 2.6 during this period, as opposed to 0.6 for inflation. Thus, arguably gold has been four and a half times more volatile, in relative terms. If this is correct then in the circumstances it is hardly surprising that very long time periods are required for the moving averages to come together. So, the evidence seems to suggest that if you are investing money for your infant grandchildren (or, better still, great-grandchildren) and hedging inflation is your only concern, then gold might be a wise choice, but that it cannot be relied upon to fulfil this function in the short to medium term.

It should also be noted that in the case of gold, measuring volatility on year end values does not always convey the true picture. It is arguably a valid approach for long term investors who are going to adopt a "buy and hold" approach, but it does not fully express the full range in the fluctuation in the price of gold during the year. For those who pursue a short term, tactical approach to asset allocation then this intra-year volatility will represent a major issue.

Gold as a Safe Haven

Traditionally people have seen gold as something to take into their nuclear bunker with them in the hope that, into whatever sort of world they re-emerge, gold will still be accepted as a universal currency. Gold has a long record as a "safe haven" investment and benefits from the fact that it is portable and virtually indestructible. Jewish families fleeing Germany in the thirties often tried to convert their possessions into gold first. How does this arise?

In part it has to do with liquidity. With the possible exception only of cash itself, gold is the most liquid asset in the world, instantly convertible into cash and with its value established beyond doubt or argument by its weight. Thus, when even cash itself may lose all of its value (as it did in Germany in 1945 or in the Confederate States of America in 1865) then gold stands out as the ultimate investment of choice. There is also apocryphal evidence of a flight to gold in the panic-fuelled run up to "Y2K". Thankfully, war, genocide and global disaster (real or imaginary) are far from the normal state of affairs, however, and we need to examine why gold should still be seen in this way by many people as part of a "normal" investment scenario.

The answer to this probably lies at least in large part in another unique quality of gold, and one which is often over-looked. It is said by some to be probably the only investment asset in the world that does not have a corresponding matching liability of some kind.

A share, for example, carries the liability that the creditors of the company can come against the share of the company's asset which it represents in the case of liquidation. A bond is subject to default risk, the risk that the liability of the issuer to redeem it may prove impossible to fulfil. Derivative positions, by definition, are subject to liabilities both of the holder and of the counterparty. Property investments are subject to the liability of the property owner to keep the building in good repair, fully insured, etc. (the last itself being subject to counterparty liability), and to the liability of the tenant to pay the agreed rent. The same can be said of just about any other investment. Investment in oil, for example, can usually only be accomplished by physical ownership or synthetic ownership. Physical ownership will be subject to liabilities under bills of lading, charterparties, contracts of marine insurance and supplier contracts. Synthetic ownership is achieved through derivatives, which by definition always carry a liability and counterparty risk.

Yet, though this analysis is probably technically correct, there is probably an easier way of expressing it. Gold may be the only investment that can never have zero value. Currency can have zero value if the government issuing it falls or becomes bankrupt. A share can have zero value if the company goes into liquidation. Even commodities can theoretically have zero value in certain situations, for example when a cargo arrives in the middle of a market glut and the costs of discharging it are greater than the price anyone is prepared to pay for it (and what about a long-delayed cargo of whisky arriving in the US in 1921 after the introduction of prohibition?).

Gold can never suffer this fate because there are various conventional uses for gold that will always create demand for it, and indeed a certain proportion of every day's gold trades are to satisfy this demand. The chief two are jewellery and dentistry, although gold is also required in various specialist electrical applications. These would even survive the disappearance of the basic instinct, born of things like cultural economics and emotional decision making, that gold somehow *must* have some intrinsic value.

For, as with all investment matters, we come down ultimately to behavioural finance, and it is undeniably the case that, whatever the scientific analysis, investors feel a certain confidence in gold, a sense that it provides some measure of ultimate security, that they simply do not feel with regard to any other asset. Given the overriding importance of behavioural factors in investment then it is this, more than anything else, that drives the flight to gold in nervous times.

Had one followed those instincts in 1929, the year of the last great crash, then one would have been well rewarded. The purchasing power of gold grew by 17 times in the next five years. Similarly in the 1970s, as the oil crisis unfolded and the UK went bust (coincidentally under a Labour government) having to call in the IMF, the purchasing power of gold was multiplied 15 times.[1]

However, timing would have been everything. Gordon Brown, for example, showed his financial acumen by deciding to sell half of Britain's gold reserves between 1999 and 2002. The average price of gold during this period was $270 an ounce. However, since it had come down from a previous high of $850 an ounce, it seemed reasonable to assume that this represented a low point in gold's fortunes.[2] Brown disagreed, and sold. The price of gold subsequently went to over $1000 an ounce. (From 2002 to 2008, gold rose on average over 18% year on year.)

However, in ascending from the specific to the general then, due to gold's very high volatility, which we have already noted, it is very difficult to measure the trade-off between demand and price movements with any precision. The increase in demand for gold in the run-up to Y2K has already been mentioned. It was said also to occur in Japan in 2002 when investors became fearful that the government there was about to withdraw the central guarantee of bank deposits. Certainly there were some investors (including the author) who moved out of equities into gold in the last quarter of 2007. However, as we will see, fluctuations in genuine underlying demand can often be masked by short term speculative pressures.

---

[1] Analysis from BullionVault's Gold News.
[2] Mark Dampier of Hargreaves Lansdowne, quoted in the *Daily Telegraph* 11 May 2009.

Gold as a Hedge against US Dollar Weakness

One thing does seem to be the case, which is that gold provides a reasonable hedge against the dollar, particularly when the dollar is doing badly. Measured against the dollar, on a trade weighted indexed basis, gold tracks it very closely for the 15 years to 2005. However, gold holds up well as the TWI dollar heads into decline between 2001 and 2003 and then, as the TWI dollar languishes from 2005, gold heads upwards.[3] This is consistent with various claims in the past that gold provides excellent downside protection against US dollar exposure, particularly so when the value of the dollar falls relative to other countries. There have been various hedge funds that have constructed positions based on this belief, and these positions have in turn undoubtedly contributed to the measured volatility in the gold price, which is not properly shown by measuring it purely on a year end basis (see above).

This is undoubtedly due in part to the dollar and gold having been inextricably linked for so long due to the historic reasons we examined earlier. While it is now possible to have gold prices quoted in other currencies, these are effectively just reached by way of a simple conversion calculation from the dollar. Interestingly, this may be yet another example of behavioural finance. If an investor wants or needs dollar exposure, then when the dollar is at historically low levels it would surely make sense to sell gold to buy dollars, whereas the pricing dynamics seem to suggest that the opposite happens.

Gold as a Diversifier

So it would seem that gold makes a good diversifier within a portfolio, particularly if you are a dollar based investor, since it seems to have negative correlation particularly against the dollar when it does badly relative to other currencies, and with US quoted equities, against which its correlation grows more strongly negative the worse the US stock market performs.

Measured since 1986 it has negative correlation with just about every other asset type, save only the broad basket of commodities represented by the DJ-AIG index and oil. Even in these two cases, however, it is only about +25%; other than that it is steadfastly negative. Against the FTSE index, for example, it is −20% and against UK property as measured by the IPD index it is just below zero.

---

[3] Analysis from Bloomberg data quoted in a World Gold Council report in October 2008.

It used to be thought that an asset class which exhibited consistent negative correlation with others was unlikely to be an attractive long term investment. This was on the cosy old assumption that most asset classes tend to go up in value most of the time, if only because of the effect of inflation. On this basis, then anything which shows negative correlation is likely to go down most of the time. The classic example which used to be cited was Japanese equities, in respect of which this did of course hold true for many years.

However, the comfortable old certainties no longer apply. Times change and we change with them.[4] It is now possible to find asset classes which can exhibit both negative correlation and high returns. Some sets of active currency data, for example, strongly suggest this. Even the much-maligned Japanese stock market rallied at one stage during 2008. At the very least, it is certainly no longer possible to reject something on the grounds of negative correlation, though this should still be grounds for considerable caution.

We also need to be aware of the effects, usually unpredictable, of mixing different assets together. It is rather like improvising a chemical reaction by mixing two or three different chemicals at random and waiting to see if it produces an evil smell, a charming colour effect or an explosion. There is research, for example, which seems to establish that investing in single commodities is unlikely to produce consistent out-performance, whereas aggregating a basket of them together may. Likewise, we see in the chapter on energy that by mixing oil and natural gas together in the same portfolio we can arrive at both a higher return and a lower volatility figure than for either of them individually.

Returns

As noted above, it seems that over a very long period we can expect gold to produce a real return of zero, matching inflation more or less perfectly. This would raise an obvious question: if you are looking for an "inflation plus" return, why would you have gold in your portfolio at all, particularly as you could hold government bonds instead, which (provided you are a non-taxpayer) could be expected also to return roughly the rate of inflation, but with much less uncertainty (since gold returns have much more volatility than bond returns).

---

[4] Surprisingly, the maxim *tempora mutantor nos et mutamur in illis* is attributed to a seventeenth century Welshman who liked to astound his friends with his ability to speak Latin. Perhaps after Welsh anything is an easy language to learn.

First there is the point referred to above. Gold can never sink to zero value, whereas it is theoretically possible that government bonds could. So, in constructing a "nuclear bunker" type portfolio gold would be high on the list if only for its intrinsic value. However, in normal conditions this would clearly be outweighed by the desire for certainty.

There is another interesting point here, which can be argued either as positive or negative depending on your point of view. It is often said that "gold doesn't have children"; in other words, it produces no yield, but offers only the possibility of a capital gain or loss. Given this, it is strange that its returns have not been much more volatile than they have against the return on quoted equities, since the latter produce a dividend yield which (particularly in the UK) have provided the major part of equity returns and have a smoothing influence on downside periods.

Those planning for the doomsday scenario will argue that this is actually a strength rather than a weakness. With many bonds a large part of their value may derive from a discounted running yield, and if the source of those coupon payments was to dry up then that large part of their value would fall away. For those of a less nervous disposition, it will appear as the disadvantage that it undoubtedly is. For investors who need to generate high cash flows in the short term to meet liabilities, for example, then an income producing asset will be attractive in principle, and a non-income producing asset[5] less so.

Second there is the fact that, once again, when we talk about gold returns regressing to the inflationary mean, we have to talk about very long periods indeed; quite possibly a century or more.

Gold Doesn't Have Babies

There is one point about gold returns that is so obvious that it often gets completely overlooked. The nature of the investment return earned by gold is completely different from the returns of, say, equities, bonds or property. All of these assets enjoy some element of running yield (dividends for equities, a coupon for bonds and rental payments for property); gold does not.

Investing in gold consists of buying it and then selling it at some later date; there will be no intervening cash inflows. This has some important implications.

---

[5]The epithet NIPA, pronounced "nipper", was once applied to a hapless member of one of the City of London's corporate finance teams.

First, we cannot simply compare the percentage movement in the price of gold with, say, the percentage movement in the S&P100 index. This is not a valid comparison since, though it tells us all we need to know in the case of gold, it tells only part of the story in the case of the S&P100. In order to make a valid comparison we need at the very least to take dividend yield into account, and arguably, in the case of a "buy and hold" situation, the reinvestment of dividends too, so as to arrive at a true total return measure. When this is done, a very different picture emerges.

Second, because of this, there is a very real argument here as to the best measure of returns. Yet again we are faced with a situation that some sort of compound measure, such as an IRR, may give a more accurate representation of real life than a simple series of periodic returns. An IRR calculation of a holding in equities will give due expression of the time value of money to the dividend payments, and also to the eventual sale proceeds, whenever these may be received. A series of simple periodic returns, or an "annualised" return calculated from these, will assume that the impact of every year is the same, and thus will favour gold unfairly.

Third, if an investor has outgoings for which to provide (and any institutional investor will, if only to cover their running costs), then gold cannot be relied upon for this purpose, and unless due provision is made for this then the investor risks turning cash flow negative. We will discuss in more detail elsewhere the need to model both investment and operation cash outflows when planning asset allocation.

FIXING THE GOLD PRICE

We discussed earlier the various bases upon which pricing and/or valuation mechanisms work for different asset types. The price of gold is fixed twice a day in London, in what might perhaps be described as a more private version of open outcry. Under this process a number of market-makers come together under a chairman, who declares an opening price. The market-makers then attempt to buy and sell between themselves at this price. If there is a surplus of buyers over sellers, the chairman moves the price up and they try again. If there is a surplus of sellers, the price moves down. This process continues until there is a balance (defined as within 50 bars) between buyers and sellers at which point the chairman declares the closing price "fixed".

There are by tradition (since the present system began in September 1919) five market-makers involved. These days each one is part of a major international bank, the fix occurs by way of a conference call, and it is fixed in three different currencies (dollars, sterling and euros).

So far, so good, but let us examine the system in a little more detail. Each of these market-makers is trading in the "room" as a principal, buying to and selling from the other participants. However, if you look at the substance of what is happening rather than the form, they are effectively buying and selling as intermediaries, since as soon as the fix is completed they will straight away buy and sell the same gold to their customers to settle the contracts which they had when they went into the room.

This leads to a practice known as spoofing, which is rather like playing poker, whereby a participant with lots of sell orders will hold off from selling straight away, hoping that by so doing the price will rise to a high enough level that he can sell on more advantageous terms. This can probably be explained away as bringing the market into equilibrium, at least within limits, but where there is an overall surplus of buyers or sellers it can lead to large swings, as there is no disadvantage in spoofing high, or low as the case may be. This is one reason why, at least on a day to day basis, the gold price can exhibit high degrees of volatility.

The market maker will take a small commission for having executed the order against your contract. What you will not see is the price at which they bought or sold the gold which is now being bought or sold to you. It seems reasonable to assume that they are able to make a profit on this, or they would not survive very long as professional gold dealers. This is something you will never know. You will pay the closing price of the fix, but you will almost certainly be trading at a different price to that at which the market-maker traded that gold during the fix.

So, as we will see again when we look at gold futures, there does seem to be a definite insider advantage when it comes to gold. If you are investing in gold over a long term then these anomalies become relatively unimportant, but beware that if you are planning to invest tactically in gold then there are these various factors which in effect constitute additional dealing costs.

HOW TO INVEST IN GOLD

There are a number of different ways in which one can access gold as an investment, and we will look at each in turn:

- Gold shares
- Physical ownership (which can itself be broken down)
- Synthetic ownership
- Indirect ownership

Gold Shares

This was for a long time the only practical way in which many investors could access gold and, just as with similar situations in property, commodities and infrastructure, it is subject to a very obvious drawback. Just as in their cases, one is not buying indirect exposure to the underlying asset, but a share in a business which operates upon that asset. In this case, a share in a gold mining company. There are two separate but related problems here.

The first is that the value of a company's gold reserves (the extent of which may in any event be a matter for some dispute) makes up only a part of the valuation of the company which is expressed by the share price. Just as with any company share, an equity analyst's view of its appropriate price will be based upon a supposedly scientific view of discounted future cash flows (dividends), but will be strongly influenced by his view of the quality of the company's management, and of any company specific issues, such as cash reserves, exploration and extraction programmes, takeover prospects, competitive positioning, currency matching, etc.

In other words, in buying the share you are not taking a punt on the price of gold but (largely) on the perceived quality of the company's management and the collective market consensus view of the company's prospects. This can result in two different mining companies having two very different valuations, expressed by very different price/earnings ratios. This should by itself be enough to give the game away. Any time you have to think about a price/earnings ratio then by definition you cannot be buying something which is priced according to underlying asset values.

Of course, you could seek collective exposure to the gold mining sector as a whole, looking to diversify away the so-called "specific risk" of holding any one individual company. This will undoubtedly have a smoothing effect, but does not really resolve the basic problem; we are looking for direct exposure to the gold price but what we are being forced to buy contains some element that is derived from the price of gold, but also another, very significant element, which represents business operating and financial risk.

The second problem is that because these are shares in public companies then they form part of a particular stock exchange, and will to a certain extent go up and down with the stock market rather than by reference to the price of the underlying asset (gold) or even necessarily to the state of the company itself. If the stock market drops 25% then there is a very good chance that the share price of a gold mining company will also drop significantly, regardless of what may be happening to the price of gold. This is of course the classic "systemic risk", often referred to as stock market beta, so beloved of traditional finance.

Without wishing to labour the point, this is particularly unfortunate in the case of gold, which is after all widely seen as a defensive investment which will hopefully provide comfort and protection when it is most needed – in really dire stock market conditions. Unfortunately, experience of 2008 suggests very strongly indeed that it is precisely in these abnormal conditions that the pull of stock market beta becomes dramatically stronger, thus making it less likely than ever that a share in an asset related company will provide some sort of proxy for the underlying asset itself. On the contrary, the share will instead tend to be strongly influenced by the movement of the stock market – exactly what we are seeking to avoid.

Physical Ownership

Investors can buy gold directly either in the form of jewellery, coins or bars.

Jewellery has the advantage that it can be easily bought, plus the non-financial benefit that people enjoy wearing it. Indeed, in some cultures the amount of gold someone wears is an overt status symbol; showing one's wealth by wearing it.

Sadly these are about the only good things that can be said about owning jewellery. Firstly, there is the obvious security risk; you wear it in the street at your peril, and cannot keep it at home without some sort of safe in which to keep it (and even this is unlikely to deter a professional thief). It was once customary to have paste imitations of your jewellery made, and consign the genuine article to the depths of a bank vault for this reason.

Secondly, there is very little equation between the value of a piece of jewellery and the value of the gold which it contains. Even in the gold souk in Dubai, where gold necklaces and bracelets are allegedly sold by weight, a significant premium is charged over the market price. In fact the value of most expensive jewellery is represented not by gold, but by the jewels mounted upon it and, to a lesser extent, by the quality of the workmanship.

So, jewellery is not a practical option from an investment point of view.

Coins fall into two categories; those which had some genuine historical interest as coins (and will be sought by coin collectors) and those which are of interest and/or value simply because of the amount of gold which they contain ("bullion coins"). We will ignore the former variety as they probably fall into a different category which perhaps they share with other "collectables" such as stamps, medals, share certificates, etc.

All modern coins issued in recent years are almost pure gold – a difference from the former variety since pure gold would be too soft to be cast as a coin for everyday use – and there are widely available tables showing the weight and fineness of gold contained by each type. This, coupled with a ready availability of dealers around the world, makes them a genuinely "dealable" form of gold, so much so that various governments have at different times placed restrictions on their ownership and transport by private individuals.

However, there is a downside here too, namely that professional dealers clearly have to make money, and in this case they do so by always selling a coin at slightly too high a price and buying one at slightly too low a price. This "spread" effectively constitutes a dealing cost and, while there is no general agreement as to how much it may be, estimates range from 7% to as much as 15%.

So, a better bet than jewellery but still hardly ideal.

The thought of gold *bars* conjures up exotic visions of bank vaults and treasure ships. In fact, bars can be quite small and suitable for wealthier private investors; the variety often seen advertised in airline magazines, for example, are usually 1 kilogram. The standard size used by banks and professional bullion dealers though are about 12 times this size, equating to 400 troy ounces.[6] In other words, if gold was trading at $1000 an ounce, one of these would be worth $400000. It is at this level that physical ownership of gold becomes meaningful for the professional investor.

Since there are few investors around the world who possess a high security vault in which to store gold bars, or an armoured car and military escort with which to transport them, physical ownership is usually effected by opening an account with a bullion dealer, who for a modest fee will take care of all these tiresome details for you.

Even here there is a distinction, however, between genuine physical ownership and that which normally prevails. The normal situation is a "gold pool account" where the bullion dealer will simply make an entry in their accounts showing that you are entitled to ownership of a certain quantity of gold and then whenever you wish to sell it, simply sell a corresponding amount to your buyer from their stock; again, this transaction may in turn be a "paper" one. This is often referred to as "unallocated" gold.

---

[6]Those accepted without question by banks and bullion dealers are usually known as "London good delivery" bars.

A version of this, with accounts being operated online, has also become known as "e-gold", "digital gold" or "Digital Gold Currency" (DGC). While these arrangements have the benefit of immediacy and convenience, investors should be aware that DGC providers are unregulated and thus not subject to the same external audit regimes of a bank, investment manager or bullion dealer (should any investor still derive comfort from such oversight).

Those of an untrusting disposition, however, harbour dark suspicions that a dealer might sell more gold to clients than is actually sitting in their vaults, and insist on true "physical" ownership, with the serial numbers of particular gold bars being allocated against their name.

Most bullion dealers have arrangements with banks who will provide a "buying short" facility, which is essentially a margin loan arrangement. However, given the highly volatile performance of the price of gold, buying short can only be described as a highly risky activity.

Synthetic Ownership

Both futures and options contracts are available on the gold price (determined in accordance with the "fix" described above), and these are used both for hedging and as a substitute for physical ownership.

In the first case, a holder of physical gold might be concerned that the price will fall, and that they will be forced to sell the gold, perhaps to meet a liquidity need, before it recovers. In this case, they may choose not to sell the gold but to hold it, and short the market instead. In the second case an investor may have a view that the price of gold is likely to rise in the short term, but buy a derivative contract as an easier and less capital intensive (since the price of the derivative will be much less than the price of the gold) alternative to buying gold itself. This sort of activity is frequently indulged in by hedge funds. If, for example, you had consistently shorted the CDO market and gone long the gold price throughout 2007 you would have made a very considerable amount of money.

Again, there are some things to watch for here.

First there is the *carrying cost* of a future, often referred to as the financing cost. This arises through an investor only having to pay a small part of the total value by way of a margin. If you think it through, the principle will become obvious. If you wanted to buy gold today, you would have to pay for it today. You would either have to borrow that money, in which case you would have to pay interest on it, or you would lose out on the opportunity of earning interest on it with a bank. In either case there is a cost. There is of course no running yield with gold, so you earn nothing on it during your period of ownership.

In a notional world there will be a counterparty on the other side of your futures contract who has given up the opportunity to sell their gold in the market today, thus giving up the chance either to pay back the money which they borrowed to buy it, or depositing the money to earn interest upon it. Thus, there will always be an advantage to the buyer and a disadvantage to the seller, based upon the notional cost of financing.

If this imbalance was not corrected then we would be living in an irrational world. The pricing of futures contracts recognises this by factoring the financing cost into the price calculations. Thus, as the futures contract nears maturity, its price will adjust closer and closer to the actual gold price. This is why futures contracts are priced differently to the current price in the first place; this financing cost is built in. Some investors fail to recognise this and are therefore disappointed when an apparent profit on which they are sitting is steadily eroded as expiry approaches.

Second, there is the question of *artificial volatility*. This can arise in various ways; we have already seen one example, when a preponderance of buyers or sellers can push the fixing price much higher or lower than would seem to be justified by simple supply and demand. In the world of futures there are two specific instances when it can occur.

Gold futures all close on a particular day of a particular month. Thus, as the expiry period of a particular futures contract approaches, there can be frenzied market activity as investors try to close out particular positions; while there is no empirical data to support this belief, it seems likely that this has been exacerbated in recent years by hedge funds trading highly leveraged positions. If one or two investors with very big holdings try to brazen it out to the last moment, particularly rapid swings can occur. In the last few days of these expiry periods, it is almost certainly the state of the futures market which drives the fixing price, rather than vice versa.

We saw earlier that a small margin is all that it is usually necessary to pay in order to take out a futures contract. In the case of gold these can be much lower than those traditionally demanded elsewhere (for example, in the case of quoted equities), and sometimes as low as 2%. Naturally, where possible an investor will normally be allowed to top up the margin should the price move against them but there are circumstances where a margin call just may not be practical, for example when the price moves rapidly and significantly. A futures contract will therefore usually have an automatic stop-loss built into it, allowing it to be closed out if that level is reached, without the need first to obtain the investor's permission.

Traders will seek to take advantage of this when market trading volumes are low. If a large trader suddenly offers to sell at a low price, this may be sufficient to shift the price downwards so that brokers start triggering stop-losses, thus pushing the market down even further. Now the trader can buy back their gold and more at a good price. This also works in reverse, with a trader first offering to buy at a high price and then looking to sell a larger amount.

These stop-loss arrangements mean that we are not dealing with a perfect market here. In a perfect market, heavy buying triggers selling as the price moves up, and vice versa thus leading to a natural force in favour of market equilibrium. In the gold futures market, the opposite can happen, as heavy selling forces more heavy selling under stop-losses, thus pushing the price lower rather than higher.[7]

Gold is a highly volatile asset. This is even when measured on a year to year basis, when artificial volatility of the sort referred to above would not logically play a part, so investors should note that the actual volatility intra-year and day to day may be significantly higher than year on year figures indicates. Again, this suggests that gold is best viewed as a long term investment, and that anybody using it as part of tactical asset allocation needs a strong nerve.

Third, there is what is sometimes referred to as "roll-over psychology". Gold futures expire. When they do, if an investor wishes to have continued exposure to gold then they have to take out a new future, a process known as "roll-over". First, there is obviously a financial cost to this.[8] Second and more importantly, there is also a psychological cost. Every few months the investor will be faced with a fresh buy decision, an ordeal which the holder of bullion does not have to undergo. Basic principles of behavioural finance suggest that it may become increasingly difficult for an investor to maintain their exposure to gold in a falling market, since it becomes progressively more difficult to "re-up" after each negative period, in respect of which they will have actually lost real money on their futures contract.

Indirect Ownership

Access to many asset classes has been transformed in recent years by the rapid proliferation of Exchange Traded Funds (ETFs), which offer the opportunity of indirect ownership. Briefly, an ETF operates like a public company, with its securities quoted on a stock exchange, but

---

[7]This is what is thought to have happened on Black Monday in October 1987 in the quoted equities markets, as computer-driven stop-losses ("program trading") kept kicking in and driving the price still lower.

[8]Discussed in earlier chapters – see page 160.

representing underlying assets. For example, an ETF which was designed to give coverage of the FTSE 100 would simply take all the money that had been subscribed by its investors and use that money to buy the various constituents of the FTSE index pro rata to their capital weighting. Thus, although an investor had invested in the ETF, they would effectively be investing in the FTSE index.

ETFs generally charge relatively low costs and have come to represent an obvious means of access for investors seeking passive exposure to a particular market, sector or asset class. Their workings are explored in more detail elsewhere, particularly with regard to oil, but here let us content ourselves with saying that there are basically two different ways in which exposure to gold can be gained through an ETF.

Many gold ETFs on the market operate on an unallocated basis, so that entitlement to gold is shown by a paper trail. This works very well, and there have been no recorded causes for concern. However, many investors take the view that as gold is being bought as a "last resort" investment then it makes sense for an ETF to hold physical gold in the form of specific, allocated gold bars. There is, therefore, a distinction between physical gold ETFs and others.

Interestingly, there are now also some futures based gold ETFs, which offer collectivised exposure to the gold market in this way. These will be subject, at the fund level, to exactly the same issues outlined above. However, the presence of an ETF should take away the problems of roll-over psychology, since the ETF has no option but to re-up; after all, it is designed to track the underlying gold price as closely as possible. Please note though, that unless and until the underlying derivative contract (usually a Contract For Difference or Total Return Swap) becomes an exchange traded instrument, rather than a private Over The Counter arrangement, then such vehicles will obviously be subject to the same issues of counterparty risk which we have already discussed in earlier chapters.

SUMMARY

Gold offers an excellent hedge against inflation over a very long period, but over shorter periods, even 25 years or so, can actually exhibit negative correlation with inflation.

Though gold should over a very long period provide a return roughly equivalent to inflation, in the short term it is highly volatile and therefore offers the opportunity from time to time for significant gains (and losses).

Gold appears to be negatively correlated with quoted equities in general, although there are periods when they move in similar fashion.

Though the data is not conclusive, various reports suggest that gold tends to provide downside protection against both the dollar and US equities.

Shares in gold mining companies do not provide a good proxy for gold itself, since they represent, at least in part, operational business risk.

Physical ownership of gold may take the form of jewellery, coins or bars. The first two are subject to various limitations. The latter is the purest form of physical ownership, but has a significant cost hurdle.

Synthetic ownership is achieved by derivatives, usually futures. These may be adversely impacted by artificial volatility and are also subject to the stress of roll-over psychology.

Indirect ownership is accomplished by Exchange Traded Funds (ETFs), which can be either allocated (physical), unallocated or futures based.

10
Active Currency

Around the end of the Second World War, the United States and Great Britain, then representing at least ostensibly the two strongest economic blocks in the world (though in reality Britain had been effectively bankrupt since 1941) drew up a new global monetary system which became known as Bretton Woods, after the small town in New Hampshire where the delegates met. Actually, no less than 44 allied nations were represented, but of these many were small and had entered the war very late (only a few weeks before VE day in the case of Argentina and Chile) and the US and Britain were effectively running the show.

Within this pairing, it was very much the Americans who called the shots, despite the British delegation being headed by no less a personage than John Maynard Keynes, widely recognised as the world's leading economist. The Americans were officially led by Secretary of State Cordell Hunt, who would go on to win the Nobel Peace Prize as one of the founders of the United Nations, but in fact Hunt was gravely ill at this time, which meant that events were left in the hands of America's two most powerful civil servants: Harry White and Lauchlin Currie.

Incidentally, both White and Currie were later accused of being Soviet agents, allegations which, though unproved at the time, were probably true, as both were apparently named in compromising material found in Russian archives after the collapse of the Soviet Union. White died dramatically of a heart attack a few days after being quizzed by the same House Committee that unmasked the spy Alger Hiss. Currie survived the experience, but later had his US passport taken away and ended up living in Colombia. Incidentally, lest it be thought that this was exclusively an American problem, Anthony Blunt, Guy Burgess and Donald Maclean were all active at this time within the British Secret Service, and its Middle East department was being run by a terribly nice chap called Kim Philby, who was being tipped as a possible future Head of the Service.

White and Keynes had very different agendas. Before the war, the British Empire had formed a huge, protectionist trade block and the pound had been effectively the world's trading currency of choice. Britain obviously wanted to preserve this, and Churchill had watered down some of the provisions of the Atlantic Charter in 1941 to try to preserve some wriggle room, but the reality was that Britain was finished as a great power, and her economy was just as much in need of American help as anyone else's. White wanted not only an end to the importance of the "Sterling Area" and the balanced playing field which this would produce in emerging Asian markets for US manufacturers, but more besides: the opening of European markets, without access to which the great economic growth which had occurred in the US as a result of rapid wartime expansion could not be sustained.

Effectively White won, as it was always inevitable that he would. Keynes had wanted all national currencies in the world to be pegged against a notional measure made up of a basket of the world's leading currencies, which would in turn be pegged to the price of gold. What emerged was a system of fixed exchange rates, with each currency being pegged to the dollar, which was then pegged to the price of gold at $35 an ounce. White and Currie had, at a stroke, made the US dollar the world's reserve currency. Henceforth every central bank in the world would have to maintain stocks of dollars with which to enter the market where necessary and support their own currency in order to keep it at the agreed exchange rate. There was more besides, but it is this aspect of Bretton Woods which is relevant to any consideration of active currency as an alternative asset.

Obviously were we still living in a world of fixed exchange rates then discussion of buying currency as an investment would be academic, so it may be worth considering briefly how Bretton Woods fell apart. Ironically, it was Britain which was to prove the catalyst.

We saw above that there was more to Bretton Woods than the establishment of fixed exchange rates. It also worked to move dollars from America to Europe by deliberately running a US trade deficit. American companies made large profits trading in the newly-opened markets in Asia and South America. Some of these dollars were then passed to Europe in the form of Marshall Aid, being used to rebuild European industry which could in turn sell its products in the US, thus moving more dollars to Europe.

It was not until the 1960s that things started to go badly wrong. The cost of the Vietnam War badly unbalanced American public finances. The dollar began to be seen as over-valued against the mark and the yen, two of its main trading rivals, making US companies less competitive in export markets. Speculators began sporadically to attack various currencies, most notably the pound. Large international banking groups grew in size and influence, moving huge amounts of currency around the world every day. Worst of all, however, was the gold problem.

Gold was officially pegged at $35 an ounce, but there was still a private, non-government market for gold, in which people could trade at whatever price they liked. The US tried to limit the size of this market; US citizens, for example, were banned from owning gold for many years, and later the US government would refuse to exchange dollars for gold to governments who dealt in the private market. In the end, they decided to try and manipulate it instead, setting up the London Gold Pool in 1961, the idea being that governments (chiefly the US) would sell gold into the market to meet private demand and thus keep the price at $35, buying it back when the situation reversed and there was more supply than demand. In reality, this latter situation almost never happened (during the Cuban Missile Crisis, for instance, the price of gold hit $40 in the private market), and all that transpired was a long, slow, steady draining away of US gold reserves. Britain could afford this even less.

In 1967 the Wilson government, faced with a run on the pound and the prospect of Britain's remaining gold and foreign currency reserves disappearing in a matter of days, devalued the pound from $2.80 to $2.40. It later emerged that an alternative plan proposed by the Bank of England, involving radical spending cuts, had been rejected; much later, actually, as Wilson buried the relevant documents under the Thirty Year rule. Perhaps this helps to explain the resignation of the future Prime Minister Jim Callaghan, then the British finance minister "on a point of honour".

This effectively marked the end of the Bretton Woods regime which had given the global finance system relative stability for over 20 years. After another run on gold, the London Gold Pool surrendered to market forces and was dissolved in 1968. A fully private gold market and floating exchange rates subsequently became the norm, creating the investment environment within which we operate today.

HOW CAN AN INVESTOR MAKE MONEY BY INVESTING IN CURRENCY?

There is a simple answer to this question and a much more complex one. Let us start with the simple one.

Because the exchange rates of one currency against another now fluctuate from one second to another, an obvious way to make money is to exchange one currency for another, and then subsequently re-sell the one you bought at a more advantageous rate. This can be done either in the spot market or by synthetic exposure, most notably the purchase of put and call options. Since we have already examined these sorts of instrument in reference to other asset types, the reader will already understand how they work.

Another way in which money can be made is by looking at a number of variables which all impact on the same investment situation, at least some of which are currency related. This sounds terribly complicated, but can be easily explained by way of an example.

Suppose that a German company, whose equity is denominated in euros, issues a bond denominated in US dollars. It would be possible now for someone such as a hedge fund to build a mathematical model into which could be plugged many inputs. One of these obviously would be the euro/dollar exchange rate, but it would also be necessary to consider the prospects for both interest rates and inflation in both countries, together with assumptions about stock market beta, the alpha of the individual share, the fundamentals of the company's trading and the market within which it operates. So currency rates might make up just one part of an investment opportunity; an important part, certainly, but still only a part. We will see an example of this when we consider the carry trade.

The more complex answer is the response to a slightly more complex question. How can an investor make money by investing currency – surely it's a zero sum game, isn't it?

Are the Currency Markets a Zero Sum Game?

A zero sum game is one in which any gain made by one player can be achieved only by another player suffering an equal loss. Sharpe uses the assumption that equity trading is a zero sum game in his famous demonstration of the theoretical inferiority of active equity investment, compared to the passive strategy of simply buying the market.[1] In a zero sum environment, says Sharpe, if you put all the investment managers in a room together so that they can only trade with each other, at the end of the day half of them will have made a loss and half of them a gain. If you separate out those that have made a gain and ask them to come back again tomorrow, and so on and so, then, says Sharpe, you do not have to wait very long for the odds against consistent outperformance to become overwhelming.

The "zero sum" argument is an objection which is constantly levelled at the idea of using currency as an investment class. If the currency markets really are a zero sum game, then surely, as Sharpe argues, no

---

[1]Given the prevalence in modern equity investing of leverage, short selling and derivative exposure, does this assumption necessarily still hold ...?

manager can ever consistently deliver an alpha return; the odds are heavily stacked against them. However, currency markets are *not* a zero sum game.

For just as with gold, there are a considerable number of market participants every day who are not there because they want to be but because they have to be. Put another way, they are not trading currency as an investment, with a view to making a gain, but as a part or extension of their normal business activities, either because they need foreign currency, or because they need to hedge a foreign currency liability.

A good example of the first would be the companies which own the foreign exchange kiosks which one sees on the streets of every major city. They are actually using currency as their stock in trade, and will need to be constantly in the markets selling where they are long and buying where they are short. An example of the second might be a non-US airline which knows that it needs to buy fuel in dollars on particular dates and decides to try to hedge against undue uncertainty in the prevailing exchange rate on those specified dates by buying some options, thus effectively locking in the actual sums which they will have to pay in their own currency.

As with gold, it has been estimated that at least half the total trades in any one day may actually take the form of this "business" activity, and this makes a big difference for those active currency dealers who are operating alongside them. The business traders want to get the best deal they can, but this is not as vital to them as it is to a professional investor. In particular, most of them are committed to buying or selling a particular amount of a particular currency on that day, and waiting for another day may not be an option, either because of immediate business demand or simply as a matter of management policy. So they will take the best deal they can get, regardless of whether that deal might actually represent the best possible outcome that could be obtained with more flexibility, and perhaps with a better understanding of the overall picture.

This flows through into the respective mental approaches and methodologies. Business users go into the market to buy and sell, whether currency or options, at the best price reasonably available. These market trades are designed to match the specific day to day and known future currency requirements of their organisation. It is as simple and straightforward as that. Active currency investors, on the other hand will be consciously pursuing one or more of three broad strategies, and often particular strands within them.

This distinction also holds true in the way in which the world's institutional investors approach currency.

INSTITUTIONAL APPROACHES

Risk Management

Traditionally, investors saw currency in slightly the same way as those "business" market participants we have just been examining. The word "slightly" is important though, for in the case of investors they will usually be concerned not with actual liabilities but with potential exposure. For them, currency is seen not so much in terms of currency hedging, but as part of an overall risk management programme.

So it is true that, like those business users, they are not approaching currency as a source of investment gain in its own right, but there the similarity ends. They are not interested (usually, though it does sometimes happen) so much in matching a particular outflow or inflow as in looking at their overall exposure to various risks, of which foreign currency risk is obviously one, and trying to balance this, to keep it within acceptable levels. A simple example might help to explain this.

Suppose that you decided to make an allocation to commodities, and to access these through ETFs. As we saw in an earlier chapter, the instant issue which arises here is that commodity ETFs are routinely denominated in dollars, and even where they may not be then the underlying commodities are, which means that the mere fact that the fund itself is not denominated in dollars provides no protection at all; fund pricing each day will be a simple matter of dollar conversion to the fund currency.

So, what do you do about the fact that you now have a great deal of dollar exposure in your portfolio that you did not have before?

You might begin by asking how important it is. If you have made a very small allocation, say 4% or 5%, then you might take a view that this is just something that you can live with. If, however, you have read the right books,[2] you will be making sensible, significant allocations in a range of about 15% to 25%, so this comfort will not be available to you.

You are now in a situation where dollar risk may significantly impact your overall returns. If commodities go up 10% over the year, but the dollar goes down 10% against your own currency you have just seen what would have been a very acceptable result turned into a disappointing flat position. In some cases, dollar risk might even turn a nominal profit when expressed in dollars into a real life loss when expressed in local currency.

There is only one way in which you can try to manage this risk, and that is by running a short position on the dollar. You might decide, for

---

[2] *Multi-Asset Class Investment Strategy* and *Pioneering Portfolio Management* already referenced.

example, to make your commodities allocation and review it after one year, and at the same time as buying your commodity ETFs you buy a put option on the dollar, or perhaps a dollar swap.

When the review date comes around, a number of outcomes are possible.

If the dollar exchange rate is the same as it was originally then you will make whatever return you would have made anyway on commodities, but you will have lost the cost of your option. This is a classic hedging situation; you are paying a price (the cost of the option) for something you want (certainty of outcome).

If commodities have gone up but so has the dollar then you have lost the cost of your option, but this will hopefully have been off-set by the gain in local currency value which the stronger dollar has delivered. Result: hopefully local currency neutral.

If commodities have gone up but the dollar has gone down, then the profit you make on your option should hopefully off-set the loss in local currency value caused by the weaker dollar. Result: hopefully local currency neutral.

If commodities have gone down, and the dollar has also gone down, then you will make a profit on your option which will off-set some of the local currency loss caused by the weaker dollar. Result: hopefully local currency neutral.

If commodities have gone down but the dollar has gone up, you will lose the cost of your option but this will hopefully be off-set by the local currency gain created by the stronger dollar. Result: hopefully local currency neutral.

So, it can be demonstrated that by shorting the dollar you can remove some or all of the uncertainty of outcome which dollar risk represents. Be aware, though, that there is no free lunch here. As stated earlier, you are buying something (certainty) for which there is a price (the cost of the short position). The cost of that position will always be present in the calculation, always operating as a drag on your returns. It will hopefully be obvious that nothing can match the situation of having no dollar hedge and experiencing both positive commodity returns and a stronger dollar, or even positive commodity returns and an unchanged dollar exchange rate.

This, then, is the way in which investors have traditionally approached their dealings with currency, and any time you hear someone talking of "a currency overlay" this is often to what they are referring, though this can be somewhat misleading and in some cases investors themselves are confused by the term. For an overlay can go well beyond hedging a position, often involving some discretion for the manager to speculate, and there are even such things as "pure alpha" overlays. In the interests of clarity and simplicity, we will not consider overlays further but concentrate on hedging, pure and simple. For just as each investor has a portfolio of assets, so also they have a portfolio of risks. Here, they are essentially looking to smooth away some of the peaks and troughs in their overall risk profile.

For the sake of completeness it should be noted that there are some who regard an investment portfolio with no currency hedge as one which contains unrewarded risk, a concept with which we dealt in an early chapter of this book. Without going into excessive detail, it seems questionable whether this is true. "Unrewarded risk" describes an inefficient portfolio where an unnecessary amount of risk (historic volatility) is being taken in order to target a given level of returns; in other words it would be possible to construct an alternative portfolio which should deliver the same rate of return for a lower level of risk. Is this the case here?

It is true that an unhedged portfolio must be inherently "riskier" than a hedged one, in the sense of there being greater uncertainty of outcome. However, the potential for a higher return is also present. If, continuing the above example, commodities went up *and* the dollar went up, then an unhedged portfolio would obviously deliver a higher return than a hedged one, since the hedged portfolio would have been diminished by the cost of the short position on the dollar, which is now worthless. It is as if you have paid a premium on an insurance policy without having needed to claim on it.

Most of the proponents of this point of view (who just happen to be currency overlay managers) usually give the game away sooner or later by saying something like: "of course, over a period of about twenty years or so the currency probably all comes out in the wash, but you will suffer much higher volatility in the meantime". The idea that risk and volatility are the same thing is never far away.

In a sense, this discussion is academic. Nobody would deny that an unhedged portfolio offers greater uncertainty of outcome than a hedged one. On the contrary, the whole point of hedging a portfolio is to reduce that uncertainty. The decisions for the investor to make are just how fearfully they view that uncertainty (bearing in mind that it could have a good outcome as well as a bad one) and, if appropriate, whether they are prepared to pay whatever the price may be of reducing it to less fearful proportions.

Active Currency

To move from using currency overlays to viewing currency as an investment class in its own right is a major step, and one which many investors around the world have so far felt unable to take.

Active currency managers seek to generate real returns from currency trading as an asset type in its own right, and regardless of a client's own currency risks (though in some managed account situations, clients can prohibit particular types of exposure where these may "double up" a risk already present in their own portfolio). It is therefore every bit as legitimate an investment activity as, say, quoted equities or hedge funds.

Mention of hedge funds raises an immediate issue. Currency exposure is part of the methodology of many hedge funds, particularly of the global macro variety, and thus many choose to classify active currency not as an asset type in its own right but as one tilt within the hedge fund world, or even perhaps as part of the investment approach of several different hedge fund tilts, none of which are actually called "active currency".

Again, we risk getting bogged down in semantics. At the end of the day, it does not really matter what an asset or asset type is called, but only how it is likely to perform within your portfolio in terms of return, volatility, correlation, etc. There is, however, no doubt that being labelled as "hedge funds" has delayed the adoption of active currency managers by institutional investors, fearful perhaps of headline risk.

It is true, also, that the legal structure of many active currency funds is more or less identical to that of hedge funds operating in other or related areas, which means that the co-investor risk of other investors suddenly demanding their capital back at the most inopportune time is ever-present, and one which the intelligent investor will wish to consider.

Liquidity

However, on the other side of the coin, investors crave liquidity, and what could be more liquid than money itself? In fact, this is a slightly specious argument, since many active currency managers will be invested not in currency itself but in swaps and options, but at least the latter of these are themselves liquid instruments, quoted and traded.

So certainly compared to some of the other alternative assets, active currency is liquid. Those who remember the events of September 2008 will probably even conclude that it is more liquid than certain fixed income instruments which were ostensibly held because they were "liquid".

Volatility

Another "pro" in favour of investing in active currency is that the Deutsche Bank (DB) active currency index (of which more below) exhibits very low volatility since 1989. Remember that volatility is something of which investors live in mortal fear, since they view it as "risk" and want to eliminate it from their portfolios as much as possible. Active currency would seem to be a prime candidate here, delivering less volatility of return than any major asset category except market neutral hedge funds. When you pause to consider that the reason why investors buy market neutral hedge funds is precisely *because* they promise low volatility, then this is a very strong argument indeed for including a meaningful allocation to active currency.

Correlation

Should you be pursuing a rather more grown-up approach to investing then you will be concerned with correlation, particularly correlation with quoted equities, which are likely to make up the bulk of any legacy portfolio. Here, again, active currency scores highly. It shows no correlation at all with the FTSE 100 index, for example; in fact, slightly negative correlation. This holds true across most asset types, save only for global macro hedge funds and UK real estate, with which in both cases it has about 60% correlation of annual return.

The former is easy to understand. Many active currency managers *are* global macro hedge funds and may therefore end up in both indices. Even if not, then one of the three main active currency strategies, which we will examine below, forms a major part of what many global macro managers do.

The second is less easy to understand, and seems to be one of those things that just *is*, without necessarily any smart financial explanation. The only thing which these two asset types have in common is low correlation with inflation, but that is true of many others as well.

ACTIVE CURRENCY STRATEGIES

There are three distinct strategies which are pursued by active currency managers, one of which may be further sub-divided into two different ways of approaching the same "tilt". In practice, though one particular methodology can predominate at any one time, many managers will use a mix of the three.

They are: the carry trade, momentum (also called trend), and value (the latter being usually broken down further into fundamental and quantitative).

The Carry Trade

The carry trade is rather unusual as an investment approach in that it works best if everything stays absolutely the same. With just about every other type of investment, the investor is hoping that something will change, whether it be a price, an exchange rate, an interest rate or whatever.

The carry trade works on a very simple principle. First you find a currency which has very low borrowing costs. Then you borrow in that currency. Then you lend the money on in a different currency, which carries a higher rate of interest. A traditional pairing here used to be the Japanese yen, where the government was keeping interest rates very low to stimulate growth, and the New Zealand dollar (the "kiwi"), where the central bank was keeping rates high to discourage inflation. However, some bolder souls borrowed the yen and then lent it into emerging, high growth economies.

It may surprise you to hear that in today's sophisticated financial world, with analysts in hedge funds and investment banks constantly modelling every possible combination of economic and investment factors, something so straightforward could be successful, but indeed there have been lengthy periods when the strategy performed very well. However, when the "kiwi" peaked against the US dollar in the summer of 2007 and then started to decline, the yen/kiwi carry trade, along with various other things, started to unravel.

The way in which the carry trade is usually executed is that you open a short position in the low interest rate currency and go long the high interest rate currency. This has the practical effect described above. You have to pay interest on the short position, but earn interest from your long position. Everything goes swimmingly unless and until something changes, most notably of course the relevant exchange rate.

During 2009 the focus of the carry trade switched to shorting the US dollar against either the Australian dollar (the "aussie") or the kiwi. Even the Canadian dollar (which for reasons never explained to the author is known as the "loonie") came into play. However, in 2010 the yen was once again being tipped as a currency to short.

In truth, though it is difficult to find any publicly available numbers, it is probable that much less money was deployed in the carry trade from 2008 onwards, as a result of investor nervousness and manager uncertainty. Things were not helped by various carry trade managers having some combination of open counterparty trades, custody positions and even cash balances with Lehman Brothers in London. When Lehman collapsed, it created a situation which may make various lawyers a great deal of money, but which has already caused a great deal of trouble to a number of investors.

It seems likely, though, that money may be starting to creep back into this area. Given, however, that it thrives on stability and there is general agreement that we are likely to see more, rather than less, uncertainty in future, then the carry trade should be treated with caution.

There are grounds for slight concern in the area of correlation, too. Mergenthaler (2009)[3] analysed the various constituents of the DB index and found that in the case of the carry trade (1) correlation with quoted equities appeared to have increased steadily in recent years, (2) correlation increased at times of high volatility in equity markets and (3) in particular, correlation increased when equity markets fell sharply. Given what we have considered earlier about the phenomenon of man-made correlation during flights to liquidity, we should be careful to avoid reading too much into these headline findings, but they do bear out the fact that, at the very least, the ongoing performance of carry trade managers should be closely monitored.

Hopefully it goes without saying that investors may find this difficult if they invest in active currency without first finding out how it works. The writer has come across situations where investors had given a mandate to a manager not only without understanding how the carry trade worked, not only without having asked the manager exactly which strategy they would be pursuing, but also without knowing what the carry trade was, or even that it existed at all.

Momentum/Trend Investing

Momentum investing, otherwise known as trend investing, can be very simply stated. You look at what other people are buying, and copy them. In other words, where there is demand for a currency and its price is moving upwards, then momentum investors assume that this will continue to be the case for some time, just as when there is weak demand for a currency so that its price is moving downwards.

For anyone who believes that finance is a hugely complex area of study, and believes in analysing the fundamentals of any investment situation, it is a depressing truth that momentum investing has for long periods been very successful. It could perhaps be compared to having had a permanent long position in quoted equities from 2003 to 2006.

Mergenthaler (2009)[4] showed that in down markets, momentum investing seems to maintain low correlation with quoted equities,

---

[3] J.P. Morgan Asset Management.
[4] Already cited.

whereas the carry trade correlation seems to increase. This suggests that as quoted markets head down, active currency investors would do well to reduce their exposure to the carry trade and increase the other two approaches accordingly. This idea should be treated with caution, however, as it may well be that there are external economic or monetary influences at work which influence the figures, and it would be interesting to see the result of further research here. For example, while momentum and the carry trade seem usually to be negatively correlated against each other, this reverted to almost perfect *positive* correlation during the period covered by the Asian Crisis.

Value Investing

As its name suggests, value investing involves finding currencies which are undervalued when measured by certain metrics and models or, equally, identifying those which appear to be overvalued. One then goes long the former and short the latter.

This is partly a matter of digging into economic factors, such as GDP growth, interest rates, inflation, etc. However, valuation is not just absolute but relative as well. So, if one can identify a currency which seems to be fairly valued against one currency but perhaps undervalued relative to another, this would also present an investment opportunity to a value manager.

Incidentally, it is here that we start to find a blurring of the boundaries between asset types, since these techniques are also used by global macro and various other hedge fund managers. It is difficult to propose firm principles in such a grey area, but usually active currency managers will only invest in currency related instruments, whereas hedge fund managers will cast their net more widely. For example, if both a hedge fund manager and an active currency manager believed that a country's interest rates were too low, and would need to be raised in the near future, then the active currency manager would probably go long the country's currency, whereas the hedge fund manager might just as well go short the country's fixed interest government bonds.

Value investing is in turn technically divided in two, though most managers will effectively practise a mix of both. Quantitative approaches look purely at financial and economic data as processed by very complex "black box" type mathematical models. Just as with "quant" equity investing, a quant manager would simply go long or short whatever the black box indicated. It is worth noting, however, that there is an inbuilt unconscious assumption lurking within every black box, namely that normal distribution will always apply, and that sooner or later everything will revert to the mean. Quant equity managers, for example, will be saying throughout any bull market that the market is over-valued, in the sense of being above its moving average, and will surely fall back. Of course, sooner or later they will be proved right, but they may by that time have lost all their money by shorting the market.

This is one of the problems which beset the hedge fund group Long Term Capital Management. The oil company Shell is effectively two twin corporations, Shell and Royal Dutch Shell. In mid-1997, the RDS shares were trading at a premium of anything up to 10% over their Shell counterparts. Reasoning that this was illogical, and that the two would each revert to the mean, LTCM went short RDS and long Shell. Instead of doing so, however, the premium continued to widen until at one stage it was over 20%. By this time, LTCM was hurting so badly in other areas that it had to liquidate its position, presumably at a huge loss. This bore out one of the many wise utterances of John Maynard Keynes: "markets can stay irrational for longer than you can stay solvent."

Business school students tend to spot the flaws in the quantitative approach. The assumption that normal distribution will always apply is not necessarily a sound one; certainly there are some areas, such as venture capital returns at the company level, where it does not apply at all. Even if it does, there may be outside economic or political factors operating which will skew the results, or delay mean reversion, or even force returns into a totally new pattern, to which normal distribution may still apply in the future, but operating around a different mean. Finally, of course, investment decisions can be largely emotional and pay no attention whatever to reason or financial logic, at least for considerable periods. Again, Keynes recognised this, saying that at times there were "animal spirits" loose in the markets, and that at these times logic would not necessarily apply.

So, for all these reasons, most active currency managers tend to filter the output of any quantitative model with subjective instinct and common sense. They recognise that there are some things which cannot be modelled; for example, what may now arguably be the world's leading currency, the Chinese yuan, is not freely tradable and is being held at what everyone agrees is a very significant under-value. Yet here one is in an area of political decision making, not the "normal" behaviour of financial markets. Many funds and investors are trying to find ways of shorting the renmimbi (yuan) but they will presumably be suffering losses through negative roll yield every time a period expires and they have to renew their position. Everybody "knows", so they say, that the Chinese government will revalue their currency (some analysts suggest that it may be worth at least double its official value against the dollar), but will it happen and, if so, when? The financial logic is impeccable, but something other than financial logic is driving events.

For those who believe in a more intellectual approach to investing than that afforded by momentum managers, it will be refreshing to hear that according to the DB basic index (see below),[5] value investing has been consistently the most successful of the three approaches over a long period (since 1997, at any rate), having both a higher average return and a higher Sharpe Ratio.

There is also research which suggests that applying value investing techniques consistently over a long period tends to be successful, whereas value techniques do not seem to work very well in respect of currencies in the short term.[6]

ACTIVE CURRENCY BETA

When we turn to consider the question of active currency beta we encounter a very unusual situation which is not shared by any other asset type. There is indeed a measure of beta return which is both identifiable and investable. Whether it is truly representative of actual industry performance is very much open to question. However, in this case does it really matter?

All of which sounds very confusing, and indeed *is* so for anyone coming to this asset type for the first time, so let us examine things step by step.

What is the Beta Measure We are Discussing?

The most commonly used index of active currency performance is the DB currency returns (DBCR) index; a further version of this has also been developed, DBCR+, which has a few essential differences, notably as regards the carry trade. Both versions give a composite figure for active currency as a whole, but also three separate figures for the three individual strategies.

So far so good. This is where things start to get a little bit complicated.

Every other industry benchmark we have considered has operated by means of gathering the actual performance figures of individual managers and then collating this data. In other words, the benchmark has been some sort of record, whatever the precise methodology involved, of actual performance. This is not the case with DBCR.

---

[5] According to the *basic* index. The DBCR+ index shows the carry trade as having been dramatically the most successful. However, this includes non-G10 currencies and is also largely based on back-testing, having been in operation only since February 2007.

[6] Bilal Hafeez, *Currency: Value Investing*, Deutsche Bank Research, 2007.

What is the Methodology?

DBCR operates not by gathering the performance of individual managers, but by replicating what it might be possible for them to achieve simply by following the most basic principles of their chosen strategy. Incidentally, before the crisis two or three different types of replication were also being touted in some quarters as a way of capturing artificially the performance of various hedge fund strategies, although sceptics were expressing concerns as to how such approaches might fare in abnormal and/or turbulent market conditions. Most unusually in the case of financial theory, the sceptics were very soon given an opportunity to find out, and suffice it to say that the idea of replication seems to have been quietly dropped.

Without wishing to muddy the waters, however, the way in which DBCR works is different. Whereas hedge fund replication techniques sought either to copy the sort of trades which managers were making, sometimes in arrears (hence the concerns about market turbulence), or to use ways of investing in broad economic indicators to ape the way that certain hedge fund tilts operated, DBCR captures precisely what a manager might (or, it can be argued, should) be doing.

Thus, the carry trade is replicated by ranking currencies by their 3 month LIBOR,[7] then shorting the three lowest yielding currencies and going long the three highest yielding ones. The basic DBCR restricts the available choice to the G10 currencies (which includes the kiwi), whereas the DBCR+ opens the carry trade up to emerging market currencies as well. Appropriately, since the latter would seem to involve much more risk, the extended approach yields a much higher notional return.

The word "notional" is an important one in two respects. First, as we have just seen, neither DBCR measure is recording real performance that has actually occurred, but rather theoretical performance that *would* have occurred *if* a manager had been slavishly following the basic principles of their chosen strategy. Second, the DBCR was only launched in 2006, and the DBCR+ in 2007, so all figures before those dates have been created by back-testing.

Back-testing is rightly regarded by institutional investors with some scepticism. When hedge fund managers come calling they always seem to have back-tested figures which demonstrate that their chosen strategy is a sure-fire winner. However, there are two main objections to back-testing, and neither of them really applies in this case. The first is that you can make your strategy fit the figures; if the figures do not come

---

[7]London Inter-Bank Offer Rate.

up with the result you want, then you can alter your tilt until you get a more favourable outcome. Second, you can make the figures match your strategy by means of subjective assumptions which exclude unfavourable outcomes. It is difficult to see that anything like that could be happening here.

The only limiting assumption which has been made is to restrict the range of currencies to the G10, and even so that is lifted (at least for the carry trade, where it is likely to have the most impact) in the DBCR+. As for changing the strategies, that hardly seems possible, for they are what they are, particularly as the most fundamental form of each is being adopted for modelling purposes.

Momentum investing is replicated within the DBCR by going long the three currencies with the highest spot prices (demand will tend to drive up the spot price) and short the three with the lowest spot prices.

Value investing is replicated by ranking the relative value of each currency by its OECD purchasing power rating. Then, fairly obviously, you go long the three most lowly rated and short the three most highly rated.

Just to make the point again, since it is such an important one, this is the only asset type which falls to be considered in this book where the beta is a replication model, rather than some sort of measure of what is actually happening to real life managers. There are measures where there is a real question of just how much of the industry they are capturing (hedge funds and venture capital would be good examples), others where they are so young that they cannot yet be meaningful (such as the non-UK property indices), and some asset types where a beta measure just does not exist yet (such as private infrastructure). However, DBCR does not even pretend to be a measure of industry performance. It sets out what an active currency manager *could* make, were they a robot rather than a human being and simply applied unthinkingly and automatically the basic principles of their chosen strategy.

This suggests, therefore, that the DBCR should be setting the base return, the floor for manager performance: which makes it rather disturbing to discover that most active currency managers actually *underperform* the index!

Of course part of this may be due to the question of fees, which the DBCR actually ignores, though they become relevant at the fund level (see below). Much more likely, though, because this is a clear demonstration of the principle of Occam's Razor,[8] there is no virtue in complexity for its own sake, and if a more simple approach can be shown to be at least as effective, it is the simple approach which should be preferred. As with so much in the world of investment, there is often little empirical evidence to show that multiple layers of complexity are not just an unnecessary complication, designed to baffle and impress the client, thus justifying higher fees for the manager.

Is the DBCR Investable?

There is an ETF which tracks the index as a whole and three others which track the individual strategies. Thus, an investor can either access the overall world of currency returns, or mix and match their own preferred combination of approaches. There are, however, a couple of points to bear in mind.

First, the ETF as originally launched was denominated only in euros. This presumably raises issues for non-euro investors, such as British or North American pension funds. For to make a significant allocation (ideally at least 15%) would mean importing into the portfolio a large amount of euro currency risk, and so you would have to take the costs of maintaining a permanent short position on the euro into account when calculating the likely net returns. Would you then wish to look beyond the index at what it was actually doing at any one time? For example, it may already be shorting the euro under one or more of the three strategies, so that you might actually be unknowingly doubling up a risk that was already being taken by the fund.

This is surely an unnecessary level of complexity, and might well prove off-putting to non-euro investors. However, it is believed that by the time this book is published Deutsche Bank will have introduced sterling, dollar and Swiss franc share classes as well.

Second, we must come back once again to the question of counterparty risk. Just as with the commodities ETFs we examined in an earlier chapter, the fund itself is exchange traded, but the underlying derivative instrument is not. For two different reasons, investors might feel able to take a more relaxed view in this case than in some others: (1) if one had to choose any non-government entity in the world against whom to have counterparty risk then surely Deutsche Bank would be high on most people's lists; and (2) the contract is rolled and settled every quarter, which means that even at worst one would never have more than three months' returns at risk (though the same practical issues as to what would happen to the assets and management of the fund in the event of default would still apply).

As we have noted before, though, there seems to be a general trend away from private and OTC instruments in favour of those which are

---

[8]So-called because first attributed to the fourteenth century churchman William of Ockham.

exchange settled or subject to a recognised clearing house arrangement,[9] and indeed the Obama administration is talking of making this compulsory as part of their proposed reform of financial markets, at least in the US. It is hoped that such an arrangement will therefore become available within a reasonable time, but unless and until it does, please remember that there *is* counterparty risk, and it is for each individual investor to decide for themselves just how significant this may be.

FINAL CONSIDERATIONS FOR ACTIVE CURRENCY

Active currency, at least as represented by the Deutsche Bank replication product, has been a strong and consistent provider of excess returns, with relatively low levels of volatility, and little correlation with quoted equities, or indeed most other asset types. In principle, therefore, it would seem an ideal candidate for a significant allocation.

In practice, however, the counterparty risk on the underlying contract is a significant issue, and should be fully discussed internally before making any decision to invest.

SUMMARY

The possibility of making money from active currency trading was opened up by the collapse of the Bretton Woods system of fixed exchange rates.

Some have argued that active currency is a zero sum game, but this is false, as at least half of market participants are business users, for whom making money by trading is not their prime objective.

There are three main active currency strategies.

The carry trade looks to borrow a currency which has low interest rates and lend it out in a currency which has high interest rates.

Momentum or trend investing looks at which currencies are being bought and sold by other people, and does the same.

Value investing tries to identify currencies which are over- or under-valued in terms of economic and financial fundamentals and sell or buy them accordingly. Most managers will employ a mix of quantitative ("quant") and more subjective techniques.

---

[9] As is happening with UK property (Real Estate) derivatives.

Currency performance is measured by the DBCR. However, this is not a record of actual manager performance but a replication model, showing what managers could achieve using only the most basic features of their chosen strategy. Interestingly, most managers under-perform the DBCR.

The DBCR can be accessed by means of an ETF. However, it is important to note that there is counterparty risk on the underlying contract.

The DBCR indicates the ability to deliver strong and consistent excess return over a long period. However, it is important to note that much of its output is created by back-testing.

11

Other Alternative
Assets

As we saw very early on in the book, the definition of just what might encompass "alternative assets" is very flexible, and highly personal. While rejecting the narrow, surely artificial approach of Anson (2002),[1] we never actually agreed on precisely where the boundaries should be drawn. A fully subjective approach might allow any asset which has the potential to increase in value, such as those described in this chapter.

For there are, in fact, many things which investors might hold in the expectation of them increasing in value, and any time this is true then surely it is permissible, and even advisable to refer to an "investment". Of those outlined below, only one, forestry, already forms part of the portfolios of many investors (certainly in North America). This asset type was felt to be not yet sufficiently recognised on a global scale to merit its own chapter, but perhaps this may change for future editions of this book.

The others are at different times referred to as "exotics" or "collect-ables". These all seem to share two characteristics: (1) a successful investment approach would logically require a high level of specialist knowledge going beyond mere investment theory and practice and (2) they generally comprise specific, individual assets which may in many cases be capable of identification and cataloguing. By virtue of the fact that they are often something for which the individual investor may already have an attachment which is purely emotional and has nothing to do with finance, these are sometimes also referred to as "passion investments", and the funds which are formed to invest in them as "passion funds".

However, three points are worth making here.

The first point, which we have already encountered several times, is that it almost certainly does not matter what an asset is called. All that should really concern any investor is how it is likely to behave within their portfolio. Two examples will suffice. First, many infrastructure projects, investments which would normally not even appear on many

---

[1] Already cited.

investors' radar screens, share very similar characteristics to government bonds, and yet usually the less likely an investor is to consider infrastructure projects, the more obsessed they are likely to be with government bonds. Second, the Yale Endowment's portfolio contains oil and gas royalties, which most investors would describe as "energy" investments, yet Yale classifies them as "real assets" and places them within the same allocation as their real estate exposure. Does this matter? Perhaps from a philological point of view, but hardly from an investment one. Certainly it does not seem to have done Yale's track record much harm.

The second point goes back to the idea of the episteme, which we examined in an earlier chapter. Asset allocation decisions must be viewed not just against the harsh light of strategic considerations and financial principles, but also against the altogether more nebulous backdrop of the prevalent zeitgeist, the spirit of the time. To do otherwise would be to ignore the unconscious assumptions which would be implicit in any such decision process.

For example, when David Swensen was putting what was to become known as the Yale Model together in the mid-1980s, institutional investors did not invest in hedge funds; these were very small by modern standards, and the exclusive preserve of high net worth individuals, sometime acting through Family Offices, but more usually in those days through private banks. Nor, apart from one or two notable pioneers such as Phil Horsley[2] at the University of Rochester, did they invest in private equity funds. Yet Swensen's proposal to the Board of Trustees at Yale was that they should allocate about two fifths of their total portfolio to these largely unknown asset classes.

It is interesting to imagine the scene. The trustees, all of whom were very eminent in their own fields but surely with little specialist knowledge of investment, being confronted by what must have seemed a wild young man (he was only in his early thirties, albeit he had served several years with Lehman) with wild new ideas – namely that they should invest the endowment's assets according to a totally new philosophy and in some totally new asset classes. We can only speculate about what was said, but it seems clear that, in addition to being a hugely successful investor, Swensen must also be a magnificent and persuasive communicator.

It is a fanciful thought, but might a modern day equivalent perhaps be trying to advise the trustees of a European pension fund to make a 20% allocation to antiques, or classic Ferrari sports cars? A tough sell

---

[2]Who shortly afterwards founded what is now Horsley Bridge Partners.

indeed. Yet perhaps the huge subsequent success of the Yale Model, and the fact that its common sense approach just feels instinctively right, blind us to the fact that initially it might have seemed a much scattier idea. Thus proving, as Swensen says in his book,[3] that successful investors seek out opportunities in less well-followed (and less liquid) markets.

The third point relates specifically to what might be called the post-crisis world. As first a huge corporate credit problem collided with a credit derivatives problem to threaten the very existence of the world's banking system, and then the huge sovereign debt problem, into which the former had been partially transposed, threatened the credibility of various governments as issuers of supposedly "risk-free" bonds, it became apparent that many of the old certainties could no longer be relied upon. At the very least, investors around the world need to reflect deeply on the true meaning of such words as "risk" and "value".

There is a scene in Michael Moorcock's *Copernicus Quartet*[4] which depicts an extended party in London which lasts for several weeks, during which time the pace of socio-economic events is artificially speeded up.[5] During the life of the party, the caterers who supply it first stop accepting cheques because they have lost faith in the banks, and then cash because they have lost faith in the government; finally they will accept only gold. By this time, anyone who can afford to do so has left London and converted whatever they can salvage of their "wealth" into farm land in Scotland, recognising that it is only real assets, such as land, timber and farm produce which have any true value.

This is undoubtedly a nightmare scenario, but one which a growing number of observers are beginning to wonder about. It is certainly one possible outcome of the present situation, though admittedly an extreme one, that 2008 may have marked the beginning of the slow but inexorable collapse of a financial system built upon apparently inexhaustible corporate credit and sovereign debt, paper currency and politician's promises.

Whether or not such apocalyptic events actually come to pass probably does not matter, at least not yet. What *does* matter is that some investors are beginning to question the ability of the present system to provide a safe and suitable environment within which to grow and preserve the value of their assets. Perhaps what we are actually witnessing are the beginnings of a new episteme starting to coalesce out of the turmoil, one in which the automatic holding of government bonds will

---

[3] Already cited.
[4] Phoenix House, London 1993 (collected edition).
[5] The book is at least partly science fiction.

no longer be seen as a "risk free" option, and one whose inhabitants may well look upon the holding of real assets much more eagerly than might have been the case before 2007.

FORESTRY

Returns and Correlation

One of the reasons why one is reluctant currently to afford forestry a chapter of its own is the difficulty encountered in finding any reliable industry data on long term investment returns. For what it's worth, there are figures[6] which state that over almost 20 years from 1990 US forestry showed an average annual return of 12.7%, with very low correlation with the S&P.

We need to be a little careful of these figures. For one thing, they are annualised returns rather than compound returns over time, and the latter are likely to be significantly lower since, given the nature of forestry investments, an early outflow is likely to be followed by a long barren period with no inflows. For another, they cover only the US and are from a commercial source rather than a specialist data provider. They do, however, strongly suggest that forestry is indeed a valid asset class for a long term investor; most important of all is the low correlation, which is after all the main reason for seeking out exposure to alternative assets in the first place.

Another important consideration is that, like private equity, it is difficult to see how any industry beta could exist, and so passive investing is out of the question. Any investor wishing to break into forestry will need either to hire managers for direct investing or to choose funds for indirect exposure. Either way, manager risk is unavoidable, and any attempt at benchmarking performance should be seen in that light.

Forestry is an interesting asset to classify. Is it real estate because it is grown on land and can be (and is) bought and sold as such? Or is it a commodity since it is a natural product and, once harvested, is used as a building material? Probably the truth is that it is neither, but an asset type (perhaps even an asset class) in its own right.

For a start, it exhibits one important difference with agricultural commodities. A coffee crop must be harvested at a particular time; you can vary the date by a few days, or even weeks, one way or another, but there is no escaping the fact that there is an optimum time for harvesting, always during the dry season of the local weather pattern, and

---

[6]From Timberland Investment Resources.

that after this date the crop will gradually start to fall off and spoil. There is also the question of operational economics to consider. In Brazil, for example, the entire coffee crop is harvested at once, even though typically 25% of the beans are unripe and must be picked out and thrown away. There is thus no way of escaping the swings and roundabouts of seasonal supply, demand and pricing.

With forestry, by contrast, one can simply choose not to harvest the crop but to allow it to continue growing for another year, or even several years if there was a sustained slump in timber prices. For trees do not diminish in value, but grow, since each year adds further radius to the trunk. Arguably the same is true of industrial commodities such as metals, but here the periodic operating costs are much higher and so cutting back production significantly (much less entirely for one or more years) would carry very serious financial implications. So, if forestry is to be considered as a commodity, it is the only one which is fully flexible as regards production timing, even over a long period such as several years.

Direct and Indirect Forestry

It is possible to buy patches of forest from professional forestry managers. This is subject to the same potential drawback of investing directly in real estate, in that it is very difficult to build a properly diversified portfolio. This is more of a problem with forestry, though.

Forestry is subject to two mains risks: fire and disease. In order to reduce these through diversification it is vital to be able to hold a range of locations and species (some species are prey to certain diseases and pests while others are not); the situation is complicated still further by the fact that some species are prevalent in particular areas. For example, some Asian forestry sites contain only teak. Thus, global coverage seems to be strongly indicated, so that either a global forestry manager or a number of different local ones would be required.

Further diversification still is required. As well as geography and species, age is important. Some types of commercial timber can take 30 years to come to maturity. So, again, a mix of ages would seem desirable otherwise there could be a long wait for any cash inflows. Most investors deal with this by targeting a range of new plantings and established trees. This might be thought of as a sort of primary and secondary forestry investing, and again the two are not always available together on a single site.

Indirect exposure is possible by way of ETFs, but here we run into the same drawback which has already been described in relation to other asset types. Forestry ETFs do not invest in forestry. Each one is a basket of equities, shares in companies which are in the forestry business. They are not a good substitute for holding forestry itself, since they carry business operating risk and must to a certain extent go up and down with stock market beta.

The remaining options are funds which *do* invest in a range of actual forestry assets. Just as with various other alternative assets, a favoured approach seems to be a closed end private vehicle such as a limited partnership or an OEIC. Given the illiquid nature of the underlying assets, and the greater tax flexibility involved, a limited partnership would seem the favoured option here, making this another member of the class of private assets.

It seems difficult to understand why forestry has been ignored for so long by so many of the world's institutional investors, and safe to predict that this state of affairs will not long continue. There again, it seemed both easy and safe to predict that the world's institutional investors would all make significant allocations to private equity in the mid-1990s, so maybe forestry will after all be preserved from their attentions for a while yet.

A further consideration is the environmental one. The logging industry came in for a bad press during the 1980s for their alleged wholesale destruction of various areas, such as the Amazon rainforest. Closer examination shows that this criticism was not necessarily entirely justified. In Brazil, for example, most deforestation has occurred as a result of land clearance for cattle ranching and large scale agriculture. At the smaller end of the scale there is also the "slash and burn" of subsistence agriculture, doubly tragic because this land tends to become infertile within a few years, prompting yet further forest clearance. The forestry industry claims that its activities can actually reverse the overall trend of deforestation by buying land that would otherwise be cleared; even when trees are cut down, others are planted in their place.

Incidentally, deforestation, though a tragedy, is nothing new. The galley-building programme of the Venetian Republic (and the subsequent attempts of the Ottoman Empire to match them in an early example of a naval building race) resulted in the complete disappearance of southern Europe's hardwood forests during the fifteenth and sixteenth centuries.

GEM STONES

There is an understandable allure to the idea of holding precious stones as an investment, which harks back to the days of pirates haunting the Spanish Main. While it is true that even in Napoleonic times some noble families did indeed carry a large amount of their personal wealth around with them in the shape of gems and jewellery (particularly when fleeing war or revolution), those with images of *Treasure Island* type hoards of glittering diamonds and rubies in mind may be disappointed to learn that many of the gems held for investment purposes around the world are in fact uncut and unpolished, and may closely resemble small, dull pebbles.

There are, in fact, two stages at which gems can grow significantly in value. The first is when they are sold by a primary dealer to a secondary dealer, and the latter then cuts and polishes the stone. This is the first drawback for an investor. They will naturally want to buy from a primary dealer and pocket some or all of the uplift in value. However, to do so they will need to select a good cutter to work for them, and here is an instant source of risk. A good cutter can greatly enhance the finished value of an unremarkable stone; a clumsy one, or even a good one on a bad day, can do exactly the opposite.

The second stage is when the finished stone is turned into jewellery by being set in worked precious metal, such as gold. There are thus two options open to an investor at this stage; either sell the finished stone to a jewellery manufacturer, or joint venture with one and then sell the final product.

As stated at the outset, specialist knowledge is essential here. As anyone who has seen *Place Vendôme* will know, an uncut diamond can resemble nothing so much as a grain of crystallite sand, and to gauge its potential as first a finished stone or stones and then when set as jewellery can take a lifetime's experience. This is what comes into play when gems are "graded".

By common consent, this is a difficult area for investment. The market can at different times be highly illiquid, with a large gap between buyer and seller pricing expectations. There are many clever forgeries in circulation. A good gem-cutter is essential, but will not unreasonably demand a correspondingly high fee for their services. Both supply and demand can be sporadic. Science can be an enemy as well as a friend; a while back someone invented a way of turning white topaz (which was very common) into blue topaz (which was very rare), which was bad news for anyone who had carefully built up a collection of blue topaz.

Of course gems appeal to our emotions. Like the precious metals they have an undeniable intrinsic value. During the last hours of freedom for the Dutch Republic in 1940, a team of British secret agents successfully snatched most of the contents of the Amsterdam diamond market from under the noses of the invading German forces. A few years previously, many desperate Jewish families had tried to turn their wealth into diamonds, since they were easier to carry and conceal than gold as they fled Germany and Austria.

Unless you are yourself a gem dealer or cutter, however, this must surely be one of those areas where the heart says "yes" but the head says "no". The benefits are elusive and uncertain, while the dangers are only too clear, and the latter seem heavily to outweigh the former.

WORKS OF ART

Many institutions around the world have significant art collections, though whether these have been bought expressly as investments is often a moot point. At one stage in the 1980s one major German bank was rumoured to have valued its collection of modern art more highly than it had its investment banking subsidiary, which employed several hundred people.

People do invest in art, however, and the word "people" here is deliberately chosen, since most of them are very high net worth individuals or families. As yet, it is difficult to identify many major institutional investors (though see below) who have taken the plunge, though there is no reason why this should not change.

The potential benefits are obvious. Good art will appreciate in value over time, particularly once the artist has died, so that no further supply will be forthcoming from that source. Scanning historic prices achieved at auction suggests that art will at the very least keep pace with inflation, and probably do significantly better. The British Rail Pension Fund, for instance, made a very small (2.5%) allocation to art in the 1970s (a time of rampant inflation in the UK) with precisely that stated objective.

Particular opportunities exist to buy works by artists who are currently unfashionable and/or underrated; until about 30 years ago, for example, it was possible to buy paintings by the Scottish Colourists very cheaply indeed.

If the potential benefits are obvious, however, so too are the potential drawbacks. Very high prices for individual works by established painters makes putting together a collection a very expensive business, and can drive some purchasers to make riskier, speculative investments in artists who are as yet currently un-established. There is no guarantee that these decisions will turn out to have been sound ones, and, even if they were, the "Scottish Colourist" effect can take decades to work its way through the system. Works by major Impressionists, for example, did not really take off astronomically in price until about the 1960s – getting on for a century after some of them were painted.

Investing in art is a serious business, and in the US there is a concept of "investment grade" art which focuses largely on an artist's background. First there is the educational side of things, which will normally include an MFA (Master of Fine Art) degree. Then there is the artist's professional background, which comprises their exhibition history. Once an artist is having solo exhibitions in major commercial art galleries, they are definitely "established", while having a work somewhere in a museum is the icing on the cake. Anything less than this, such as group exhibitions, or exhibitions in small local galleries, becomes a question of degree, and therefore involves greater risk (though as Peter Drucker is reputed to have said "there are no threats, only opportunities in disguise").

There are in fact a number of art funds in existence already. Signs of growing sophistication include the creation of the first art indices, such as the Mei Moses,[7] the AMR[8] Post-War Art 50 and the AMR Art 100, and at least one index tracker fund. Where there is an index, of course, then synthetic coverage may surely follow, as seems likely increasingly to be the case in real estate. Who will be the first to take the plunge and offer a total return swap on an AMR index, which would in turn make possible the first art ETF ...?

Finally, it should be noted that there are numerous devotees of the "art as a safe haven investment" school, who believe that institutional investors may shortly turn in significant numbers to works of art as providing a safe store of long term value. Could art be the new gold?

MUSICAL INSTRUMENTS

Peter Drucker's words could perhaps be aptly applied to the world of fine violins. Beginning in about the fourteenth century and reaching something of a peak in the seventeenth, Europe suffered what has since become called "the little ice age", in which cold wet summers, and even colder winters caused famine and starvation, not to mention unpredictable military events; during one particularly bitter winter the Baltic Sea froze and the Swedish army marched across it to attack Copenhagen.

Though Europe's little ice age caused appalling suffering throughout the continent (the population of Iceland halved, while that of Greenland vanished almost completely), it was to prove a great benefit to others, allowing three gifted families from Cremona, the Amati, Guarneri and Stradivari, to produce the best stringed instruments, particularly violins, which were a relatively new instrument at the time, that have ever been made. The secret of their success? The little ice age had dramatically slowed the rate at which trees grew, thus resulting in their rings being

---

[7]Developed by the Stern School of Business.
[8]Art Market Research.

packed much more tightly together, which in turn produced a glorious sound.

Since it is not possible to find such trees today, it is impossible to create new violins which match the originals, and there are thus a finite number of these in the world. Prices have risen steadily and on the rare occasions when such instruments come to auction they typically fetch well over a million dollars.

Thus it was that attendees at investment conferences a few years ago were treated to presentations on a violin fund, just one way in which investors can access this interesting market. The market, and thus the size of the opportunity, is relatively small, however, so this is not an area in which a large institutional investor could be active. The only alternative would be effectively to establish a private museum some- where to house a collection of instruments, but treating them like com- mercial stock in trade, to be bought and sold as seemed advantageous, and it is difficult to imagine anyone being prepared to go to these sorts of lengths.

By the way, lest any musicphiles should be disturbed at the thought of all these fine instruments vanishing into dusty bank vaults, relax. They are actually leased to performers who would not otherwise be able to afford to own them, and played regularly on the world's concert platforms.

ANTIQUES

Investing in antiques, too, is probably an activity best restricted to private individuals, amongst whom it has become very popular, as witnessed by the number of prime time television shows dedicated to this subject.

The antiques market is, however, a fickle and potentially treacher- ous one. Auction prices can vary wildly between time and location according to which dealers are present, and what their current stock situation might be. In the case of less well recognised items, percep- tions of value, and therefore price, are unpredictable. Finally, skul- duggery abounds, whether in the shape of replacement drawers for a desk, the top of one table being put on the legs of another, or downright fakes.

It is probably also true to say that for many who deal in this area, the thrill of attending an auction, of trusting their judgement against that of the experts, and perhaps even of gradually building up a small collection, outweigh baser instincts of profit and loss. In much the same way the fun of actually attending a horse racing meeting is for most people greater than the avaricious desire for a big payoff on a winning bet.

That said, there are some generally recognised principles for success (or at least for hoping to avoid failure).

The first is to buy only those items which appear to be in perfect condition. Any time that obvious restoration work has been performed, the value of an object will drop, sometimes dramatically, from what an owner might expect an item in perfect condition to fetch. This is a risk which can and should be avoided, though it will significantly increase the amount of capital which you have to deploy. If necessary, buy low priced items in perfect condition, rather than high priced items in need of work.

The second is to target items which have a provenance, a verifiable history, documented if possible. There are three very good reasons for this. First, it will help you to avoid items which are fake. Second, it will help you to avoid items which have been stolen. Third, items with a provenance can be markedly more valuable, and more easily saleable in a difficult market, than those without one. In much the same way one of two identical houses can command a higher price if it can boast of a famous resident in the past.

The third is to specialise in one particular area, preferably as narrowly defined as possible, and become as expert in that field as you can. There is a wealth of books available, and having read them an avid collector or dealer will then also visit various museums, to get a feel for what items in perfect condition actually look like.

The fourth and last is to start at home. Just what might be hidden amidst the "junk" in your attic or garage? Still more, what might emerge during a house-clearance exercise for some recently deceased elderly relative? While your chances of discovering a long-forgotten Monet painting are remote, the most surprising objects can actually command quite high prices at auction. Old toys would be one good example, particularly if still in their original boxes.

WINE

Anyone who appreciates wine will have thoughts of establishing a cellar as their wealth expands. Perhaps first just a few shelves under the stairs, but eventually (as happened in California during the dot com bubble) whole caverns beneath the house, drilled and dynamited out of the rock, and equipped with temperature control equipment. Not content with this, some collectors also rented dedicated storage space in wine warehouses.

The problem with all this is fairly obvious. Even with determination, enthusiasm and a willing and supportive partner, it is difficult to drink more than about 365 bottles of wine a year, and there are some who would find even this number grossly excessive (interestingly, many who took up the new craze of wine collecting in California had been previously virtually teetotal).

Obviously much is bought to be drunk not instantly but in later years. However, this is less so than in the past, since many red wines are specifically designed now to be drunk at a relatively young age, while, with the exception of certain Chardonnays and dessert wines, most whites are for more or less immediate drinking and will actually start to deteriorate quite quickly if kept for any length of time.

Whatever the case, there comes a point at which you can no longer reasonably expect actually to drink all the stuff, and to compound the problem you are now probably being courted by several different wine merchants, and yielding on a regular basis to their entreaties to buy a case of a certain Amarone which is particularly hard to come by, and will be drinking sensationally in about five years' time. At this time you will have become a genuine collector – but is this necessarily the same thing as investment?

If the above analysis sounds even vaguely familiar to you then you will have drifted into being a collector almost by accident. It is a big step from there to buying cases of wine specifically for profit, in the precise hope of being able to re-sell it (or even sell it back to the dealer from whom you bought it) at a later date.

As with other forms of investment, you could choose to appoint a manager to do all this for you. Most wine dealers will happily buy and store wine for you (on either a discretionary or non-discretionary basis, but usually with an advisory role). Given that wine futures are now also available, then it is tempting to enquire why institutional investors have not put even a very small toe in the water here.

Wine futures are very special animals, however. They relate to a particular harvest of a particular wine in a specified year and what actually happens is that the wine is bought *en primeur*, that is, while it is still in casks and has not yet been bottled. The theory is impeccable; at each stage of its life the value, and thus the price of the wine should increase. The 2000 Chateau Latour future price went from about $220 a bottle in 2001 to about $650 a bottle in 2006. However, it does not always work out like this; the 1997 vintage actually *declined* in price over time.

In other words, wine futures are not really "futures" at all in the financial sense. Instead of making a commitment now to enter into a transaction in the future, you are entering into a transaction now and paying for something which you will only receive some time in the future. Nonetheless, it would be theoretically possible to write either an option or a total return swap around such a transaction, and it will be interesting to see if any investment bank decides to take up this opportunity.

It is difficult to see that exposure to wine could ever be truly synthetic, though. For one is talking about a physical product which would still need to be stored somewhere by someone, even while awaiting possible delivery under a futures contract or option. Gold would perhaps be a good analogy, but the storage costs of wine might be even greater than in the case of the physical storage of gold, in which case all the traditional futures theory about holding costs would come into play.

There is another reason why gold is not a precise parallel. Gold is fungible, that is one ounce of gold is exactly the same as another ounce of gold, just as one barrel of Brent Crude is the same as any other barrel of Brent Crude, and any ounce of gold or barrel of oil could be tendered as good delivery against any contract. Wine, however, is not.

As any wine drinker will know, even different bottles within the same case can taste very different, and wastage is higher than many might imagine. Even ignoring the obvious risk of breakage when dealing with glass bottles, some wine aficionados believe that as many as one bottle in eight might actually end up being presented for drinking in less than perfect condition. If one is dealing in dozens of cases bought *en primeur*, then this might be of less consequence, but there is a very different market which exists for single bottles or cases of very high value vintage wine.

So, it would certainly be possible in theory for institutional investors to invest in wine, though some would presumably be prevented from doing so by religious or regulatory concerns. Whether it is really a market which is suitable for institutional investors, at least at the moment, is however a very different question.

In the absence of satisfactory synthetic exposure, the only way in which this could be done would be by taking delivery of and storing physical assets. As we have already seen with gold, this is not necessarily a difficult thing to arrange, though there is obviously much more counterparty risk with a wine merchant than there might be with a regulated bullion dealer. At the very least, an investor would presumably need to see that their wine was being stored and accounted for separately. It is easy to imagine, however, that if the wine merchant were to go into liquidation then the liquidator may well take a lot of persuading to release the wine, regardless of what it said in the company's records.

In terms of "investment" we would presumably only be talking about the world's very best wines, once the preserve of Burgundy and Bordeaux but now under increasing competition from high class production elsewhere. Even so, it is difficult to imagine the quantity of suitable wine being able to support investment appetite of, perhaps, $100 billion a year or more, particularly since even at present levels of demand many of these wines are already priced well beyond the reach of most drinkers.

All in all, the drawbacks mount. Prices can be dramatically affected by economic or investment bubbles, as happened with Californian wines from about 1997 to about 2001. Wine is subject to breakage and biological frailty. Specialist storage is required and thus holding costs are high. No proper synthetic market yet exists. Incidence of financial failure or market intermediaries, or at least the risk of it, is a significant factor. Sadly, even cases of fraud have been known.

All of which makes it difficult to justify wine as an asset class for an institutional investor, though this is a judgement tinged with personal sadness. However, should a synthetic market spring up which is sufficiently cost-effective, representative and robust (as is trying to emerge, for example, in the case of UK real estate) then this view might be revised.

CLASSIC CARS

The late 1980s were a heady time to be in the financial services industry, particularly in the City of London after Big Bang in October 1986. The Thatcher revolution was in full swing. Women wore shoulder pads, short skirts, black stockings and high heels. Men wore striped shirts, coloured waistcoats and red braces. Everyone drove a black 3-series BMW. Barrow Boys and Sloane Rangers rubbed shoulders (and quite a lot else besides) in City champagne bars after getting a Japanese bond issue away or finalising a big commercial real estate deal.

While it is impossible for anyone who lived through that time to look back upon it with anything other than a strong sense of nostalgia, many of the things that were then thought desirable have come to be seen in the cold, grey light of New Labour day as little more than part of the prevailing zeitgeist of Thatcherism, a time when it was possible to work hard and enjoy oneself at the same time. Among them was a fixation with classic cars.

With sudden new-found wealth came a desire to find things upon which to spend it and, sad to relate, if these things could reflect one's status and pull a few chicks then so much the better. Classic cars were a natural candidate – a craze waiting to happen. Travelling to investor meetings in Menlo Park, the home of US venture capital, at the height of the dot com bubble ten years later, the author was able to give a wry smile, while parking in a neighbourhood car park, at the sight of ten or more brand new red Ferraris lined up side by side in reserved parking lots. This was, however, still America, not Europe, and there was no sign of any of the extra-curricular activities which used to occur in City of London car parks before the days of CCTV.

Since there was a finite supply of classic cars in the world, prices rocketed. To give but one example, the price at auction of a *concours* (perfect) condition E-Type Jaguar rocketed from about £15 000 to about £100 000 within a couple of years. To put this in context, the most exciting British production car at the time was probably the box-like Rover Sterling, while Ford's European division was producing what were known in City wine bars as "Dagenham Dustbins".

Given the sudden ramp in demand, and thus prices, it was perhaps inevitable that various investment vehicles should spring up offering a pooled collection of classic cars which could be stored and maintained against the day a few years hence when they could be sold at a significant profit. Incidentally, this is one area in which the author can validly claim world-leading expertise since, as a young investment banker, he was responsible for writing the Prospectus of one such investment company which floated on the junior market in London in 1989. Sadly, for reasons which will become rapidly apparent, it is not an expertise which can currently be put to any practical use.

The basic idea was in fact sounder than it might at first appear to a modern reader. Investors really were buying brand new Ferraris and Lamborghinis and storing them in vaults with zero miles on the clock swathed in bubble-wrap. For the less well-heeled sports car enthusiast there was at this time a seven year waiting list for a new Morgan (the author was on it, while driving a second-hand yellow one). The word "bubble" proved prophetic, however. The year 1990 saw negative returns on stock markets on both sides of the Atlantic, accompanied, at least in London, by a slump in the property market which had driven much of the rapid growth. In America, Michael Milken went to prison, Drexel Burnham went bust having also pleaded guilty to racketeering charges, and a major slump in both bond and debt markets ensued, threatening to bring down even the great RJR Nabisco buyout of 1988. The party was over, at least for the time being.

As with all bubbles, the prices of classic cars fell just as quickly as they had risen, leaving a lot of investors with some very over-valued sets of wheels. The investment vehicles which had been set up faded away, and have not been seen since.

With the perfect appreciation provided by hindsight, it had perhaps all been very predictable, for this had been a genuine bubble. In the 1970s it had been possible to pick up even pre-war Bentleys for a few thousand pounds. High petrol prices and taxation under the Labour administration which had preceded Thatcher, coupled with a genuine dwindling in the number of enthusiasts, had forced prices artificially low. When the sudden demand came, many old crocks were dragged out of garages and hastily renovated; some of them even got sold in time to make their owners some money.

From 1990, though, a different reality prevailed, one in which employment in the City was precarious, and one's first priorities were those traditional enemies of classic car ownership: mortgage payments and school fees.

There have been periodic attempts to revive the idea of investing in classic cars, but it seems unlikely than any institutional investor will find the idea appealing. A pity, for the basic idea is not without its attractions. Like musical instruments, there are a finite number of the very best cars, and most are individually known and logged. As with antiques, a provenance can add significantly to the value; there has always been, for example, a specialist market in former racing cars which have been driven by particular drivers.

As with musical instruments, however, the finite nature of supply can work against you, since that supply is also relatively small, and so any increase in demand might quickly distort pricing. However, to show what can be possible, a Bugatti Type 57C was sold at auction in America in May 2010 for "at least $30 million", having been bought by its previous owner, a doctor, for $59 000 in 1971. Just to demonstrate the time value of money, you might like to try to guess the 40 year IRR. The answer is given in a footnote below.[9]

On balance, this is an area probably best left to the individual investor, who can at least have the fun of driving their Lotus Elise behind the family 4×4 while the wife and children, safely ensconced in an air-conditioned, computer controlled environment watch resignedly in the rear view mirror for those first few tell-tale signs of white steam (from the front) or black smoke (from the back).

OTHER COLLECTABLES – COINS, MEDALS, STAMPS, MILITARIA, SNUFF BOXES, PERFUME BOTTLES, ETC.

These are all existing passion investments, and in some cases investment funds already exist. One coin fund, for example, floated on the

---

[9] 17%. Were you even close? Be honest. To demonstrate the dangers of only thinking about returns in one particular way, the "annualised" (average annual) return would be about 1200%, since you have made about 500 times your money over 40 years, or about 12 times your money every year.

junior market in London (sound familiar?) in 2006 and went on to buy the only Edward III gold coin known to be in existence outside the British Museum for £400 000.

Perfectly valid arguments can be advanced for all of these areas as asset types, though, as with most of the others which we have examined, an advantage (a finite supply of usually well-identified single items) could quickly become a disadvantage (a sudden and dramatic supply/demand imbalance) if any real weight of capital was directed into the space.

Even with postage stamps, for example, a Stanley Gibbons estimate in 2006 reckoned that the total market was only about $10 billion annually, of which only about $1 billion could truly be categorised as "rare". By way of guidance, that is probably only about half of 1% of the total assets of just one large investor (CALPERS[10]), so any significant institutional involvement would seem impossible without causing a massive price bubble. Just such a bubble in fact occurred in the UK in the 1970s (largely driven by the desire to find a safe haven at a time of high inflation and high taxation).

It is sad to end this chapter, and indeed this book, on a negative note, but it must also be pointed out, in the interests of a fair and balanced account, that there have been instances of fraud in what is essentially a private, unregulated and non-transparent market. In the 1950s a scheme run by an Irishman who claimed to hold a PhD from a mysterious university in Bratislava (at that time part of Czechoslovakia and inaccessible behind the Iron Curtain to Westerners) collapsed when the fund's entire stock was allegedly "stolen". Though charged with fraud, the good Doctor was acquitted and promptly disappeared, never to be seen again (just like, coincidentally, the stamps). More recently, two Spanish stamp investment schemes were closed down in 2006 when police raided their offices, alleging fraud, embezzlement, money-laundering and tax evasion.

YET MORE ...?

Even this list is not exhaustive. In particular there are a number of funds, both actual and proposed, which offer access to the international shipping market, media rights, longevity based instruments and the potential profits of litigation. These are all avenues which would reward serious consideration by institutional investors. If experience has taught us anything of investor behaviour it is surely that the very worst enemy

---

[10]Reuters, 28 February 2010.

of good performance is a closed mind, and closed minds have unfortunately been a constant within the world's investors, with only a few honourable exceptions.

At least some of tomorrow's mainstream assets are today's alternative assets. The ongoing search for uncorrelated returns more or less guarantees that. Logically, tomorrow's alternative assets are today's "exotics", or at least some of them. Investors have a choice. Do they wish to be, as David Swensen was, one of the first to the table while the choicest cuts are still available, or one of the last, fighting over the scraps? Always remember, it matters not what an asset is called, but only how it is likely to behave, and what it can provide for your portfolio.

CONCLUSION

This final chapter has been written deliberately in a way which is hopefully enjoyable and interesting, since it describes asset types which are themselves essentially enjoyable and interesting, particularly as at least one of them will probably already be a "passion" of each reader.

It is generally a sound principle to keep one's pleasures and one's investments apart, however. Even where you may believe that your specialist knowledge is such that it rivals that of a professional expert, it is essential to adopt a sensible approach, not least in the matter of having a properly diversified portfolio.

For most institutions, the very small size (by their standards) of most of these markets makes accessing them an unrealistic option, even if they wanted to. However, for smaller institutions such as Family Offices there may well be some interesting opportunities, and Family Offices, in particular, may exhibit the required levels of both open-mindedness and investment sophistication. Of forestry, in particular, we shall certainly hear more since it is already regarded by some of the world's most successful investors as an established asset class.

Of private individuals, however, it is to be hoped that they will heed the words of advice set out above. Collecting wine in order to drink it is a straightforward and enjoyable activity. Buying it as an investment is not necessarily either of those things. Similarly with classic cars. The writer suffered a significant loss on his yellow Morgan, and it might have been worse still had he not resorted to the caddish expedient of selling it to a girlfriend. As the reader may have guessed, she became an ex-girlfriend shortly afterwards.

SUMMARY

The precise definition of "alternative assets" is essentially loose and subjective. It is possible to argue that each one of the asset types described in this chapter falls under that description.

Forestry is already an established investment class, at least for institutional investors in North America. It is included here simply because it is not thought, at least as yet, to merit its own chapter.

Various well-established methods of institutional access to forestry already exist, whether direct or indirect.

The others are referred to as "exotics", "collectables" or "passion investments". These all seem to share two characteristics: (1) a successful investment approach would logically require a high level of specialist knowledge going beyond mere investment theory and practice and (2) they generally comprise specific, individual assets which may in many cases be capable of identification and cataloguing.

In some cases investment funds exist, but these will typically be quite small, in line with the markets in which they operate. In these cases, institutional involvement would be difficult.

There is some interesting potential for possible synthetic exposure in the future, notably in the case of wine (by way of writing options or swaps over wine futures) and art (by writing synthetics such as total return swaps over a selected AMR index). However, these do not currently exist.

While all these areas pose difficulty and complexity for any investor seeking to give them serious attention, current unease about the true and enduring value of financial assets provides an impetus to examine them as closely as possible.

Index

Index compiled by Annette Musker